The Story of an Auction:

For the Glory of God

Author & Compiler
Vivian S. Ziegler

The Story of an Auction: For the Glory of God

Library of Congress Control Number: 2009908985
International Standard Book Number: 978-1-60126-198-4

*Cover photo: The "Woodland Butterfly" quilt sold at the
2008 BDRA for $10,000*

Cover designed by Kathy McClure.

Masthof Press
*219 Mill Road
Morgantown, PA 19543-9516
www.masthof.com*

THE STORY OF AN AUCTION:

For the Glory of God

Contents

This book is dedicated . . .

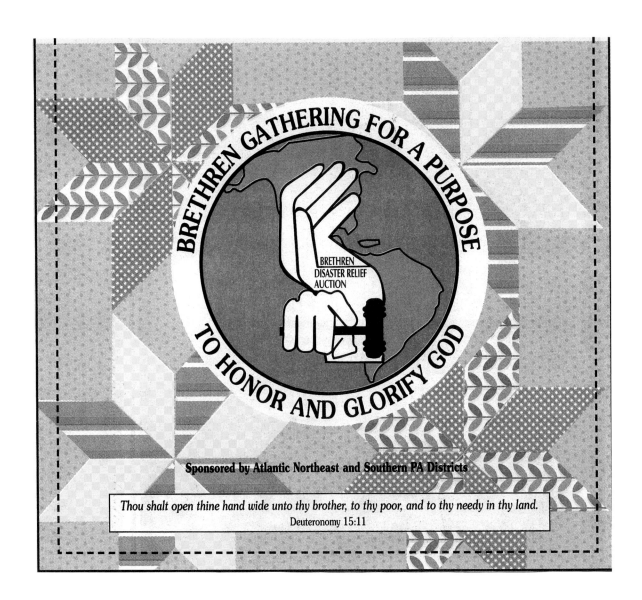

BRETHREN GATHERING FOR A PURPOSE

TO HONOR AND GLORIFY GOD

BRETHREN DISASTER RELIEF AUCTION

Sponsored by Atlantic Northeast and Southern PA Districts

Thou shalt open thine hand wide unto thy brother, to thy poor, and to thy needy in thy land.
Deuteronomy 15:11

An Explanation of the Logo

On the sale bill for the very first BDRA in 1977, the logo, showing two hands and designed by Marilyn Sanko-Ebel, was already in use. The upper hand has a two-fold meaning: Pointing upward to give praise, glory and honor to God, it is open because it is helping those who have experienced disaster and tragedy.

Underneath the hands were the words, "A Gathering with a Purpose." Dave Sollenberger explained that the Committee at that time wanted to set apart this auction from those where people went primarily to get bargains. The goal was (and still is) that people would come to the BDRA not to get but to give!

By the time the first sale book was printed in 1987, the logo was enclosed within the world globe, signifying that the relief-giving extends to where it is most needed anywhere in the world. The word, "Brethren" was added to precede the phrase, "Gathering for a purpose," since it had the approval and endorsement of the ANE District of the COB and the denominational headquarters in Elgin, Illinois. In 1989, the SOPA District was added as a joint-sponsor. The explanation of the purpose for why the Brethren were gathering was put in words: "To honor and glorify God."

The auctioneer's gavel represents the method being used (an auction) to accomplish the tasks represented: To give honor and glory to God and help to those in need, locally and world-wide.

The Brethren Disaster Relief Auction Is:

B rethren gathered together sharing and caring.

R allying together to help many victims of disasters.

E njoying the day at the Lebanon Fair grounds.

T eaching the spirit of love through giving.

H onoring God by showing compassion for our neighbors.

R especting the well-being of others.

E ntering into a peaceful, sharing attitude with other Brethren.

N ewly aware of what God has done for us.

D esiring to help many unfortunate people.

I nvesting something of ourselves in this ministry.

S haring out of our bountiful resources.

A uctioning of quilts, comforters, painting, woodwork, crafts.

S eptember's annual reservation for the gathering.

T otal made from Auction given to relief.

E ver striving to give all glory to God.

R eaching the monetary goal, a wonderful challenge.

R everencing God with our gifts and talents.

E ating the bountiful food that is supplied.

L etting God direct our efforts on this day.

I nteresting stories being passed around.

E ternal gratitude for the many blessings we receive.

F ortunate to have opportunities such as this Auction.

A ssociating with brothers and sisters as we minister.

U nable to fully comprehend some of the tragedy.

C onvinced of God's love and care for us.

T ogetherness for a full, inspiring, wonderful day.

I nviting and welcoming each one to take part.

O ne way to sense God's Spirit is through our giving.

N ow, come one, come all, to the Brethren Relief Auction."

- Candy Myer, Conestoga COB, 1993 SB, p. 48

Introduction

The goal in creating and circulating this book about the Disaster Relief Auction sponsored by the Atlantic Northeast and the Southern Pennsylvania Districts of the Church of the Brethren is threefold.

First: *"To God be the glory, Great things He has done!"* The idea of using an auction to raise funds to aid those stricken by man-made or natural disasters was God-given. However, the originators never dreamed that it would grow into the large and powerful fund-raising and beneficiary-helping organization that it is today. In Mark 10:27, Jesus said: *"With men, it is impossible, but not with God; for with God all things are possible."* (KJV)

Stories and testimonies abound showing God's hand at work at every step of the process—from the conception of the BDRA to those nameless volunteers who worked behind the scenes to make it happen, those who donated of their best (skills, time, livestock, crafts, produce, baked goods, etc.), those who made purchases, those who served on disaster response teams, and those persons, local and worldwide, who received the help. Since the BDRA will observe its thirty-third year of existence in 2009, some feared these stories would "fall through the cracks" and be forgotten. This book is an attempt to pull them together and show how the hand of God has gently guided the planners through the years in each step of the process of growth and service.

Second: *"Many hands make light work."* As you read this book, keep in mind this only shows the "tip of the iceberg" of what has made the BDRA a success. Persons mentioned are representative of many like them, who have served just as faithfully and well, and who are not mentioned. Through the years, literally thousands of people have worked together anonymously to honor God through the BDRA and its services. Even though some people have served on the BDRA Board or Committees, or have donated valuable and beautiful items for sale for many years, it was impossible to include everyone.

Third: *"If he or she can do it, I can do it also."* After reading what one person after another has done to help others, perhaps you'll be inspired to attempt great things for the Lord. Note that to accomplish His purpose, God uses persons of all ages from the very young to those over 100 years old. God includes all races, faiths, walks of life and vocations: farmers, teachers, carpenters, musicians, housewives, prisoners, artists, auctioneers, business leaders, able-bodied and those physically or mentally challenged. Since God has given each of us one or more gifts, He expects us to use them. In doing so, the unanimous testimony is that people are blessed with a satisfying sense of accomplishment, a deeper understanding of life's purpose, a closer relationship with God and…pure joy. It is hoped that you, too, will step out in faith and try it, because when you do, you'll probably discover that you like it! In the words of a poster that hung in our son's bedroom when he was a teenager: *"What in the world are you doing for heaven's sake?"*

- Vivian S. Ziegler, Author and compiler
September 2009

List of Abbreviations

The following abbreviations will be used throughout this book:

ANE = Atlantic Northeast District of the COB
BDRA = Brethren Disaster Relief Auction
BVS = Brethren Volunteer Service
COB = Church of the Brethren
COBYS = Church of the Brethren Youth Services
HPI = Heifer Project International
KJV = King James Version of the Bible
NIV = New International Version of the Bible
NOAC = National Older Adult Conference (COB)
p = page
pp = pages
pp = per person (in context)
SB = Sale Booklet
SDDA = Shenandoah District Disaster Auction
SERRV = Sales Exchange for Refugee Rehabilitation Vocation
SOPA = Southern PA District of the COB
STATE = Abbreviations according to the Postal Code
TLB = The Living Bible
TURF = The United Relief Fund

CHAPTER ONE

"To God Be the Glory"

"Great things He hath taught us, great things He hath done,
And great our rejoicing thro' Jesus the Son;
But purer and higher and greater will be
Our wonder, our transport, when Jesus we see."

- Fanny J. Crosby, blind hymn writer

BORN WITH DOWN'S syndrome, Doran Mummau, 56, is a "regular" contributor at the BDRA, seated every year at a card table near the caramel popcorn makers. His specialty is colorful woven potholders, and he usually has a pile of those he has finished beside him while he works adeptly at intertwining the looped materials on a small, pointed frame.

Starting at age sixteen, Doran has made potholders for 40 years, and has long ago lost count of how many he has woven. Since he doesn't put a price tag on his creations, he simply has placed a box for donations on his work-table. Passers-by are welcome to take one or more pot-holders, whatever they can use.

Often, his mother, Jean Mummau, is sitting quietly eight to ten feet behind him, and she has observed that some people put $20 in the box, some put $10 in the box, some put $5 in the box, and some simply take one or two potholders without putting anything in the box! In spite of that, his parents estimate that his contributions to the BDRA the last few years have amounted to between $400 and $450 each year.

In 2007, his father, Cassel Mummau, donated to the BDRA a picture of Doran with his pot holders which had been put in a frame made by Bill Longenecker with wood gathered from the burned-down Risser covered bridge near Mount Joy. It was sold twice at $500 each time to Clarence Wenger, Quarryville.

By weaving potholders, Doran Mummau contributes to Disaster Relief.

Doran travels each week-day by van to his work at the Occupational Development Center where he is assigned varied tasks, such as sorting and packaging screws. In his leisure hours, he enjoys traveling, watching preachers on television, doing latch hook and putting puzzles together. The largest puzzle he ever put together had 4,000 pieces. If he puts a puzzle together and then pulls it apart, he can reassemble it in half the time! To have a hobby like this requires much patience, and Doran has plenty of that—except, his mother notes with a chuckle, on those mornings when his van driver isn't on time!

Why have we begun this first chapter with this story about Doran? When I asked Belinda Graybill, who with her husband was a BDRA Coordinator in the late 1980s, what impressed her the most in her association with the auction, she shared this incident:

One Saturday afternoon, as the sale was closing down and vendors were packing their things away, Doran did the same. He packed up his potholders that were left, his frame, his extra loops of material, everything. Then he took his "earnings," all the contributions that people had given him that Friday and Saturday to the cashier and literally plopped the money on the table in front of him and said just three words, "All for Jesus!"

THAT is why the BDRA is held each year. All the hard work, all the hours of making tiny stitches on a quilt, polishing wood to make a beautiful table, carrying and setting up chairs to seat 1,000 persons, all the planning meetings, cooking for Kick-Off dinners, etc., all of it is *for Jesus*, to give glory to God, to show our thankfulness to God for His blessings.

Some people can't understand it, but obviously, Doran "got it!"

"As we gather together, we sometimes need to be reminded of the goal of the BDRA. All of the work and all of the proceeds are for a single purpose: To honor and glorify God by sharing His good news while helping those in need."

(Duane & Tina Ness, 2005 SB, p. 2)

"'Our goal is to bring honor and glory to God.' This has been our committee's response literally hundreds of times a year when asked, 'What is the BDRA goal this year?' This response usually shocks people a bit—we live in such a quantitative, 'bottom line' society. Dollar totals are expected to be the final verdict of every project's success. Yet this is how God measures a project's success—in dollars and cents? What 'total' could impress a God who owns the cattle on a thousand hills?

"God's vision and objectives reach far beyond ours. He desires our praises. He wants to be given glory and honor. He desires to be acknowledged as the center of our very existence and sustenance. He desires to have *His* people helping those in need in *His* name, for *His* glory, not ours. He wants our true thanks. He wants His promises to us fulfilled."

(Thom & Sue Keller, Coordinators; Dave & Belinda Graybill, Assistant Coordinators. 1987 SB, p. 1)

"Christopher Sauer was an important printer in colonial America who resided near Philadelphia and was an early leader in the COB at Germantown. The motto adopted by Sauer for his life and his business was 'TO THE GLORY OF GOD AND MY NEIGHBOR'S GOOD.'

"The primary goal of the BDRA continues to be: 'TO BRING HONOR AND GLORY TO GOD.' A secondary goal of this year's [1990][1] auction is to raise $300,000 for disaster relief to victims of disasters around the world. …

"The auction is more than producing finances, it is also a means of promoting faith and praising our Father in heaven. The spiritual dimension of the BDRA has been evident in the prayer support and sacrificial giving which many persons have offered over the past thirteen years. A small group of auction leaders has

---

[1] Note the dates at the end of each quotation because many of the dates and numbers mentioned in this book were correct at the time the quote was written but are no longer true today.

> *"To help the poor is to honor God."*
>
> *Proverbs 14:31b (TLB)*

met for a time of prayer before the beginning of the auction for the past several years. At noon on Saturdays in the main auction building… all the auction crowd is engaged in singing of hymns and prayer.

"This year a worship service will be held in the main auction building at 6 p.m. on Friday for all those who want to gather together for a time of prayer and praise. This time of worship is an appropriate way to begin the auction and affirm the primary goal of bringing honor and glory to God.

"Worship has occupied a central place among the people of God throughout the ages. In our worship of God we take the focus off ourselves and our efforts and focus upon the power, majesty and mercy of God. In our time of worship at the auction we want to seek the Lord's blessings for all the efforts surrounding the auction, and give God the glory He deserves. Through our songs of praise and our prayers, we seek to acknowledge our dependence upon God for the success of our auction efforts.

"Whether or not we attain the financial goal of the auction is not the measure of success or failure. Our faithfulness to God in honoring Him needs to be foremost. Sharing our finances is an important part of the auction, but sharing our faith through the auction is even more important. If we are faithful to our primary goal of bringing honor and glory to God, then the auction will be a success regardless of how much money we raise.

"Psalm 67 states it well: '*God be merciful to us, and bless us; and cause Your face to shine upon us; that Your way may be known upon the earth, Your saving health among all nations. Let*

the people praise You, O God; let all the people praise You.'"

(Robert D. Kettering, Associate ANE District Executive. 1990 SB, p. 12)

"At the beginning and to this day, the BDRA has had one purpose. Money is only one thing, but the main, MAIN purpose, and I can't overemphasize it, is to glorify God. We absolutely have that as our big motto. For, you see, without God you may as well forget it. Fold it in and take all that you have tried yourself. I can talk from experience, by not thinking that I needed God as I grew up, that I, I, I, I, and I could do it without Him. It's just not that way. I couldn't, and you can't; don't try and kid yourself!"

(Jay M. Witman. 1994 SB, p. 56)

"We really see we are doing the right thing with God's help and our willingness to be a servant, sharing in an auction as this to help those in the disaster areas near and far. We can see 'our faith and deeds are putting God's word into action.'"

(SDDA Coordinating Committee, 1995 SB, p. 37)

"When I was a child, growing up on Maple Avenue in Hershey, PA, our next door neighbors were Orie and Fannie Grove, members of the Spring Creek COB. I can still see through

> *"Ministry is when Divine resources meet human needs through loving channels to the Glory of God."*

follower of Jesus. And there on the porch step of her home on a humid summer afternoon, Fannie led our unchurched mailman to faith in Jesus Christ. That mailman became one of the outstanding Christian leaders in our community—all because Fanny Grove witnessed to her faith in word and deed. She literally gave our mailman a glass of cold water, and he received the living water of Christ Jesus….

"I have shared this story on many occasions, ever grateful that I had a neighbor like Fanny Grove who knew that *a Christian is meant to be a doer of the Word and not just a hearer only!"*
(From an article by Robert Kettering, Lititz COB. 2005 SB, p. 51)

my child's eye the image of Fannie Grove struggling to get Orie into her car as he shuffled his feet and as his hands trembled and his speech was slurred as a result of Parkinson's disease. Fannie waited upon her husband day and night as his caregiver, seldom leaving their home. If ever anyone could have been excused from witnessing about her faith in Christ, it could have been Fannie Grove as she was confined to her home, and opportunities for interacting with other people were very limited.

"I remember those hot summer afternoons on Maple Avenue in the days before air conditioning. Each afternoon the mailman would come up the hill on our street with the mail, and on those sultry summer afternoons, Fannie Grove had a glass of cold water for the mailman. I can still see him pausing on her porch step, taking off his hat, wiping his sweaty forehead with his handkerchief and sipping that cold water and engaging Fannie Grove in conversation.

"One day the mailman questioned Fannie about how she could remain so joyful despite her circumstances as the primary caregiver with her infirm husband. Without hesitation, Fannie Grove shared the hope that was within her as a

"From my childhood days I recall an unforgettable traumatic experience. My father returned from the hospital after visiting my gravely ill mother who was given up to die by the most experienced doctors in Lancaster. He told the story to my four brothers and my maternal grandmother. Sitting in her rocking chair, grandmother responded by saying, 'But David, what does the Master-Healer have to say about Elizabeth?' She went to the shelf in the kitchen, located the family Bible and turned to James 5 and with commitment read the passage to us. Mother was anointed the next morning and again that same evening by I. N. Musser and a deacon from Mountville. After that she rallied and lived for another 67 years, going to her Heavenly Home at the age of 91. Quite a Christian legacy!

"The last week in January 1995, I experienced a T.I.A. innovation (inadequate supply of blood to the brain) while driving. This result-ed in intermittent moments of consciousness. Stopping the car along the highway, I inquired of God, 'What is happening?' Driving cautious-ly twelve miles to my home, and being grateful for God's care, I called for the Anointing Service by my pastor, Galen Hackman. Following this service, my family doctor directed me to the Hershey Medical Center where I was given a multitude of tests and treatments. After spend-ing a week there, I was transferred to the John Heinz Rehab Center in Wilkes-Barre adjacent to the hospital where our doctor son is a staff member.

"After three weeks of therapy, a Neuro-Psychiatrist physician interviewed me for dis-charge. He emphasized that I was fortunate to have experienced an unusually speedy recovery. This gave me the opportunity to witness to him about the anointing experience.

This sparked some intense questioning. My response was simply, yet profoundly, to give credence to the 'Book of Life' which contains the formula for potential healing for the human family as provided by our Creator. To God be the Glory!"

(Excerpted from an article by Robert S. Young,
Conewago COB. 1996 SB, p. 7)

"Anyone who thinks that a pastor leads a static, staid, boring life will change perspect-ive by following my wife and me on twelve interims after retirement. A pastor never re-tires. A Christian never retires. Whoever thinks that life is only a matter of inhaling and exhaling can catch the Spirit in a lively church and find a long and good life, even into age eighty-one."

(John D. Long in 1995 SB, p. 23)

"The date was Monday, January 6, 1992. I remember it like it was yesterday. I was driv-ing south on Route 81 from Harrisburg to my home in Mechanicsburg. A debate was going on in my mind. My daughter, Eva, was scheduled to return to college in Pittsburgh the following day, and I wanted to make some sour cream cookies, her favorite kind, for her to take back to school.

"Mentally, I ticked off the ingredients I would need. I had everything but the sour cream. Where, I wondered, should I stop to pick up sour cream at 4:30 in the afternoon? The grocery store closest to our house is situated at a corner where four roads meet. It is always difficult to get in and out at that time of day. The store at the other end of town promised long lines at the cash register and a long wait to complete my purchase. Then I thought of the Handy Market, located on the way into town. Perfect, I thought. I can stop, make a quick pur-chase, and be on my way.

"There was only one car in the parking lot of the Handy Market when I arrived. I thought I'd be in and out of there in no time. Inside, I noticed one man looking at the videos to the left of the cash register, and three young boys looking at the magazines to the right. When I passed one of those boys, I heard him say, 'Don't take it now; she might be watching you on the monitor in the back.' That comment didn't re-ally register with me until much later.

"I located the refrigerator section in the back of the store, found the sour cream, opened the door and took it out to check the expiration date. Then I noticed that the back of the refrigerator section was open to the stock room of the store.

"A young woman appeared immediately on the other side of the refrigerator section and said, 'Lady, you've got to help me. I'm in a lot of trouble here. I'm locked in the back room and can't get out! Behind the cash register is a phone. Please go over there and call 737-1234. When they answer, ask for extension 100. Tell the person who answers that you're at the Handy Market and the clerk is locked in the back room and can't get out. Do whatever he tells you to do.'

"I returned to the cash register area. The three boys looked wide-eyed, as they asked me if I worked there. I responded that I was going to help the clerk for a while. Immediately, they lined up to pay for their hot dogs and sodas, and left the store to make a hasty exit on their bikes.

"I called the number the clerk had given me and was surprised to reach a local motel. When a man answered at extension 100, I told him, 'I'm at the Handy Market and the clerk is locked in the back room and can't get out. She asked me to call you and find out what to do.'

"The man was immediately defensive. 'How do you know that?' he asked.

"'Well," I said, 'I came in to buy some sour cream and when I opened the refrigerator door, the clerk came to the other side and asked me to call you for help.'

"Just then, the man looking at the videos came to attention as he heard my story. 'Oh,' he said, 'I used to work here, and I know just what to do. If someone comes in while you're in the back room and trips the safety lock from this side, you can't get out. I'll go let her out.' He did that, and left the store.

"The clerk came out shaking so badly she could hardly stand up. She took the phone and spoke to the man on the other end, assured him she was okay, and hung up. I put my hand on hers and said calmly, 'Now, take a few deep breaths. You're okay now.'

"Slowly, her story came out. It was her first night to work alone. She had gone to the back room to get something. Then the three boys came in, intending to take something, she guessed. When she went back to the door, she couldn't get out as it was locked. She panicked. Then I came in and opened the refrigerator door. She said, 'When I saw you, I knew you had an honest face. I thought I could trust you.'

"I smiled. 'Well,' I said, 'I'm a pastor, and I hope I have an honest face. I'm glad I could be here for you.'

"Immediately tears streamed down her face. 'You're a pastor!' she exclaimed. 'So God really did send someone to help me after all.'

"'He usually does,' I affirmed.

"I stayed with her a bit until she was calm enough to stay on her own, and then left with my sour cream. Suddenly, my busy schedule was no longer quite as important as before.

"About a week later, I stopped back at the Handy Market to pick up a few things and check on my friend. When I went in, she said, 'You're the woman who helped me, aren't you?'

"I smiled and admitted, 'Yes, I am.'

"'Now, wait a minute,' she said. 'I want to get my husband. He wants to thank you.'

"Then their story came out. It had been her first night to work alone. When I called, he was skeptical, but he was ever so grateful that I had been there when she needed help. He thanked me profusely. Then he asked, 'Say, my wife said you were a minister. What denomination are you with?'

"'Church of the Brethren,' I responded.'

"He looked at his wife. Fresh tears streamed down her face. 'Well, how about that!' he said, amazed. 'When my wife was a little girl, she was raised by a Brethren family in Lancaster County, and when she needed help, God sent a Church of the Brethren minister to rescue her!' We stood for a few minutes and talked, marveling at the wisdom of God in sending His servant at just the right time.

"When Jesus said, *'Go into all the world and preach the good news…,'* (Mark 16:15 NIV), surely He meant to preach it in your own neighborhood as well as the far corners of the earth. Or, as Saint Francis stated it: *'Preach the Gospel at all times. If necessary, use words.'*"

(From an article by Jan Custer. 2006 SB, p. 12)

"When you see me the next time, probably dressed in a white suit and standing on a podium for Brethren Disaster Relief, remember one thing: my goal is, yes, to create money to help the poor. But my *biggest* goal is to somehow get the spiritual application out to others. If we did 18 relief auctions in my lifetime, I hope we could say we had 18 people learn to know Christ much better. The $3 million we earned doesn't mean anything in eternity, but their souls mean a lot."

(Jay M. Witman in a message given at the Myerstown COB January 30, 1994, anticipating the 18th Annual Auction to be held September 23, 24, 1994. 1994 SB, p. 56)

"D. L. Moody was once criticized by one who said, 'I don't like your method of evangelism.' Moody said, 'I've got questions about it too. What's your method?' The man didn't have any. Then Moody observed, 'I believe I like my method of doing it better than your method of not doing it.'"

(Quoted by Bill Longenecker, Stevens Hill COB. 1995 SB, p. 38)

"We are doing a much better job as the Good Samaritan than we are as the evangelist. It is far more important to save the spiritual part of man than the physical. The physical is here for only a short time, while the spiritual part of man, (which Jesus said is worth more than the whole world), will live on throughout eternity, either in Heaven or Hell. After Peter reminds us of the coming 'day of the Lord,' he says, *'Dear friends, while you are waiting for these*

things to happen, and for Him [Jesus] to come, try hard to live without sinning; and be at peace with everyone so that He will be pleased with you when He returns. And remember why He is waiting. He is giving us time to get His message of salvation out to others.' 2 Peter 3:14,15 (TLB)"

(Olen Landes. 2004 SB, p. 65)

"The bumper sticker, *Honk if you love Jesus*, is a meager substitute for a personal conversation with a friend about your faith and trust in Jesus. *Honk if you love Jesus* can't hold a candle to working side by side with victims of a devastating hurricane to restore their home. *Honk if you love Jesus* can't measure up to a compassionate hug when personal tragedy beats down your health door. *Honk if you love Jesus* may evoke a 'beep' on the road; however, it rarely stirs a passing driver's heart to make the decision to follow Christ.

"So … honk if you're in a hurry and need to pass me. Other than that, keep sticking to the basics—love your neighbor, serve those in need, and then drive the message of Jesus home so that those closest to you will see that He is real to you."

(By Craig H. Smith, ANE District Executive in the 2006 SB, p. 38)

"What is most valuable is not what we have in our lives but WHO we have in our lives!"

CHAPTER TWO

The Joy of Giving

"The test of generosity is not how much you give,
but how much you have left." (Unknown)

W HY DO PERSONS who live in town go to a Brethren Disaster Relief Auction (BDRA) and buy a calf and then say, "Sell it again?" Why would ten people, who are normally rather frugal, bid a pie up to $100 or more and then one after another say, "Sell it again?" Why would a person spend countless hours building a roll-top desk or a Grandfather's clock, using the best wood possible, carefully constructing, staining and polishing—and then donate the finished masterpiece to the BDRA?

The BDRA operates out of the principle of loving, caring and sharing. We love because God first loved us; we care because we have been cared for; we share because, having been given much, we too must give. We are called as Christians to make a difference! How do we accomplish this?

Allow the love and sharing spirit of Mrs. Lizzie Longenecker to speak to us. Lizzie is 97 years old[2] and a life-long member of the White Oak COB. She cared about the flood victims in West Virginia, the hungry people in Ethiopia, the earthquake victims in Mexico, the drought-stricken farmers in Georgia, and the typhoon victims in the Philippines. So she (with the aid of a granddaughter) personally visited a shop, purchased the material, and sewed together 1,800 patches

---

[2] Ages, dates, job titles, location of church membership were all correct at the year of the respective Sale Booklets from which the quotes were taken, but are not necessarily correct today.

that were integrated into a quilt called *"Around the World."* At the 1986 BDRA, she was introduced to the crowd of bidders and spectators. A lively exchange followed, and when the auctioneer's gavel pounded the desk as he yelled the word, "Sold," Mrs. Longenecker then knew that her loving, caring and sharing amounted to $7,000!"

(Earl K. Ziegler, COB ANE District Executive. 1987 SB, p. 30)

SEEK THE BIGGEST BARGAIN!

There are probably three main reasons for attending the usual auction. One reason may be that there is a sale of property belonging to a good friend or relative. Another reason may be that the announcement listed some items that we would like to have. And then there is the strongest reason of all: a chance to save money by picking up items at ridiculously low prices.

When it comes to the BDRA, the motivation is quite different, though again there are probably three main reasons: One reason may be to meet old friends and be together with a lot of brothers and sisters in Christ. Another reason may be to share in raising money for the relief of those who suffer disaster. And then there is the strongest reason of all: *to honor and glorify God.*

Those two sets of reasons are in sharp contrast. The usual auction calls for the bargain hunter; the BDRA calls the disciple. Somehow, that reminds me that I cannot serve both God and money. Now, I don't find bargain hunting to be wrong. If I save money in a bargain, I may have more to give to the work of Jesus, though

it would not be quite honest to pretend that is why I want the bargain. Still, where can one find big bargains and *at the same time* honor and glorify God? The two don't seem to go together, yet at the BDRA they do!

What it comes down to, I think, is answering the question, "Which is the bigger bargain?" I think I know the answer, and it doesn't lie in saving money! Let me illustrate. The bidder gets a ground-cherry pie for, say, $25. Then he gives it back to be sold again. He gets the bigger bargain: instead of purchasing a pie, he has purchased genuine help for some suffering people.

A woman buys a chicken pot-pie dinner, but presents it for sale, and it sells for $280. Who gets the bigger bargain? Instead of feeding just one person, she may have helped to feed fifty or more! What a bargain!

That is probably why I am bothered by bargain hunters who wait until late in the day on Saturday to buy baked goods or produce. Real bargains! They often go for half-price. I confess that I have taken advantage of those bargains, too. But God has been nudging me. Wouldn't it be a bigger bargain–in terms of results–if the buyer would not only pay full price, but even double price? My suggestion: *At the close of the day, double the price of everything so we can seek the bigger bargain!* Wouldn't that be closer to giving honor and glory to God?

(Charles M. Bieber. 1998 SB, p. 39)

"Giving to the Auction is a way for us to worship God, because whenever we do something

to thank God or praise Him, it's an act of worship."

(Olen Landes, 2007 SB, p. 5)

❖ ❖ ❖

Disaster has hit the economy of the United States plunging the nation into economic recession. The job market is tight, unemployment is high and the amount of money available for charitable work is not abundant. Many relief agencies are feeling the pinch of the economic crisis at home on the one hand and the enormous amount of need abroad due to war, famine, earthquakes, typhoons, tornadoes and volcanoes.

The past twelve months have been a time of unprecedented disaster around the world from the famines of Ethiopia and Sudan to the plight of the Kurdish refugees, from the victims of volcanoes in Japan and the Philippines to the hundreds of thousands killed as a result of the typhoon in Bangladesh. While the United States and allies experienced limited casualties as a result of the Persian Gulf War, the number of casualties and innocent victims of the war in Iraq are staggering, and the suffering, disease and hunger continue. Massive relief efforts have been undertaken to help these victims, but much more remains to be done.

The only thing limiting this aid is financial resources to accomplish the relief efforts.... While economic hardships may be upon us in the United States, compared to the enormous suffering around the world, we are most blest. … All of us can share of our resources, whether large or limited, to help meet the cries of suffering people around the world.

(Robert D. Kettering, COB ANE Associate District Executive. 1991 SB, p. 47
—but doesn't this sound as though it could have been written in 2009?)

❖ ❖ ❖

In the fall of 1996, the organization, *People of the Golden Venture*, invited people to host refugees being released from the York County (PA) prison. We received two men, one from China, Frank Gao, and another, Abbdou Tsedey, from Monrovia, Liberia.

I picked Abbdou up from the prison and then proceeded to purchase some "ethnic" food as well as essential clothing. (Jail food for three months had been rather bland.) At a local bank we cashed a check that amounted to all of Abbdou"s worldly assets. As we exited the bank, Abbdou counted out ten percent of the money.

"This amount belongs to God," Abbdou exclaimed. "Give it to your church."

"I think you need it more than our church does. You have nothing," I responded. "At least keep this amount to help you get a new start in life."

"No," countered Abbdou. "*You* don't understand. I have been giving back to God a portion of all that I earn. My family has done this for as long as I can remember." (Abbdou's parents had been shot to death one night when his village in Liberia had been raided by a marauding band of rioters.)

The following week our church received Abbdou's "tithe" offering for the Community Outreach Fund. Abbdou, having nothing, *first* gave to support the ministry of Jesus Christ.

Abbdou, having nothing, *had everything*! He had the love of Jesus in his heart and then gave generously and faithfully as a result of that love. May his tribe increase! *(Joe Detrick, SOPA COB District Executive. 1999 SB, p.5)*

(Postscript: Abbdou lived with the Detrick family for five months and was a real blessing to them. In the fall of 1998, Abbdou was struck down by a hit-and-run driver while riding his bicycle on the way to work. Abbdou was able to return to his apartment in York following a long hospital stay. His injuries have not yet allowed him to return to work. Still, Abbdou continues to praise God, being thankful every day for the gift of life. Amazingly, Abbdou holds no ill will toward the person who struck him down. "God has forgiven me, a sinner. I must forgive others also, just as God has already forgiven me. What good does it do to be vengeful? I must continue to love, yes, even my enemies, even as God loves His enemies." What a testimony of faith!)   *(1999 SB, p. 5)*

I gave a little talk in church last week. I said basically that God has been teaching me about thankfulness, about not taking for granted the gifts He has given me, like family, friends, church, good health, and clean water. I thought perhaps He wanted the people here to learn about thankfulness—children need to learn to say "Thank You." (If ours forget to say "Thank You" for a gift, they must give it back.) Spouses need to thank each other—husbands to wives for their cooking, clothes washing, child care, and wives to husbands for their work and wages. People need to be more appreciative of

the doctors and nurses for their hard work and good care. We need to thank our pastors and pray for them. We need to thank God for His faithfulness and blessings."

(Doreen Bieber Miller, missionary doctor in Ahuas, Honduras. 1998 SB, p. 30)

Two memories from past auctions tie together for me the relationship of family and giving in Jesus' name to those in special need. In the late sixties, my grandfather purchased a clock at a charity auction. The clock's builder did his part by creating this work in chestnut. My grandfather did his part in the purchase of the timepiece. Today, each time that I see that handiwork in my home, I am reminded to do my part to help many who are not as blessed.

The other memory that speaks to me was my father's purchase of a quilt for my mother. The quilters did their part by creating a masterpiece. My father did his part by honoring my mother, his sweetheart, with the quilt as a token of his love. And simultaneously, somewhere, someone in need, someone less fortunate, would benefit from a greater, God-given love.

That's Brethren. We preach the Gospel. We have a burden for the souls of the lost, but we also are a *doing* people. We do the work of Jesus, and therein lies the excitement, the blessing, and the worship associated with the Auction. While we are working, fellowshipping and bidding, while we are eating a Moravian sugar cake or buying a heifer, or while we are singing a hymn or considering which craft to buy, we are also providing for someone who is hurting.

We are blessed even as we become a blessing to others. Let's continue to encourage each other to make a difference in Jesus' name.

(From an article by R. Edward Weaver, COB SOPA Moderator. 2002 SB, p. 60)

❖ ❖ ❖

I command you to be openhanded toward your brothers and toward the poor and needy in your land. (Deuteronomy 15:11, NIV)

❖ ❖ ❖

THE REWARDS OF GIVING

Every ministry that I felt good about, that I could conscientiously support, whether I could give one hour a year or one dollar a year, I would do for them whatever I could. I've always been a firm believer in giving pledges to ministries as I feel it takes real faith to pledge money without knowing how you're going to get it. Of course, there are limits to everything, but it was so spiritually rewarding. The most frequent question that I got asked was: "Why do you *do* all this?"

After I had entered the prison ministry as a volunteer, I took a friend along to a Dairy Cooperative meeting one time and mentioned that I had been in the prison the night before. He was aghast and asked, "Why in the world would you waste your time doing that?"

"I'll quit if you will answer this one question," I replied. "You have three teenage boys: 15, 18, and 19. If you get a phone call at 3:00 in the morning saying your 18-year-old son did something stupid and he ends up in jail, should we do what you just said—throw him in jail, lock him up, throw the key away and let him rot? If you tell me to, I will quit tomorrow."

"Victor, keep up the good work," he responded.

"It makes a difference if it is *your* son, doesn't it?"

End of conversation. I'll never forget that. He never challenged me again.

There is nothing that gives more pleasure than being able to rescue a child, pick him up out of the gutter, giving a second chance to someone who is down, or even helping an elderly person who did something that everyone should have enough sense not to do. You know that he just wasn't thinking of the consequences and something went wrong, either emotionally or Satan had a foothold. I am so thankful that I can be the one helping instead of being the one *needing the help*!

(Victor K. Ziegler in "On My Way to Heaven… Traveling with Grace," p. 271. 2008 SB, p. 59)

❖ ❖ ❖

In a culture that cries out for "how much we can get," it [attending the BDRA] is a great day to be among the people of God who give prayerful consideration to "how much we can give."

(Craig H. Smith, COB ANE District Executive. 1998 SB, p. 5)

❖ ❖ ❖

Tell them to use their money to do good. They should be rich in good works and should give happily to those in need, always being ready to share with others whatever God has given them. By doing this, they will be storing up real treasure for themselves in heaven—it is the only safe investment for eternity! And they will be living a fruitful Christian life down here as well. (1 Timothy 6:18, 19, TLB)

Some years ago I invested in some stocks. I didn't know what I was doing, but left it up to the broker. It was not a good investment. They have gone down in value. I believe that this text clearly implies that the money we give toward disaster relief is a "safe investment for eternity." I do not know what the returns will be, but I am sure they will be something grander than anything we will ever experience during this short span of life.

(Olen B. Landes. 2001 SB, p. 6)

I plan to exercise some of my buying power at the 25th Annual BDRA. It's not because I need anything. I really don't. But, I understand that others do. I understand that sometimes things happen in life that are disasters—unavoidable—crushing—overwhelming. I understand that these events often leave persons in need. And, I understand that we can help. I understand that our gifts fix, furnish, finance, and fan the flame of hope for those in serious need. I understand that my small bit of buying power, plus your bit of buying power, equals a buying power that extends God's gift of help and hope to those who need a hand up.

Most importantly, I understand that this is done in the Name of the One whose buying power is unlimited, the One who counted the cost, the One who purchased my salvation with His own blood. The One who paid it all—the full price at Calvary—the One we call Jesus.

(By Craig H. Smith,
COB ANE Executive, 2001 SB, p. 11)

THE "I AM RICH" MENTAL EXERCISE

Just imagine …

1. Take out all the furniture in your home except for one table and a couple of chairs. For a bed, use blankets or pads.

2. Take away all of your clothing except for your oldest dress or suit, shirt, or blouse. Leave only one pair of shoes.

3. Empty both the pantry and the refrigerator except for a small bag of flour, some sugar and salt, a few potatoes, some onions, and a dish of dried beans.

4. Dismantle your bathroom, shut off the running water, and remove all the electrical wiring in your house.

5. In fact, take away the house itself and move your family into your storage, garden, or tool shed.

6. Place your new "house" in a Shantytown, with hundreds of others exactly like it.

7. Cancel all subscriptions to newspapers, magazines, and book clubs. This is no great loss because now you have to imagine that none of you can read, anyway.

8. Imagine there is only one radio for your entire Shantytown.

9. Move the nearest hospital or clinic ten miles away and put a midwife in charge instead of a doctor.

10. Throw away your bank books, stock certificates, pension plans, and insurance poli-

cies. Leave the family a cash hoard of ten dollars.

11. Give the head of the family a few acres to cultivate, on which he can raise a few hundred dollars of cash crops—one-third of which will go to the landlord and at least one-tenth to the money lenders.

12. Take your average life expectancy and lop off twenty-five years. At least.

Now you are living in the same conditions in which well over one billion people on the planet live. How rich we are, indeed! Use that wealth responsibly and with compassion.

(Written by Economist Robert Heilbroner and circulated on the Internet)

Continuing in a similar vein of thought, consider these facts:

- 90% of the people on earth do not have an automobile.
- Millions of refugees in Pakistan, Mozambique, and Sudan live day by day on fruits, nuts, and on broth made by boiling tree roots.
- More people have a life span of less than 45 years than there are people who have a life span of at least three-score and ten.
- More mothers of the world see half of their offspring die in childhood than there are mothers who see their children reach maturity.
- While we search the refrigerator for an extra serving of dessert, many search daily to find just a bit of food to survive. While we search for an unneeded Christmas gift for a friend, many search for the bare necessities for their families. We feel handicapped without electricity for two hours, but many people in the world will never have access to electricity–for even five minutes!

One of the great truths proclaimed in the book of Proverbs is this: *"He that hath pity upon the poor lendeth to the Lord; and that which he hath given will He [the Lord] pay him again"* *(Proverbs 19:17, KJV).* Those who help the poor and unfortunate are lending to the Lord—and He pays a wonderful interest on the loan! God blesses peoples' generosity with His generosity! Money and material aid, given to those in distress, is *not* gone forever.

(Excerpted from an article by Harold S. Martin, Pleasant Hill COB, 2008 SB, p. 22)

Nobody made a greater mistake than he who did nothing because he could only do a little.

(Edmund Burke)

"I don't believe in luck; I believe in opportunity, and it's up to each one of us to take advantage of the opportunities we have." These are the words of Wayne A. Nicarry (December 15, 1919 - May 29, 2005) who took advantage of the opportunities in his life and used them to make a difference in the lives of others. His wife, Frances (Oberholzer), played a big role in helping him take advantage of those opportunities. Being the family caretaker and homemaker, she played a big part in raising their sons, Ronald L. and Wayne F. "Somebody is behind the success a person achieves, and she was that person for me," Nicarry said of her.

On January 17, 1947, Wayne Nicarry, Dwight Grove and John Grove started Grove Manufacturing Company in Shady Grove, PA. The company became an international success, growing from one employee to over 8,000 employees, with annual sales exceeding well over a half billion dollars.

The three men started in a rented garage in Shady Grove, selling their wagons to area farm equipment dealers. They had to supplement their income by doing side jobs. To help them move heavy steel to production areas, the partners invented a mobile, hydraulic crane. Word of the crane soon spread, and they added it to their expanding product line. It was the crane that turned the company from a small business to a national and international success story.

The Nicarrys have strong roots in the COB, having met through the church and married at age nineteen. At one time, Wayne considered becoming a full-time minister. Ordained as a free minister in 1946, he served the Chambersburg (PA) COB as full-time pastor from 1949 to 1954.

"The church is really what has formulated my fundamental principles of business," said Nicarry. "As a businessman, I make contacts with people all over the world, and as a minister, I'd like to think that I have influenced some of them as a result of my philosophy of life and commitment to humanitarianism," he added.

As a youth, he "desperately" wanted to attend Elizabethtown College, but was unable to because of the Depression and his family's need for help on the farm. However, because

he strongly believed in church-related colleges to help young people develop strong values, he served on the College's Board of Trustees from 1960 to 1996, and in 1996, the college bestowed on him an honorary Doctor of Science degree.

Along with the college, the Brethren Home, Bethany Theological Seminary, Greencastle Medical Arts Center, Greencastle Golden Age Center and the Church of the Brethren have all received support from the Nicarrys.

Nicarry said he never expected to make a lot of money. However, as his assets grew, so did his conviction that they really belong to God. Mindful that many people contributed to his success, he believed that he, in turn, needed to share by helping others. His guiding philosophy was: *"It's not how much one gives but how much one keeps for himself."* Then he added, *"God knows why you keep it."*

(Karen Edwards in 2000 SB, p. 31)

A frequent response to Brethren fund raising efforts is "What I have accumulated will all go to my children." One writer penned these words, "It is good to be well descended, but that glory belongs to the past." There is certainly nothing wrong with giving good things to our children; even the world does that. And that is just the point.

Christians are accountable for far more than the world. *"What doth the Lord require of you but to do justly, love mercy and to walk humbly with thy God"* (Micah 6:8, KJV). Brethren Christians bear no small responsibility. Beyond our immediate church buildings and programs are the needs of persons dealing with disasters, the homeless, the frail elderly, troubled youth, missions, etc. …Our calling is to be responsible with whatever level gifts we have been blessed, and return whatever we can to God. The time to act on this issue is now, above all times, **now.**

(*Robert S. Young and Martha Douple Shaak, 1995 SB, p. 56*)

❖ ❖ ❖

Shortly before his death, Patrick Henry wrote: "I have disposed of all my property to my family. There is one thing more I wish I could give to them, and that is the Christian religion. If they had that and I had not given them one cent, they would be rich. If they have not that and I had given them the world, they would be poor."

❖ ❖ ❖

The BDRA puts into practice the words of *1 John 3:16-18 (NIV): "If anyone has material possessions and sees his brother in need but has no pity on him, how can the love of God be in him? …Let us not love with words or tongue but with actions and in truth."*

❖ ❖ ❖

James 2:14 (NIV) says, *"What good is it if a man claims to have faith but has no deeds?"* A boy was without food and shoes. In his plight he approached a woman whom he thought would be sympathetic and asked her for help.

The woman replied cruelly, "If God loved you, wouldn't He send you food and shoes?"

"God did tell someone, but he forgot," the boy replied.

Will we forget? In the name of Jesus Christ, we shall remember and give.

(*Earl K. Ziegler, COB ANE District Executive. 1988 SB, p.5*)

❖ ❖ ❖

Your bank doesn't want your change. Beginning in 2008, the BDRA is equipped to handle all of the loose change that you can find. Just bring your jars, boxes, or bags of loose coins, and we'll help you unload it. It will be counted on the premises. Our goal is to have TWO TONS of coins by Saturday afternoon.

"A poor widow came and put in two very small copper coins, worth only a fraction of a penny. Calling His disciples to Him, Jesus said… "This poor widow has put more into the treasury than all the others…. She, out of her poverty, put in everything—all she had to live on" (Mark 12:42-44, NIV).

❖ ❖ ❖

We want you to know about the grace that God has given the Macedonian churches. Out of the most severe trial, their overflowing joy and their extreme poverty welled up in rich generosity. For I testify that they gave as much as they were able, and even beyond their ability. Entirely on their own, they urgently pleaded with us for the **privilege of sharing** *in this service to the saints. And they did not do as we expected, but* **they gave themselves <u>first</u> to the Lord** *and then to*

*us in keeping with God's will.... Just as you excel
in everything—in faith, in speech, in knowledge,
in complete earnestness and in your love for us—
see that you also excel in this **grace of giving**. (2
Corinthians 8:1-5, 7 NIV)*

CHAPTER THREE

Looking Back to the Beginning

During the noontime singing at the 1989 BDRA,
a woman standing near the stage asked someone:
"Why do all these people know the same song?"

How did the Brethren Disaster Relief Auction get started anyway? To answer that question, we will look at (A) **The History of the BDRA,** (B) **Brief History of the Church of the Brethren,** (C) **When Did the COB Begin Its Disaster Response Program?** and (D) **What is the BDRA like today?**

A. THE HISTORY OF THE BDRA

To begin, let's look at an article that was printed in the 2001 Sale Book and summarized the first 25 years of the BDRA.

TWENTY-FIFTH YEAR OF BRINGING HONOR AND GLORY TO GOD
(By Charles M. Bieber)

It was God who brought the first disaster relief, coming in Jesus Christ to relieve us of the disaster of our sinfulness. It was also God who inspired the institution of the BDRA in 1977. Inspiration, however, came twice before 1977. A flyer distributed in early 1948 announced a "Public Sale for World Relief," on February 7, at Root's Auction sponsored by the Eastern District Men's Work.

In the late 1960s, it was Eastern District COB Youth who once again launched an auction for relief. Selling mostly household goods and other contributed items, their sale was held for several years, also at Root's Auction, averaging about $5,000 annually. However, as youth leadership changed, the auction was discontinued.

Auctioneer Sells Own Coat for Foreign Relief at Sale Here

Auctioneer Paul Sanger, Lebanon, offers a broom to the highest bidder today at the Church of the Brethren auction in East Petersburg. Sanger sold his overcoat for $50 to help raise funds for foreign relief. (Photo 1948)

Then, in early 1977, inspiration struck again. From old minutes, it is clear that Jerry Greiner, who had been on youth cabinet earlier and in 1977 was chaplain at Elizabethtown College, was the first coordinator, serving through 1980. The first committee included a number of persons who had been involved as youth: Henry Reist; Jim Gibbel, who served as treasurer; Marilyn Sanko (-Ebel), designer of the logo, which continues with only minor changes; Mark and Marty Hershey, next coordinators; Jay M. Witman, who pushed for bigger goals; Jacob Ruhl, who provided a great deal of business and organizational know-how;

and others active in interpretation such as Bob Young, who had helped plan the men's work auction in 1948.

The District Executive Committee endorsed the auction and approved solicitation from congregations. The auction, however, remained an independent entity. The fact that 1977 was the year of the Johnstown Flood, with need for extensive near-local assistance, gave added impetus to interest and support. Congregations quickly responded to requests for help, and it is clear that women's groups, in particular, became involved, as implied in Greiner's report of that first Auction, which opened like this:

The first Atlantic Northeast District Disaster Relief Auction is now history. The Committee, in planning this event, hoped to provide an opportunity for Brethren to celebrate their caring heritage by raising money for a worthwhile purpose. Following the initial announcement of our intent, congregations throughout the district responded quickly; first by making Afghans and quilts and later by donating items, including some valuable antiques. Others were encouraged to prepare special food items, such as chow-chow, homemade root beer, etc., while still others brought to the Auction some of their handmade crafts. The gathering of approximately 2,000 people at Lebanon County Fairgrounds gave indication of the tremendous initial response to this first annual Auction of the district. Those 2,000 expended almost $12,000 for food and other items which were on sale. By all appearances, this event allowed the church to celebrate its unity and in so doing raise a substantial sum of money for disaster relief.

Treasurer Jim Gibbel, in his final report, announced receipts of $2,751.40 for foods, $884 for arts and crafts, $7,510.65 from the Auction, and $364 in donations, against expenses of $1,767.64. It was Gibbel's privilege to send $9,946.32 to the Brotherhood Disaster Relief Fund with the request that $3,729.87 each be used for the Pineville, Kent., Disaster and the Johnstown Flood Disaster, and the balance go into the Brotherhood Disaster Fund.

From the outset, the Auction has been a family affair, both in arrangements and in participation. In 1977, Auction day closed with a Youth Jamboree of folk games on the fairgrounds. The youth helped in setting up for the Auction and cleaning up afterward. In different

DISASTER RELIEF AUCTION

"A Gathering with a Purpose"

Saturday, Sept. 17, 1977
10 A.M.
At Lebanon County Fairgrounds

Sale Sponsored by the Atlantic Northeast District of the Church of the Brethren. Proceeds for emergency Disaster Relief.

A partial sale listing to include - Antique wheat cradle, old school desks, tables, milk can, new bicycles, record player, lawn chairs, electric toaster oven, shrub trimmer, wooden benches, old Bibles in German and English, afghans, numerous handmade quilts and comforters, flower arrangments and shawls.

Craft exhibits and sales to include paintings, stuffed toys, decoupage, cross stitch, macrame and crochet items.

Homemade food to include - soups, pies, ice cream, root beer, apple dumplings, chow chow. Breakfast served beginning at 7 a.m.

Those wishing to donate items should bring them to the Fairgrounds beginning at 9 a.m. on September 16.

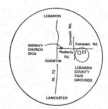

Located 3 miles South of Lebanon at intersection of Rockerty Road & Cornwall Road. Watch for sign on Rt. 72 at Rockerty Road.

years they shared Christian joy as "Clowns for Christ," distributing helium-filled balloons to children, made and sold funnel cakes and hot pretzels, sponsored an "Alternative Gift Giving" booth, and provided a hot potato bar. Children with coaster wagons delivered purchases to buyers' cars. Especially for the children have been

PUBLIC SALE
for WORLD RELIEF
SATURDAY, FEBRUARY 7th, 1948

The District Men's Work Council hereby announces that a Public Sale for Relief Purposes will be held all day Saturday, February 7, 1948, beginning at 10:30 o'clock at Root's Auction, located between East Petersburg and Manheim, ½ mile west of Route 72.

The purpose is to raise money for relief in foreign countries. All proceeds will be transmitted to the General Brotherhood Board, Church of the Brethren, Elgin, Illinois.

Elder R. P. Bucher, of Quarryville, Pa., will have the invocation and state the purpose of the sale.

Food will be served by the following Churches: MECHANICS GROVE, CONESTOGA, EAST FAIRVIEW, EPHRATA, LITTLE SWATARA and EAST PETERSBURG.

200 Cakes and Pies will be sold by Women's Work and Ladies' Aid. Hand-made articles (quilts, aprons, crocheted pieces, etc.).

Council of Men's Work wishes that more donations of money and merchandise be given. HELP MEET THE FOREIGN RELIEF NEEDS.

Signed, JOE W. KETTERING, President   M. ALEXANDER GLASMIRE, Vice-President
WILLIS S. NOLT, Secretary-Treasurer   GUY SAYLOR   ROBERT S. YOUNG

Livestock

One Beef Heifer; 575-lb. Bull; 1 Registered Holstein Bull (3 wks. old); 4 Holstein Heifers; Pigs; Ducks; Chickens.

Household Goods

New and Used Breakfast Sets; Used Living Room Suite; Walnut Table; Rocking Chairs; 2 Wardrobes; Baby Stroller; NEW PHILCO RADIO; Dishes; Pictures; 4-Burner Oil Stove with Oven; Iron Bed with Spring; "Bengal Queen" KITCHEN RANGE; Large Size HEATROLA; 2-piece PARLOR SUITE; Kitchen Cabinet; and many other items not mentioned.

Farming Implements

SEVERAL TRUCK LOADS OF FARM IMPLEMENTS

Farm Trailer; Farm Wagon; One No. 71 Eight Row John Deere Tractor (New); Mounted Duster for A. B. or H Tractor; Plant Jr. Riding Cultivator; McCormick-Deering Riding Cultivator with Fertilizer Attachment; Steam Cleaner; Ground Roller; One No. 32 John Deere Disc Harrow; 25 Gallon Ready Mixed Red Paint; 50 Gallon Black Roof Paint; 2 New Garden Seeders; 1 Garden Cart; 1 Buggy; Horse Cultivators; Harness.

2 TONS BRAN AND WHEAT   HAY AND STRAW

Miscellaneous Items

60 Pieces of Lebanon Bologna and Baum's Home-Made Bologna; Flour; Potatoes; Apples; QUARTER OF BEEF.
CANNED GOODS AND MEATS

Pocket Calculator; 12 Diamond Point Hoes; Range Shelter; Butcher Furnace; Butchering Tools; Copper Kettle, etc.
NEW AUTO TIRES, Size 6:00 x 16

TERMS CASH: All items must be removed on the day of sale. Bring all merchandise to sale grounds Friday, February 6th, or Saturday morning February 7th, before 10.00 A. M.

Conditions of sale will be made known by S. CLYDE WEAVER — Telephone Lancaster 7469.

Auctioneers: HENRY SNAVELY   Clerks: JACOB RUHL
PAUL SANGER   ALLEN MILLER   M. D. HERTZLER   JEROME BRUBAKER
ELMER SPAHR   GEO. H. BOWERS   H. F. KING   JOE W. KETTERING

ITEMS FOR RELIEF SALE—Notify Men's Work Officers of Your Church.
$510.00 in Cash has been donated by one Congregation apart from items for sale.

pony rides, a petting zoo, face painting, and even, for several years, a special Children's Sale. With 5,000 to nearly 10,000 attending, it is obvious that persons of all ages enjoy coming together.

Jake Ruhl sells a quilt in the early 1980s surrounded by left to right: Randy Kline, Jay Witman, and Harvey Weik on the right. Note that Jay Witman is already wearing his white suit.

The first motto for the Auction was very simple, yet meaningful. It was, "Coming Together for a Purpose." It soon seemed important to add "Brethren" at the beginning. By 1984, in order to define the purpose more clearly, the important clause was added, "To Bring Honor and Glory to God." Even in the hilarity of an Auction, there are frequent interruptions of the sale for hymn singing, prayer, and worship. Funds for relief is a driving force, but consistently recognized as a *secondary* purpose.

Still another mark of the Auction is the openness of the committee to change and innovation. Publicity in early days came through announcements to congregations, newspaper and radio announcements and, later, even a Willard Scott television recognition. Volunteer coordinators were each assigned a group of congregations. Small brochures, four–to–eight-page folders, were distributed at the sale, listing quilts which had been contributed, giving information about sale sites and food availability, and listing the names of contributors. The first sale booklet appeared in 1987. Doubled since then to tabloid size, the booklet pays for itself through advertisements and provides not only all the basic information about the Auction itself, but a variety of articles lifting up Christ and Christian service.

At first the Auction was a one-day event. As interest grew, it became necessary to hold two, three, or even more simultaneous auctions, and the number of auctioneers grew from two to eighteen or more. One of the coordinators, Clair Kreider, observed that women, with their sewing and cooking skills, were the larger contributors. Wasn't there some way for men to be involved? There was. A heifer sale was instituted, at first on Friday evening. It grew to be both a heifer sale on Friday morning and a livestock sale (sheep, goats, pigs, horses, and llamas) that evening, and has added thousands of dollars to sale receipts.

In 1985, "Share-A-Meal" was added. Hosts/hostesses volunteer to serve a meal for a specific number of unnamed persons, who purchase meal tickets at the sale and become their surprise guests.

In 1986, the Farmer's Market began for the sale of a wide variety of donated fruits, vegetables, flowers and processed foods.

For a few years, beginning in 1987, there was a "Silent Auction" for the sale of a car, timeshares, services, and gift certificates.

In 1988, the popularity of Winross trucks was discovered, and they became a regular sale item as did, later on, especially prepared pottery, paintings and sports cards.

In 1989, two businessmen contributed $2,200 for Grow Money. Acceptors of the ten dollar envelopes agreed to use the money as an investment which would grow. It is estimated that the $2,200 has grown about a hundred-fold.

Since 1978, the SOPA District had provided relief by sharing in the canning of tons of meat. In 1989, they became full participants in the BDRA, thus adding to their long-time disaster work.

A Golf Tournament began in 1992, as did the occasional provision of ethnic foods—Korean and Hispanic.

In 1993, feeling a deep conviction that all Auction receipts should go for relief, with none for expenses, Jay M. Witman instituted a Fundraiser/Kickoff Dinner. Entirely Witman planned and financed, a dinner was served and entertainment provided for between 300 and 600 ticket holders in a huge 40-foot by 200-foot white tent on the Witman property. In 1998, the dinner moved to the Hempfield COB, and in 2000 to Yoder's Restaurant. The sale of tickets, together with an offering at the dinner and future income from the endowment promises to underwrite all Auction expenses. The Endowment Fund began in 1994 with contributions from one donor to-

taling $18,000. Later additions have brought it to about $426,000 to date.

In 1995, a cookbook was published, the result of two years of preparation. The same year the first house, for which planning had begun a year earlier, was completed and sold. A second house was built in southern PA and sold in 1997, and a third in 2000.

In 1999, the idea of Theme Baskets was introduced, and quickly took off. Baskets, anywhere from small flower baskets to waste baskets and market baskets, are filled with items pertaining to a particular theme, wrapped in clear cellophane, and auctioned.

What will be the new ideas? It doesn't matter, really. Disaster relief began with God, and these two PA districts of the COB continue to bring honor and glory to God and provide funds for disaster relief. That first year income was nearly $12,000. This year we will pass the seven million dollar mark. Aren't you grateful that God has let you be a part of it?   *(2001 SB, p.7)*

YOUTH LED THE WAY

Paul expresses this thought to his special friend, Timothy: *"Don't let anyone think little of you because you are young. Be their ideal; let them follow the way you teach and live; be a pattern for them in your love, your faith and your clean thoughts"* (1 Tim. 4:12, TLB)

And indeed the Brethren have been following and living the example that the young people of this District began with the first Auction held in the late 1960s. From the start, the vision and the excitement of the youth have greatly affected the consciousness-raising and

Sale announcement sign.

the financial contributions regarding Disaster Relief and global concerns.

Since the 1960s, the youth have remained a colorful element at the BDRA. They have been there sharing Christian joy as "Clowns for Christ," distributing helium-filled balloons to the children. They have enjoyed face painting, organizing special children's games and activities and have attempted making Funnel Cakes (which are a real art to master!). Most recently the youth… have encouraged more health-minded eating by bringing the first "Salad Bar" to the Auction.

As the willingness to come and serve remains a priority for many of our young people, 1988 will debut yet another new idea: "Alternative Gift Giving." The youth will sponsor a booth in which they plan to take monetary donations for the Auction benefit. As persons contribute an undesignated amount of money, they will receive a greeting card insert that will specify that the contributor has given a monetary gift to the Brethren Disaster Relief Pro-

gram. This insert can then be placed inside a Christmas, birthday, or other greeting card to give as a gift, i.e., the concept of "Alternative Gift Giving." Also new this year will be the "Hot Potato Bar" where baked potatoes will be served with a variety of toppings. Potatoes will be baked over an open grill.

(Janice L. Kensinger, ANE Assoc.
for Youth Ministries. 1988 SB, p. 48)

❖   ❖   ❖

In its 15th year, the BDRA was described like this:

Faithful to the Vision 1977-992

Who can say just when and how
the seed was planted years ago
In the minds and hearts of several
who couldn't say "No?"
At first, it was only a passing thought
every now and then,
But before long the three 'J's
were wondering how and when.

The little seed began to grow and grow
until it was flourishing.
A new vision was born for our District,
now it needed nourishing.
It was early 1977 when plans were made,
and the news was given:
We're having an Auction to help others
have a better living.

Committees were formed,
and congregations joined in the cause.
Many hours of "love" labor were given,

there was no time to pause.
Church members, young and old,
volunteered to be part of the team,
Making it possible all these years since
to fulfill the dream.

Each year something new is added
to the variety for all to see,
Requiring several tents to be raised
to accommodate you and me.
The Auction's theme is the focus
of all that's done each year:
To bring honor and glory to God
is clearly stated for all to hear.

Arts and crafts are everywhere,
beautifully made with you in mind.
As you walk through the areas,
beware of all you will find.
Look for a Farmer's Market
where fresh veggies are yours to buy.
There's every kind of food to eat,
why not give them all a try?

Soups, sandwiches, sodas, French fries,
popcorn and candy,
Apple dumplings, ice cream,
milkshakes and pies quite dandy,
Ethnic foods are sure to please,
and so is the homemade bread,
Weighing in the next morning
is something each of us dread.

In 1984 we added the Friday evening
Livestock Auction.
Anyone attending this event knows
it is full of action.
Bidding moves quickly,
and everyone joins in the fun

When cattle are resold a second time,
the money is on the run.

Everyone delights to see the lovely quilts
each year at the sale.
They add so much excitement
and dollar value without fail.
But even more, they represent
many hours of love given freely
By the women in our congregations,
may God bless them dearly.

As the vision grew, we distributed
"grow money" by tens to many.
We rejoice in the ways God has multiplied
these funds into plenty.
Southern District joined us in '89;
we're glad for the addition.
Helping hands have always been part
of our Brethren tradition.

The most important aspect must never be
forgotten by any of us:
As the vision continues to grow,
prayer and commitment are a must.
May we always keep in mind
the great abundance we have known
As we share with others less fortunate,
God's love will be shown.

All praise to God who touches the lives
of all who share
Of their time, talents and monetary gifts
as we say, "We care."
How wonderful it is to unite
in harmonious voices that day
As we sing, "How Great Thou Art."
What more is there to say?
(By S. Joan Hershey. 1992 SB, p. 6)

❖ ❖ ❖

B. BRIEF HISTORY OF THE CHURCH OF THE BRETHREN (COB)

The BDRA is sponsored by the Church of the Brethren denomination. Who are these Brethren, how did they get started, and what do they believe?

The Church of the Brethren was organized in 1708 in Schwarzenau, Germany. With roots in Protestantism, Anabaptism and Pietism, its founder was Alexander Mack. He and seven others, including three women, were baptized by trine immersion in the Eder River in Schwarzenau. Dedicated to a restoration of primitive, biblical Christianity and embracing a Believer's Church tradition, they were non-creedal and accepted the New Testament as their rule of faith and practice.

In addition to their mode of believer's baptism, (of triple, forward-facing immersion for which they were often nicknamed "Dunkers"), they observed the Love Feast, feet washing, the Lord's Supper and Holy Communion. Practicing anointing with oil for healing, they did not participate in war, taking an oath, or resorting to law to settle their disputes. As advocates of a simple, biblical life style, they were considered to be dissenters and were persecuted by the established churches of that day and by the government. When Alexander Mack, the founder of the Church, was asked as to how the Brethren were to be known, he replied, "By their manner of living."

In spite of adversity, the Church grew. After twenty-four years in Europe, the entire movement came to America. In 1719, Peter Becker led a group of about twenty families to Germantown, PA. In 1729, Alexander Mack, Sr., brought a second group to join them. In 1732, John Naas came with a third group to Amwell, N.J. Thus, the Church of the Brethren, (so called since 1908), became an American church.

The mother church in America was at Germantown and was organized on Christmas Day, 1723, with 23 members. On that same day, in the Wissahickon Creek, the first baptismal service by trine immersion was held, followed by a Love Feast.

By the end of 1724, two more congregations were organized, at Pottstown (now called Coventry), and Leola (now known as Conestoga). The movement spread to MD, VA, the Carolinas and westward through OH, IN, IL, and ultimately as far west as CA. The heaviest concentrations of Brethren today are in PA, MD, VA, OH, IN, and Nigeria. The present U.S. membership[3] is about 142,000 in 1,100 congregations in 36 states with mission projects around the world and the church headquarters located in Elgin, IL.

The church has either ownership or affiliation with these six educational institutions: Elizabethtown College and Juniata College, both in PA, Manchester College in IN, McPherson College in KS, Bridgewater College in VA, and Laverne University in CA. The seminary for the church is Bethany Theological Seminary in Richmond, IN.

---

[3] Membership in the COB in the U.S. in 2008 was 124,408 worshipping in 999 congregations and 50 fellowships. The average Sunday worship attendance was 59,084. Figures are from the COB Newsline, June 3, 2009. For more information, check http://www.brethren.org/ In contrast, the Nigerian church membership in 2008 was 180,000 with 300,000 attending the weekly worship services.

As one of the three historic peace churches, along with the Friends (Quakers) and Mennonites, Brethren have consistently held an official peace witness, often expressed in conscientious objection to military service. Growing out of their peace concerns have been worldwide programs of relief and reconstruction to those suffering from war, natural catastrophe and social disadvantage. Persons of all ages have participated in Brethren Volunteer Service (BVS), working without pay for one or two years in a variety of useful assignments. Heifer Project International and CROP are other agencies initiated by Brethren.

More information about the Church of the Brethren history, activities, and churches is available on the website: www.cob-net.org

*(Excerpted from articles by the late
Carl W. Zeigler, Sr. in the 1988 SB, p. 53
and the late Donald F. Durnbaugh
in the 1991 SB, p. 38 and 1989 SB, p. 34)*

❖ ❖ ❖

C. WHEN DID THE CHURCH OF THE BRETHREN BEGIN THEIR DISASTER RESPONSE PROGRAM?

Responding to the needs of others began with the founders of our denomination. Alexander Mack, a wealthy miller, the leader and founder of the church, is believed to have died a poor man because of the assistance he gave to refugees who were driven across the Atlantic from Europe because of their religious views. Likewise, Christopher Sauer, another early member, helped the new immigrants by purchasing herbs and medicines to promote their

healing as well as hosting many of them in his own home until they had recuperated from their journey and found housing.

Following the Civil War, Brethren churches in the North raised monies to be sent to needy persons in the South. In doing so, a principle was established that the funds were to be used to aid *all* persons, not just Brethren church members, and that policy continues today.

Early disaster responses were frequently on a person-to-person basis such as when Brethren helped a neighboring farmer to rebuild a burned-down barn or a storm-damaged house. In 1917, collections at local levels were approved "for relief of those unfortunate sufferers," referring to the needs of the Armenians.

In 1919, after an inspection trip in the Near East, Elder J. E. Miller reported, "We could do a wonderful work in a humanitarian way here. It would be doing what no other organization has attempted to do." The project included the support of orphanages and schools, and the reconstruction of vineyards, gardens, buildings and homes. After setting a goal of $250,000, the Brethren raised $267,265 that year to meet the needs of the Armenians and Syrians.

In 1937, Quakers, Mennonites and Brethren sent persons to minister to human needs on *both sides* of the conflict in the Spanish Civil War. In 1941, at the Annual Conference in La-Verne, Calif., a Committee on Peace and Relief was formed, which later became known as the Brethren Service Commission.

From 1942-44, the COB spent nearly $2 million in Civilian Public Service (CPS) camps where young men worked as firefighters, dairy testers, human guinea pigs in starvation experiments, and many other hospital and community development programs.

In 1946, the United Nations Relief and Rehabilitation Administration (UNRRA) asked that the COB assist them in work in China. Fifty young men were sent by the COB to China in a tractor unit to replace draft animals destroyed during the war and to train 1,000 Chinese to use the tractors, plowing over 66,000 acres in one year. This same year, HPI sent "sea-going cowboys" with animals to Europe and China, and material relief was shipped to European World War II survivors.

By 1948, international work camps began and Brethren Volunteer Service (BVS) was approved by Annual Conference in Denver, Colo. This was followed by a youth exchange program with Germany and a Polish Agricultural exchange. In 1955, a BVS unit responded to flooding in Stroudsburg, PA, and a year later to Yuba City, CA, following a Christmas Eve flooding there. During the next decade, work crews were sent to aid in flooding in Shelbiana, KY, Miami Shores, OH, and Peru, IN.

An Emergency Disaster Fund was established in 1960 to provide funds immediately for crises around the world. Consequently, the Brethren went to help when Hurricane Camille hit MS, CA had an earthquake, Hurricane Agnes damaged PA and MD in 1972, when a tornado struck in Zenia, OH, and Monticello, IN, and after the 1977 floods in Pineville, KY, and Johnstown, PA.

Jan Thompson was appointed as the first full-time Director of Disaster Response Services in 1978, and two years later the Disaster Child Care program was established.

Because disasters happen sporadically, the needs are greater some years than others. People also do not give consistently, so sometimes there are not sufficient funds to meet the needs. For these reasons, wide variations exist from one year to another. For example, in the decade of the 1980's, *expenditures* from the COB Emergency Disaster Fund toward aid internationally and locally totaled these amounts:

1980 – $389,313	1986 – $453,616
1981 – $234,437	1987 – $134,028
1982 – $213,180	1988 – $394,000
1983 – $231,408	1989 – $218,000
1984 – $428,371	1990 – $525,300
1985 – $718,974	

In the last three years for which the figures have been announced the amounts expended were: 2005—$1,468,500; 2006—$1,015,200; and 2007—$799,800. About one-third of the amount shared from the denomination's Disaster Response Funds has come from the proceeds earned at the BDRA sponsored by the ANE and SOPA.

The BDRA divides its earnings between the denomination's Disaster Funds, which are used primarily to help in national and international disaster situations and The United Relief Fund (TURF) which mainly serves needs within the two sponsoring districts. It will be discussed further in Chapter 11.

God's grace has the ability to renew and empower persons. Those who suffered from the sudden impact of a disaster experienced God's grace when they were assisted in some way through the disaster response ministry of the COB. Giving through the COB Emergency Disaster Fund has grown from $9,500 in 1962 to over $718,000 in 1985 and reached $1,468,500 in 2005. Only through the commitment, compassion and generosity of mem-

The secret of the success of BDRA: The early morning prayer meeting of the coordinator, auctioneers, and other workers. Begun during the term of Thom and Sue Keller, it has been an important tradition ever since.

bers of the COB has the growth of this ministry been possible.

At one of the BDRAs, after the noon pause in the auctioning for a short worship service, a couple with a New York accent were overheard asking one another, "Who are these Brethren – that they even *pray* at auctions?"

THE "BRETHREN LIFESTYLE"

Today Brethren have a slogan to describe their lifestyle: "Continuing the work of Jesus. Peacefully. Simply. Together." With Christ in their hearts, this should be true of them in their communities, in their churches, and within their families.

I have three simple rules for families which I first heard 77 years ago as a Sunday school kid in a tiny Brethren country church in the corn belt of Iowa:

1. "Christ is the Head of this house, the Unseen Guest at every meal, the Silent Listener to every conversation." He is The First to be addressed at the family table and to be thanked for whatever life brings. Every happening is a reason for thanksgiving when everything is recognized as a part of God's Plan.

2. Family and church endure when all else fails. I've seen banks fail and no money left. I've seen the nation under retreat in unprofitable Vietnams. I've seen society ignore human rights on matters of race, sex, national origin and religion. Yet the church does not surrender. In the Great Depression, one out of six banks failed; one out of twenty-two businesses went broke; one out of forty-four colleges closed their doors. But when you come to the churches, rich and poor, large and small, rural and urban, only one out of 2,344 churches surrendered. The church is not a manmade institution. The church has Jesus Christ as the Head.

   Likewise, a family with Christ as the Head of the home holds firm. Families change. Risk is inherent in every pattern of human relationships. Yet when Christ is The Way, human desires take their rightful place.

3. Each family is responsible for its own expectations, successes and failures. Successful families find happiness in similar ways. Every unsuccessful family is miserable in its own way. Every family chooses its way and charts its path.

   (Inez Long in 1995 SB, p. 23)

❖ ❖ ❖

WE ARE THE BRETHREN

We are the Brethren
who hate any waste.
We have been taught to clean our plate.
To "outen" the light and save the difference
So our children have a deposit
on their inheritance.

We are the Brethren
who know You came
From immeasurable wealth
to unspeakable pain.
Loving us beyond reason,
Your Body lay bleeding,
How can we fathom such deliberate abandon?

We are the Brethren,
redeemed with this blood-price.
What have I wasted, Lord,
without thinking twice?
Vigorous youth spent pursuing
hobbies of self-interest.
Great fun while it lasted
but now I've lost focus.

We are the Brethren,
not proud to admit
Those precious minutes for gossip
have taken their toll.
The time that is missing is less than the waste
Of the Father's rich blessing,
such infinite grace.

We are the Brethren
who know how to value our first dollar,
An honest day's work, lifelong friendships.
May we be Your Brethren, Lord, able to view

our neighbor the way You see him.
A person for whose soul
You have paid the ultimate price,
Remembering that the supreme waste
is that of my neighbor's soul.
*(By Jeanne Pepper, Chiques COB,
in the 2006 SB, p. 63)*

Note: Jeanne Pepper, 50, was killed in an automobile accident on February 18, 2009. An LPN, after serving with her husband for two years of volunteer service with Brethren in Christ Missions, she completed training as a registered nurse. Her desire to make a difference by serving and helping others is evident in her places of employment: Women's and Babies Hospital, Renal Dialysis nurse at the Lancaster Health Campus, and volunteering with Domestic Violence Services of Lancaster County. She was formerly active in the Florin COB and the Chiques COB, where she sang in the choir and taught Vacation Bible School classes.

❖ ❖ ❖

"HOW CAN YOU TELL IF THEY'RE BRETHREN?"

By Jean Moyer

"So you're Church of the Brethren?" said the friendly van driver who was taking several of us from the O'Hare Airport in Chicago to a meeting at the Church General Offices in Elgin. "I have an interest in the different churches. Tell me about your founder."

I had written some "Brethren History Raps" for the children's activities at the Annual Conference in Richmond, VA, and even though I felt a bit embarrassed, I just couldn't resist:

*"Well, I'm gonna tell you about a man
named Mack.
If you think it's Alexander, then you're on
the right track! ..."*

By the time I got to the closing lines of:

*"So in 1708 they went down to the river,
Where they all were baptized with nary a
shiver,
For the love in their hearts was keeping
'em warm,
And that's how the Church of the Brethren
was born."*

I wasn't sure whether the van driver was enlightened or sorry that he had ever asked the question! I thought of the simple, direct answer this same Alexander Mack gave when a neighbor inquired, "And how shall your members be recognized?" Mack's reply was terse and profound: "By the manner of their living." Now *there's* a reply that was remembered!

In 1958, Moderator Desmond Bittinger addressed Annual Conference[4] on the 250th anniversary of the founding of the Church of the Brethren. In his address, *And How Shall the Brethren Be Recognized?*, he gave three distinguishing marks of the Brethren for the next century and "the long future."

1. The Open Mind and The Open Bible

Brethren have always gathered around the open Bible, seeking truth as revealed to them from its pages. "Give me an open mind to learn Your will" is the prayer that is suggested to be a major contribution of the Brethren to

---

[4] Source of quotes from Desmond Bittinger: *And How Shall the Brethren Be Recognized?* by Desmond Bittinger, Brethren Press.

the Church and the world. This doctrine of the open mind and heart shows that we are to be seekers of God's will, even to the point of not writing a creed. Mack wanted the Brethren to have yearning minds, forever searching for the will of Christ. The ordinances of the Love Feast were to be a means of growth and grace as they were faithfully practiced.

2. The Loving Heart

The desire of Christians must be to love God with their whole heart and their neighbor as themselves. Jesus the Christ gave us the best definition ever given of our Creator: "God is love."

Bittinger speaks of the Brethren, indeed, all Christians, as those who are completely baptized—immersed in love. *"Love seeks not its own. Love goes the second mile. Love knows no stranger or enemy. Love will lay down its life for another. The simple life is always centered on love. 'For God so loved the world that He gave His only Son,' One who in turn gave His life because He loved."*

3. Serving Hands

We must be more than just "good people in a good community." Brethren must be sacrificing, self-forgetting people who seek to learn new truth, to share that truth, and to bring others into a growing relationship with God. Brethren must be those who bind up wounds, who are known as peacemakers in a world of conflict.

John Kline, whose bicentennial we celebrate this year, ministered to both sides in the Civil War and lost his life because of this ministry. We, too, must love enough to be willing to suffer.

Dan West, the COB founder of Heifer Project International, found a way to bring milk to hungry children and help to hungry families all over the world.

Multitudes of Brethren through the years, from those who put their offerings in the poor box at the first church in Germantown, PA, to those who donate time, talents and treasure to help the suffering through the BDRA and in so many other ways, reach out with their serving hands so that the peace and justice of God may come to us all.

The "Celebration Rap" taught to the children at the Richmond Conference is one in which I tried to include those responses from our heritage as to who we are as Brethren.

"Our history's great … let's celebrate –
The people and the places, the voices and the faces,
The sisters and the brothers, and all the faithful
others.
They had no creed; there was no need.
They sought to follow Christ in word and deed.
And when people asked the founder, Alexander Mack,
'How will your church be known?'
He thought awhile, and then he answered back
With a smile and a face that shone:
'You'll know the Brethren by the manner of their living:
The depth of their loving, the joy in their giving.
The open Book…The open mind,
The loving heart…The serving hands.
We want to pray and seek and find
And do all that our Lord commands.'
So, come, all you Dunkers, and join in the song.
We'll sing it together, and we'll sing it strong!
We'll live our lives as Jesus said we should:
'For the Glory of God and Our Neighbor's Good!'"
(1997 SB, p. 39)

D. WHAT IS THE BDRA LIKE TODAY?

On the fourth weekend in September, the ANE and the SOPA District of the COB,

A typical scene in the main auction hall today.

representing a combined total of 130 churches, sponsor an annual BDRA at the Lebanon, PA, County Fairgrounds. Attended by 7,000 people in 2008 and run entirely by volunteers, this auction is one of the largest disaster relief fund-raising efforts in the United States. Some church leaders claim that this is the largest annual gathering of Brethren except for their Annual Conference, a national five-day gathering for denominational business and worship.

At the hub of activity, the main auction room is where quilts, hand-crafted wooden items, pottery, baskets and other prized items are sold, but there can be as high as five auctions operating at the same time with nearly 1800 bidders! In surrounding buildings and tents, are the livestock sale barns, craft displays, theme baskets, food vendors, baked goods and farmer's market. Workers gather on Saturday morning in one building to assemble Gift-of-the-Heart kits and pack them in boxes ready for transport. A special Children's Auction, for ages 5 to 12, is held, and children also are entertained by clowns, face painters, and sometimes a petting zoo.

Although it is a busy and fun day, all are gathered on this day *for a purpose*, and that is, first of all, to give honor and glory to God. He is the One who brought everyone together, who directed the making of each sale item, who inspired the innovative ideas displayed here to raise funds, who instilled in each worker the love and compassion for others who have been struck with some natural or manmade disaster. Consequently, it is not unusual to have the auction stopped now and then so everyone can sing a hymn, have a prayer, or to hear an inspirational story about an object about to be sold. Whatever role one has as a buyer, auctioneer, cook, creator of an item, cleaning person, kit-assembler, etc., one can leave the BDRA with a feeling of having done *something* to spread the love of Christ, to show His love to others who are less fortunate—and that is a *good feeling*!

When I talked to a couple youth who have been involved with the Disaster Relief Auction, this is what they had to say:

"What I like about the auction is that anybody can get involved. It feels good to raise money that will go to specific places, and I didn't have to make a quilt or buy a cow. Everyone can contribute!" (Genee Martin).

"Last year [1989] it was neat to see people not deterred by the weather. It gave the youth a chance to hear the story of how the auction has grown and to be part of the idea of the act of giving to those who have a specific need" (Chris Dubble).

(Jim Chinworth,
ANE District Youth Advisor. 1990 SB, p. 39)

"People attending the BDRA enjoy being there. They meet old friends, and they're glad to share and happy to give! They go home at the end of the day—having eaten too much!"

(Jim Myer)

CHAPTER FOUR

God's Work Takes Teamwork!

"God never asks about our ability or our inability —
just our availability." (Unknown)

T O HAVE A successful BDRA requires the cooperation of many hearts, minds, and hands. Recognizing this, Mark and Marty Hershey, Coordinators for the fifth year of the BDRA wrote these words to their committee: "It is very difficult to be specific in expressing our appreciation to all of you and your families. All of you have done an excellent job. You are all very responsible and committed people. Many times you worked without thanks, but your work has not gone unnoticed. Many individuals will benefit because of your efforts. Therefore, what you have done has not been done in vain, and the many hard hours you worked will bring relief and hope to some persons in despair." *(2001 SB, p. 5)*

In the 25th year of the BDRA, the SB was dedicated to this diversity of persons who have worked together to make the Auction a success. On the dedication page, they are described as: "Those whose dreams and plans bore fruit, those who came up with new and exciting ideas, those who set up the facilities, those who held onto tent ropes and poles to prevent hurricane ravage, those who baked pies, bread or sticky buns, those who contributed heifers, produce, or saleable articles, those who spent hours sewing quilts, those who shouted, "What am I bid for …," those who advertised, those whose arts and crafts attracted persons and increased auction income, those who "shared a meal," and those who made bids and/or bought items." *(2001 SB, p. 5)*

On the 33rd Anniversary of the BDRA in 2009, we are still appreciative of this diverse group of people who have all worked so hard, so capably and so faithfully, giving all honor and glory to God.

Below is a partial listing of the multiple tasks that must be done, and we have probably (unintentionally) missed some.

Advertisers
Ambulance/Medical
    Staff
ANE COB Churches
Apple Dumpling Makers
Article Writers
Artists
Auctioneers
Bakers
Bidders
Candy Sellers
Carpenters
Cashiers
Child Care Workers
Clean-up Crew
Clerks
Clowns
Collectors of Change
Committee Members
Contractors
Coordinators
Crafts Persons
Dinner Planners,
    Preparers, Attendees
Directors

Disaster Response
    Workers
Distributors
Donut Makers
Editorial Staff
Electricians
Endowment Fund
    Contributors
Face Painters
Food Preparers
Garbage Collectors
Gift of the Heart Kit
    Assemblers
Golf Organizers
Grow-Money Providers
Grow-Money Users
Heifer/Livestock Buyers
    & Donators
Information Desk Staff
Lebanon Expo Staff
Musicians & Directors
Pedigree Authorities
Photographers
Planning Committees
Pop Corn Gang

Prayer Partners
Printers
Produce Growers &
    Sales Persons
Purchasers
Quilters & Preparers
Runners
SB Editors & Staff
Set-up Crew
Share-A-Meal Hosts &
    Buyers
Soft Pretzel Makers
Sound Crew
SOPA COB Churches
Tent Crews
Theme Basketeers
Toilet Cleaning Crew
Traffic Patrol
Trash Removers
Treasurer
Vegetable Canners
Volunteers
Woodworkers
Worship Leaders
Zoo Keepers

"Coming together is a beginning;
Keeping together is progress;
Working together is success."

- Henry Ford

Some of the fundraising ideas, persons who made them work and stories they've shared are listed in this chapter and the next four chapters in 26 alphabetical sections. As you read about them, remember this statement: *"Ordinary persons, touched by God, become people of power…and that's how the church grows." (Charles Bieber 1997 SB, p. 34).* It is also how the BDRA has grown to what it is today.

A. Alabaster Gifts

In the Gospels (Matthew 26:6-10, Mark 14:3-6, Luke 7:36-38, John 11:2, 12:3-8) we read that Jesus was anointed with a very expensive and fragrant ointment that was carried in an alabaster container. As a way of showing one's devotion, appreciation and love, this gift went *beyond the ordinary.*

Begun in 2005, the Alabaster Gifts auction features out-of-the-ordinary, antique and specialty donations. Since the BDRA receives a variety of unusual items each year, to keep them from becoming mundane in the crush of items being sold, they are now featured in the Alabaster Gift auction. To illustrate the type and variety of articles, note these that were sold—some before and some since the Alabaster Gifts auction was started:

• Banjo made by 78-year-old Stanley Byrd Brooks, "The Banjo Man of Jefferson, NC." With only a 6th grade education, Stanley had only one trade in his life, which was carpentry. By 1992, he had built 40 top-quality hand-

crafted banjos and included his name, date and number inside each one.

(1992 SB, p. 28)

• In 2006, the BDRA sold a set of seven wooden plaques depicting 3-dimensional golf plays. Each had a name: "Lofty Drive," "Golfer," "Bank Shot," "Chippin' In," "The 18th Hole," "In the Bunker," and "Going for Birdie." The characters were made of Finnish Baltic Birch wood from Finland and were scrolled out on a Hawk Scroll saw under a magnifying glass with light. Their creator, Merlin Gnegy, said, "I enjoyed making these plaques of golf scenes for the BDRA. To the best of my knowledge, these are one of a kind and will not be found anywhere else."   *(2006 SB, pp. 34, 35)*

(Today, Merlin, a retired farmer and member of the Sipesville COB, still enjoys woodworking and scrolling. He married Mildred Ziegler Hartzell in 2008 and together they enjoy leaving the cold weather at their home in Somerset, PA, and spending the months of November to April in Bradenton, FL)

• "Hail to the Chief" was a wall hanging donated for the 2002 BDRA. Velma Carter from the Ambler COB transferred 42 Presidential portraits from a calendar onto a 46 ½" x36 ½" navy colored cloth with tiny white stars and bound it in red. With each President were the dates of his Presidency. Grover Cleveland, who served twice, was shown once, and the

Jay Witman selling a 1923 Essex coach at the special auction in Center Hall in 2004. The selling price was $13,000.

wall hanging included George W. Bush as 43rd President. Although Velma created and donated the quilt, it was stitched and quilted by Verna Hoffmaster.   *(2002 SB, p. 35)*

❖ ❖ ❖

• A Black Granite Gravestone, 30" wide and 22" high, was presented by Weaver Memorials, New Holland, for the 2002 BDRA.

An airplane flight for four people to Ocean City, NJ for dinner was sold in 2005.

❖ ❖ ❖

• Vacation time at "The Last Resort," a vacation home in Millsboro, Del., was sold at the Alabaster sale at the 2005 and the 2007 BDRA. The home is a three-bedroom, two-bathroom rancher and contains two queen-sized beds, two single beds, and a living room sofa that opens up into a queen-sized bed.

Roots Nursery, Inc., Manheim, has donated a beautiful tree every year.

• Hand-forged "Goat Horn" iron hinges (and the boards on which they were mounted), having been removed from a barn near Akron, were sold at the 2005 BDRA. Built in the early 1700s, this barn was the place where the early COB Council Meeting was held on September 29, 1734, in which Conrad Beissel separated from the church. In the book, *History of the COB, Eastern PA,* it's written that at this Council Meeting, a rail was placed on the floor of the barn. All who wished to join Beissel were told to step to the left side, and all who wished to keep their loyalty to Michael Frantz stepped to the right. Shortly thereafter, Beissel led his group to Ephrata where they established their new church at the Cloisters.

• A twelve-foot-long pew, made circa 1915, was removed from the sanctuary of the Germantown COB in 1966 and donated to the BDRA in 2002 by Jim Gibbel, Lititz COB.

• On the 30th Anniversary of the BDRA in 2006, Patrick and David Kline, the Heirloom weavers from Red Lion, PA, donated 30 woven and dated children's coverlets to the Auction to be sold.

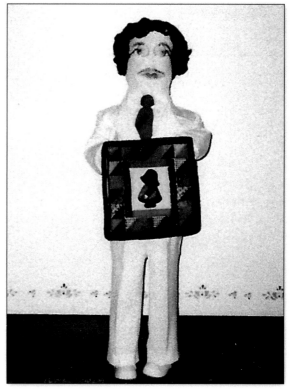

This Jay Witman look-alike doll made by Ethel Meck from the Lampeter COB sold for $500 in 1998.

• Lennox vases, R.S. Prussia China, Moravian Stars, a Ned and Gwen Foltz birdhouse and other Foltz pottery, Steve de Perrot pottery, J. Beaumont pottery, John Deere Farm Equipment, Extension tables with up to 12 boards, a Steinway piano, trees from Root's Nurseries, and even cars have been donated.

❖ ❖ ❖

• "One day in 1998, while I was making "Time-Out Dolls," I got a crazy idea which I later shared with a quilting friend in my church, Betty Kreider. "What if I would make a doll that looked like Jay Witman and donate it to the BDRA? And if I made it, who could draw the face?"

Betty encouraged me to try and suggested that I ask her daughter-in-law, Kay Kreider, to create the face. Kay agreed to help me.

So, I got to work and made a doll. Then I headed to the Good Will store and got white shoes, a white suit, shirt, wig, and tie. We had fun dressing him and taking him to the BDRA.

After active bidding on him, he was sold for $500 to my pastor, Earl Ziegler, who immediately presented the doll to his look-alike, Jay Witman. Next I was called to the platform and Jay gave me a big thank-you hug.

(By the way, he was wearing his white suit!")

(Ethel Meck, Lampeter COB)

B. Artists

The BDRA has been blessed with outstanding artists who have donated original works and prints which contributed greatly to the cause. You can get better acquainted with a few of them here:

1. ELSIE BEILER

Elsie Beiler was born in Lancaster County, PA, and has lived near Paradise since she was four years old. Enjoying art as a child, she created colorful pictures with chalk, her first medium. At the age of 13, she was given a set of oil paints. During her teen years and as a young mother, she dabbled at it and enjoyed doing creative things when she could, but she never really got serious about it.

When her children got older, she wanted another artist to do a painting of their little

Elsie Beiler and her painting of "Grace and Forgiveness" which sold for $7,600 at the 2008 Auction.

farmette and their sheep, but she couldn't describe in words what she really wanted him to do. One day her oldest daughter suggested, "Why don't you just do it yourself, Mom?"

So, at age 58, she got out her paints and brushes and began working, beginning with flower gardens, seascapes and scenes from their small sheep farm. Her only art classes had been in elementary school. In the eight years since then, she has studied books and watched art teachers on television and feels she has learned much from them. She still has not taken the time to go and get formal lessons.

Both she and her husband, Paul, had parents who grew up in Amish families but never joined the Amish church, choosing instead to be Amish/Mennonite. After she and Paul were married, they joined the Bart Mennonite Church, and now attend the Timberline Mennonite Church, a fairly new church plant also in the southern end of Lancaster County. Today the Beilers have five children and 11 grandchildren.

When the tragedy of the killing of five little girls at the Nickel Mines Amish school occurred on October 2, 2006, Elsie was deeply affected. Since she lived in that community, she knew right away that she wanted to do a painting of the school as she remembered it when she would drive by and see the children outside. She wanted to show the children playing happily the simple games they enjoyed so much. She explains, "Prayers and tears mixed with my paints as I worked with pencil and brush in hand. The parents and extended families of these dear children were heavy on my heart, along with all the courageous men and women who responded in so many ways to their emergency."

She started it about two months after the tragedy. After the old schoolhouse was torn down, she felt she wanted people to remember something beautiful about it. She called the painting, *"Happier Days,"* and says, "When I painted it, I thought that because the news of the tragedy spread around the world, perhaps tourists to Lancaster County might have an interest in this scene. After it was finished, I took it to the printer and we had maybe twelve copies made. We also made some small ones, perhaps 200 of those. I just had no idea that it would have anything to do with the healing of people, you know, with their emotional healing, and it's just been an awesome thing to watch. It's definitely been a 'God-thing,' and we've been inspired by all the people we've met and the experiences we've had. It's been such a gift."

Elsie continues, "When we took one of the first prints as a gift to Emma, the teacher, I said, 'Here it is; you don't have to take it if you don't even want to look at it. We just want you to have it if you care to have one.' But, you know, she was so delighted with it. She took it and said, 'I can give each of those kids a name.' I was amazed. Although I had made sure I had the right number of students on the picture, I didn't know the children personally."

Apparently, Emma liked the print so well that she wanted to make sure each of the Amish families had one. Elsie hesitated, but Emma assured her that they would be very interested. After they had received their print, the families asked for one to take to their friends, the officers at the Lancaster police barracks. The policemen were so delighted with this gift from the Amish that they put it on the news, and that's how people found out about the painting, "*Happier Days.*" Then Elsie had to request her printer to make more copies!

"*Friends Forever*" was her second painting in the Nickel Mines series. It wasn't reported in the news, but Elsie says ten girls were injured that day. Five survived and five died. Ten policemen responded to the call for help, and each policeman took care of a little girl until the medics and ambulances arrived. Since then, for their own healing, each officer has become a friend of the family of the little girl he had taken care of, visiting back and forth and going on picnics together. The Amish take cookies and other goodies to "their" officer at the barracks. As Elsie marveled at these new friendships as well as the special bond of love that existed between these little girls and their mothers, she also thought about the friendship that existed between the girls themselves, playing together, walking to school together, going to church together, learning together, singing together, being terrified together and in the case of five of them, dying together. From those thoughts, the title, "*Friends Forever,*" came to be.

Whenever she paints a scenic picture, Elsie likes to add birds and always paints in an odd number of them, feeling it looks better for balance. Although it is a popular interpretation, she confesses that when she placed five birds in flight above the school, she did not intend for them to represent the departing souls of the five who died.

Since the Amish do not approve of photography showing recognizable facial features, (citing the second commandment: "*Thou shalt not make unto thee any graven image, or any likeness of anything that is in heaven above, or that is in the earth beneath, or that is in the water under the earth*" *Exodus 20:4 KJV*), Elsie was

concerned about how they would feel about this picture. However, most found it acceptable because it wasn't a photograph and faces were not shown. In the light of the tragedy, some did object because it depicted little girls, but most have given her strong support in her art work.

At the BDRA in 2007, the original painting of "*Friends Forever*" was sold twice bringing a combined total of $10,100.

The third painting in this series is entitled, "*A New Day,*" and shows the newly built school surrounded again by playing children. The original of Elsie's fourth and final painting in her Nickel Mines series, showing a grieving Amish couple, was sold twice at the 2008 BDRA for a combined total of $7,600. Entitled, "*Grace and Forgiveness,*" Elsie says, "This painting speaks for itself as it shows God's grace shining on us in a difficult time, and we all have those times when we need and experience His grace."

Elsie doesn't paint every day, but when she does, it is usually for about three hours in the morning. Each of the paintings in this series took about thirty hours. However, she declares she is finished with this series, and is now eager to branch out into larger paintings, florals and landscapes. Helping children, especially her grandchildren, discover their creative abilities with pencil, crayons, or paint and brush, and teaching art classes for those being home schooled are some of her recent challenges.

Meanwhile, she also sells copies of her paintings that *look like* originals, but are in fact called giclee (pronounced ja-clay) prints and obtainable on either paper or on canvas.

Although she was familiar with the COB, Elsie had not heard about the BDRA until a committee from the Board visited her one evening. "*Happier Days*" had come out and was proving to be quite popular, and the committee explained that they would like her to paint something else associated with the Nickel Mines tragedy for the 2007 Auction. That's when the idea of doing a series was born, and she began working on "*Friends Forever.*" She said she was impressed with the goals of the Auction and how Christ-centered it was. Jay Witman explained that if she would do a painting for the BDRA, she would get publicity for her paintings and the Auction and people hit by tragedy would get the benefit—a win/win situation.

In retrospect, Elsie says, "I pray that we will always carry in our lives the *joy* and *happiness* of the children, along with the spirit of *forgiveness* shown by the parents and families of the Nickel Mines community. In learning about the BDRA, I have gotten to know a lot of really neat people, and now, every time when a disaster happens, I can feel, 'I've had a part in helping these people.' "

(Personal interview)

2. PAUL W. BRUBAKER

Red, blue and yellow. Those are the three primary colors, and all other shades and hues flow from there. That's what my grade school teacher, Hazel Ulrich, taught me. It was she who sparked an innate gift within me, encouraging me to cultivate the ability to paint.

The artistic bent within me actually comes from my dad's side of the family. I have a notebook of pencil drawings that my paternal grandmother, Emma Arzbaecher Brubaker, drew as a school girl more than a hundred years ago. Grandma passed along to my dad a love

Paul W. Brubaker

for drawing, a good eye for color, and a keen awareness of the beauty in one's surroundings. During my growing-up years, my mother would always turn to my dad to pick the paint, wallpaper and curtain fabrics. He had the gift of sensing what colors went together. From him, I also learned to appreciate the quiet beauty of a dewy meadow, the refreshing charm of a just-cultivated field of corn, and the allure of a rippling brook.

As a thirteen-year-old in 1956, I first tried my hand at oil painting. That first painting of a sailor-boy is now stashed away somewhere in the attic, but I remember exactly what it looks like. As a self-taught artist, I must say that my early paintings now look pretty crude! In the beginning, I was clueless about mixing and blending paints, as I figured red was red, blue was blue, and yellow was yellow. Only as I began to experiment with mixing and blending paints did I discover the challenge of taking the flat surface of a canvas and making it appear to be three-dimensional. Somewhere along the way, I also discovered that painting bright sunlight into my works of art created shadows. The contrast of having lights and darks side by side offers a very striking piece of work, catching the eye immediately. Consequently, bright sunlight and deep shadows have become a trademark in nearly all my paintings. After more than fifty years of painting, I think I've developed a definite style—a style that simply evolved through trial and error.

In my artwork, I'm a "realist"—I simply paint what I see. Having grown up on a dairy farm and also having had a lifelong love of local history, many of my paintings feature old houses and barns, covered bridges, and other historical buildings in rural settings. Because of being a "country boy," I've been enamored by the rustic charm of many pastoral scenes.

Even though my first painting was in oil, I later dabbled in watercolor and acrylic, but now paint exclusively in oils. One of the things I like about oil is that if I make a mistake or something doesn't look right, I can simply cover up the blunder with additional paint. Also, after a painting is dry, I love to run my fingers across the canvas just to feel the texture.

I basically paint for relaxation. When the creative juices are flowing, and I have a brush in my hand and a blank canvas in front of me, I'm in "another world." I love challenges—so the challenge in each painting is to take a piece of flat canvas and create depth through perspective and by using various hues.

Between four and five hundred of my paintings hang in Lancaster County homes and beyond. In 1987, I donated my first painting to the BDRA. Through the years I've always said to others, *"Use what God gives you!"* And I've taken that to heart personally. Since my ability to paint is God-given, why not use it for His glory? For that reason, I began donating paintings. To date, I've contributed twenty-one paintings to the BDRA—twenty of which were scenes from northern Lancaster County. Nineteen of the twenty-one were purchased by members of my local church—the Middle Creek COB. The highest price paid to date for any of the paintings was $2,100, and the lowest came in at $350, with the average being about $965 per painting. A total of $20,250 has been generated since 1987 through the sale of these paintings. An 18" x 24" painting takes me anywhere between 40 and 60 hours to complete, depending on the details and subject matter.

Painting just happens to be one of my many interests. After graduating from Cocalico High School and the American Institute of Banking, I entered the field of banking as a teller in the Ephrata National Bank in 1961. Through the years I was promoted to a bank officer, then cashier, vice president and I've been serving as the bank's executive vice president

"Covered Bridge with Swans" painted by Paul Brubaker sold for $1,300 in 1990.

and corporate secretary, as well as a member of the board of directors since 1980. On December 31, 2008, I retired after more than 47 years with Ephrata National. Now one of the tasks I face is "catching up" on the paintings people have ordered, but I never had time to do because of all my other commitments.

In addition, I have many church and community involvements, serving as a Sunday School teacher, choir member and ordained minister on the team serving the Middle Creek COB near Lititz. I'm also on the board of the Pleasant View Retirement Community in Manheim and for more than 40 years have been a member of the Historical Society of the Cocalico Valley.

My wife, the former Evelyn Hitz of Lebanon, and I reside in Ephrata and are the parents of three adult children and grandparents of six.

Through the years, I've often said, "I'd love to follow those dollars given at the BDRA and personally meet all those people who have been helped throughout the world…and if they don't know the Lord, I'd want to point them to Jesus, Who is the Way, the Truth, and the Life!"

(Paul W. Brubaker, 2000 SB,
p. 12 – plus updated data)

3. RUTH-ANNA HOPE & FREDERICK WILLIAM GREENAWALT

Living on an Amish farm in Lancaster County, Frederick William Greenawalt (Fritz) is the husband of Yvonne Armstrong Greenawalt and the father of six precious daughters: Laana,

Frederick William Greenawalt posed with a three-dimensional painting he created with his daughter, Ruth-Anna Hope.

Sonja, Hannah, Tabitha, Lydia and Ruth-Anna, as well as the grandfather of Bethany, Hannah, Nathan, Jordan and Aaron. His youngest daughter, Ruth-Anna Hope, has blended her talents with his to create 3-D paintings. In 2003, their work entitled "*The Farm Auction*" was sold at the BDRA. "*The Conestoga Crossing*," which displayed scenes along the Conestoga River beside their home, was sold in 2004.

Fritz is grateful to have had the privilege of studying under famed 3-D artist, Abner Zook, to become a painter and sculptor in the tradition of a "Dutch Master."

In addition to their artistic gifts, the Greenawalt family also loves baroque music, fine art, animals and various other crafts. Fritz has recorded a CD of hymns for Christmas and enjoys writing music, flying helicopters, experiencing freedom and reading to his family in the evenings.

Graduating from Conestoga Valley High School in 2008, Ruth-Anna Hope (Ruthi) has a keen interest in music, rodeo and in flying, having taken flight training at Lancaster Airport.

(2003 SB, p. 58; 2004 SB, p. 11,
and their profile on http://www.blogger.com)

4. BRUCE JOHNSON

Born in Allentown, PA, in 1944, Bruce began his art training at the Baum School of Art where his mother was a teacher. After earning a Bachelor of Fine Arts degree at the Philadelphia College of Art, he served three years as a U.S. Army Illustrator in Europe. Other steps in his art career included being Art Director for WITF-TV, then Executive Art Director for Armstrong World Industries in Lancaster. In each position he held, he received commendations and awards for his design work.

In the mid-1970s, as his interest in advertising design lessened, his interest in watercolor grew, and in 1979, he left the field of advertising to pursue painting and drawing, eventually building his own gallery (Gallery 444 LTD) and framing shop in Hershey, PA.

Representative of the works that Bruce has donated to the BDRA are these:

"The Picnic"
"Basic Duck Hunting Techniques"
  — *(1988 SB, p. 33)*
"Lancaster County Market"
  — *(1989 SB, p. 40)*

"The Last Straw"
  — *(1990 SB, p. 50)*
"The Great American Chocolate Factory,"
"Another Day in Lancaster County"
  — *(1991 SB, pp. 29,30)*

Bruce Johnson's art work can be seen in his one-man shows, group shows, and galleries across the United States. He was also a co-founder of the Mount Gretna Outdoor Art Show which has become one of PA's major summer events. Each year since 1980, he has combined his work, vacation and travel by going abroad to different countries to mingle with the local people and to paint, sketch, and capture the differing nuances of light, color and feeling of each culture and environment.

(From: www.bjohnsonltd.com/bio.htm
and the SB's listed above)

5. MABEL KREIDER

Living in the Manheim area, Mabel Kreider is a self-taught artist who enjoys painting a variety of subjects in watercolors and oils. Local professional artists, such as Grace Steinmetz, Ann Fields, and Al Taft have helped her along the way for short periods. Since Mabel enjoys the outdoors, it is no surprise that her favorite subjects are flowers, birds and ducks. Her explanation: "One must know the subject to enjoy painting it."

Two of her watercolors that were donated to the BDRA were: *"Blue Jays"* in 1988, and *"Mother's Iris Garden,"* in 1989.

"I thank God for the talent He has given me. My wish is that I might portray His gift of beauty and life to others of His creation,"

she says, adding, "I am glad I can use my God-given talent to benefit those in need."
(1988 SB, p. 33, 1989 SB, p. 39)

❖ ❖ ❖

6. LINEAUS W. LONGENECKER

Linn was the sixth of the eleven children born to William Sellers Longenecker and Barbara Graybill Wolgemuth Longenecker while they lived on a 113 acre farm on Risser Mill Road, north of Mount Joy. Although he was only seven when his grandfather, Sam Wolgemuth died, Linn had been told that his grandfather had taken an art course at Millersville Normal School when he was younger. Since Linn also developed an interest in art at an early age, he enjoyed studying intensely his grandfather's art assignments and sketches.

During the depression, when Linn was in tenth grade, the Union National Bank in Mount Joy offered him a job and suggested that he finish his education in night school, specializing in business. And that is what he did. He continued to work at the bank for the next 28 years, resigning in 1957 to help care for his wife, Mary, who was dying of cancer.

In 1944, he had married Mary Billow, and together they had three children: Sylvia, Robbie and Gloria. When Mary died of colon cancer in 1958, their children were between the ages of three and ten. So at the age of 79, Mary's mother, Estella Billow, became their substitute mother, raising Gloria and being greatly involved in the lives of Rob, Sylvia and Linn. She lived 19 more years allowing her the joy seeing the children grow up and graduate from college.

Linn Longenecker

By using his God-given artistic talent and without ever taking a professional art course, Linn began painting in oils when he was in his early twenties. For many years, he exhibited his paintings at the Mount Joy and Manheim Farm Shows and the Mount Joy Union National Bank. His subjects included landscapes, farms, homes, bridges, portraits and religious paintings, most of them having been commissioned.

Several of the Brethren churches having a Linn Longenecker painting gracing the front of their sanctuary include Chiques, Stevens Hill, Florin and Long Run. Middle Creek has one of his religious scenes in a room off from their sanctuary. Elizabethtown College's Anabaptist Center owns the original of his painting, "*A Seed Sown*," that depicts the origins of the COB in America. Central to that painting is the first "German Baptist" church in America, now the Germantown COB. Signed and numbered prints were made and a portion of the proceeds was contributed to the restoration project of that church that took place in the 1980's.

As fundraiser auctions, such as the BDRA, gained in popularity, Linn contributed quite a

"The Kline Meeting House," painted by Linn Longenecker, was donated in 1987.

number of paintings to help raise money for various causes. He believed and practiced the principle that *"when you give something away, you get so much more in return."* He admitted that although that principle doesn't always work, in his case, it surely did. Orders generally came in after the auctions, keeping him busy the whole next year. His painting of the *"Kline Meeting House"* brought $1,850 at the 1987 BDRA sale.

His subjects included rural scenes of farms, homes, bridges and religious paintings, all customized. "For an auction painting, I usually look for a subject which is pretty well known and which I think would interest bidders," he once told a newspaper reporter. Illustrative of this are some of the paintings he donated to the BDRA through the years:

1988 – "*The Original Conestoga Church*" (which brought $1,700)

(*1988 SB, p.32*)

1989 – "*The Brethren Heritage Collage*" and "*The Neffsville Meeting House*"

(*both listed in the1989 SB, p. 40*)

1990 – "*The Rider Building at Elizabethtown College*"   (*1990 SB, p. 50*)
1992 – "*The Star Barn*"   (*1992 SB, p. 26*)
1993 – "*The Star Barn*"   (*1993 SB, p. 26*)
1994 – "*The Hans Herr House*" (*1994 SB, p. 30*)
1995 – "*Ephrata Cloister*"   (*1995 SB, p. 31*)
1996 – "*America, the Beautiful*" – seven scenic views painted on a circular saw.

(*1996 SB, p. 32*)

When he was in his late 70s, Linn admitted he was busier than when he worked at the bank, but he seemed to thrive on the time spent at his easel. "I'm blessed with good health and this is relaxation for me. There is nothing harder on your health than putting a lot of hours in on a job you don't enjoy," he observed.

In 1993, at the age of 79, he estimated that he had completed over 1,800 paintings. Each year he did 20 to 30 paintings, many of which measured about four feet by two feet. His largest was a 20 feet high by 235 feet long mural, painted in three sections for *Sight and Sound* in their early production of *"Behold the Lamb."* Linn had painted a number of the backgrounds for the sets of the early productions of *Sight and Sound*, as Glenn Eshelman, the owner and producer, had been an art student of Linn's while he was growing up.

Admitting that he felt spiritually enriched each time he completed a painting, Linn, a member of the Florin COB, admitted, "I keenly sense a closeness to God and that He has blessed the 'gift' which He has given to me, which I feel has become a testimony of God's beautiful world of nature."

At the age of 82, Linn was suddenly stricken with debilitating health issues. His last years were spent at Brethren Village where he died in January, 2001, at age 86.

(Excerpted from "Memories of the William and Barbara Longenecker Family, 1995, by Barbara Mowrer, Sylvia Weaver, and Linn Longenecker; an article, "Tranquil Canvas Donated for Disaster Relief," by Susan Grubb Roof in the Intelligencer Journal, September 1993, and various BDRA SB's from 1987 to 1996.)

7. P. BUCKLEY MOSS

Patricia Buckley, born in 1933 in New York City, was the second of three children of an Irish American/Sicilian marriage. Since Pat had the perceptional disorder known today as dyslexia, she was perceived in grade school to be a poor student. However, one of her teachers felt that this little girl, who was "not proficient in anything," was artistically gifted. Based on that opinion, her mother enrolled her in the Washington Irving High School for the Fine Arts where her artistic abilities were encouraged.

After receiving a scholarship to New York's Cooper Union for the Advancement of Science and Art, she studied there four years and then married Jack Moss, a chemical engineer.

In 1964, the Moss's and their six children were living in Waynesboro in the Shenandoah Valley of Virginia. It was there that she came to appreciate the quiet beauty of rural scenery and learned to know the Amish and Mennonite "plain" people. Soon, she included these new elements into her art, revitalizing her career and ambitions.

In 1967, she won her first major art show prize, a one-person museum exhibition, which resulted in a "sell out," encouraging her to seriously market her work. Today she has thousands of fans who treasure her art with its distinctive look and popular appeal.

In addition to her tremendous artistic success, Pat is almost equally well-known for her work with special education groups and her generous donations to child-related charities. She has become a role model for the learning impaired and frequently is asked to speak to special education classes.

Some of the paintings which Pat has donated to the BDRA are:

2007 – *"Sharing Work and Fellowship"*
                (2007 SB, p. 36)
2008 – *"Dawdi House #15"*   *(2008 SB, p. 24)*
2009 – *"The Farm House #14"* *(2009 SB, p. 81)*

What a blessing it is to see an artist of her renown giving encouragement and support to those who might otherwise be forgotten and misunderstood and those who have been stricken by disasters through no fault of their own.

(Excerpted from www.pbuckleymoss.com and 2007 SB, p. 36, 2008 SB, p. 24)

8. TERRY REDLIN

Born on a farm in South Dakota at the end of the Depression, Terry Redlin lived in a house locals called "the dollhouse" because of its small size. For 30 square miles, nearly everyone living on the nearby farms were relatives.

His teachers in elementary school called him "Windows Redlin" and seated him near the inside walls of their classrooms. Otherwise, he gazed at the sky and the landscape outside and thought about fishing and hunting or imagined new designs for model airplanes. If he wasn't daydreaming, he was drawing.

At age five, when his dad gave up farming and began repairing cars for a living, the family moved to town. Neighborhood children played hopscotch, marbles, kick the can, built forts and flew kites. On weekends, families hunted or fished together. A childhood playmate says, "When I look at his paintings now, I realize he's captured our memories of childhood."

When he was 15, he and a friend were riding a motorcycle and were hit by a drunk driver. That was the end of his dream of becoming a forest ranger because Terry's leg was crushed and had to be amputated. At that point, knowing he was limited as to what his career goal would be, he said, "Art, I knew I could still do."

He married Helene Langenfeld when they were both 19, a year after they graduated from Watertown High School in 1955. To his amazement, South Dakota awarded him a "handicapped student" scholarship to the School of Associated Arts in St. Paul, MN. He regarded it as a gift. "The chance that they'd ever see any return on that money was nil."

After doing sketching at Brown & Bigelow in St. Paul for two years, he was homesick and missed hunting and fishing. He and Helene returned to Watertown where he landed a job as a draftsman. Six years later, he had three children. Seeing no future for himself in that small town, the family moved back to Minnesota where Webb Publishing hired him as a designer in 1967. After being promoted several times and learning new skills, such as handling

a camera and printing, things were going well for him when the company laid off several artists. He was afraid he'd be next. In April 1975, he announced to his family that he was beginning a five-year plan to become a wildlife artist. While still working at Webb, he spent all his spare hours outside, observing and photographing wildlife.

When he was ready to begin painting again, he created a studio in his basement, complete with everything needed to create prints from his paintings, mats, frames and to pack and ship them. He worked 120-hour weeks. He figured if he didn't succeed with painting, he could make it with a framing and shipping business.

After selling a few paintings to some small art stores, his first major print, "*Morning Retreat,*" for Ducks Unlimited broke the $5,000 mark at three different banquets and for more than $3,500 at a dozen other banquets. But Redlin, who had already worked 20 years as a commercial artist, did not quit his job at Webb until he was making four times his Webb salary through his paintings.

His paintings often contain buildings and landmarks, such as churches, barns, houses, cabins and grain elevators that are real, but the scenes he creates with them are all in his head. He has nostalgic, story-telling themes, rooted in Americana. When they were last on the market, Redlin paintings sold for $50,000 to $75,000. Now, they could be considered priceless, because they are not for sale. He has not sold any originals since 1985, when he agreed to his son's suggestion that he build a museum to house them. "The idea of the museum is to bring in outside tourism money for the state, to pay back what South Dakota gave me for tuition to go to art school."

The Redlin family believes in giving back, repaying people for kindness and generosity, and helping those in need. Some Redlin prints which have been sold at the BDRA are these:

2004 – "*Patiently Waiting*"   (*2004 SB, p. 68*)
2005 – "*Sunset Harvest*"   (*2005 SB, p. 66*)
2006 – "*Spring Fishing*"   (*2006 SB, p. 66*)

(From an article by Ellen Tomson in the Saint Paul Pioneer Press Express, December 17, 1995; SB's listed above, and www. redlinart.com)

9. NED SMITH

E. Stanley "Ned" Smith was born in 1919 in Millersburg, a small town on the Susquehanna River north of Harrisburg, PA. He grew up in a household that was attuned to nature; his mother was an avid birder, and his father, who managed a local shoe factory, had a passion for botany. Combining his love of natural history with an innate aptitude for art, Ned was already producing quality wildlife illustrations when he completed high school in the 1930's. A self-trained artist and naturalist, in his 46-year career, he created thousands of astonishingly accurate drawings and paintings of wildlife for books, magazines, and other publications, as well as dozens of limited edition prints.

After graduation, he began working, not as an artist, but as a lathe operator in a machine shop–a steady income for him and his new wife, Marie Reynolds, his childhood sweetheart.

He continued to draw and paint, however, spending every spare moment outdoors, hon-

ing his abilities as an observer of wildlife. In 1939 he made his first commercial sale, a cover painting for *Pennsylvania Angler* magazine. After working as a fulltime illustrator for a year for Samworth Publishing in South Carolina, the Smiths returned to PA and Ned landed a job as the staff illustrator for the Pennsylvania Game Commission. Over the years, he created nearly 120 *Pennsylvania Game News* cover paintings.

He left the Game Commission's employ in 1953 to work fulltime as a freelance artist and selling his columns, articles and illustrations to *Sports Afield, National Wildlife, Pennsylvania Angler, South Carolina Wildlife, National Geographic,* and other magazines. Over the years he illustrated 14 books, including the Peterson series *Field Guide to Birds' Nests* by Hal Harrison. In 1983 he created PA's first-ever state duck stamp, and painted a second design two years later.

In the late 1970s, he began to work in the field of art prints producing such masterworks as "*Waiting for Dusk*" and "*A Little Bit Cautious.*" During the same period, he also created several of the Game Commission's Working Together for Wildlife prints, including "*Dutch Country Bluebirds,*" one of his most popular pieces, as well as fundraising prints for the National Wild Turkey Federation, Hawk Mountain Sanctuary, the PA Federation of Sportsmen's Clubs, the BDRA and other organizations.

For many years, Ned Smith battled heart disease. In the spring of 1985, while working in the garden of their Millersburg home, he died of a heart attack at the age of 65. Since his death, the value of his work has continued to rise. Original paintings now command prices in excess of $60,000 and some popular prints have a resale value of more than $5,000. Those persons who were lucky enough to buy his prints at the BDRA in the late 1980s and early 1990s not only helped those in disasters but also made a good investment!

(From www.nedsmithcenter.org, and 1988 SB, p. 32)

10. ERMA WENGER

Born on January 25, 1932, Erma has loved art as long as she can remember. When she was just four or five, she collected different kinds of stones to draw designs on the walk, later using crayons and chalk for coloring. After receiving a gift of oil paints at age 12 from an aunt, Erma began painting with oils. Although she took art classes in high school, she has been mostly self-taught with some lessons from a few renowned teachers.

Through the next 60 years, she developed her God-given gift and created many glass and canvas paintings. She has shared her gifts with others by teaching classes in oil painting for ten years in her home and giving numerous chalk painting programs in various churches.

With her specialties being Lancaster County themes, the Amish, farm scenes and covered bridges, her original oil paintings and prints can be found throughout the USA and 20 different countries. She now sells only prints of her work, and they are available at Roots Country Market near East Petersburg every Tuesday. When she donates some of her work to the BDRA, they are always very popular items.

(2007 SB, p. 64)

11. MICHAEL L. WISE

Mike Wise, who is in his 28th year of teaching art at Hempfield high school, donated several original watercolor paintings to the BDRA over the years. They included paintings of local landscapes, wild flowers and perennials, an occasional still life and a mixed media piece. In 1990, his painting simply titled, *"Flowers,"* brought $425 and one the prior year sold for $475.

However, Mike, the father of two sons, is a busy man these days. Five years ago, he and his wife, LuAnn (Shelly), then deacons in the Chiques COB, were sent out by that congregation to begin a church plant called "New Beginnings," which meets in the Brickerville Fire Company Building. He has been serving as the lead elder there and is working toward becoming ordained. Along with his teaching, he also witnesses by opening his art room for students to hold Bible studies and Christian clubs.

12. ABNER ZOOK

When Jay Witman visited the art studio of Abner Zook in 1987, he rated his time there as being "very rewarding and stimulating," both in the wealth of historical information he received from the former Amishman/artist, and also by viewing the many examples of his 3-D carvings/paintings on display there. He found Abner to be very willing to share his tremendous knowledge of Amish barn-raisings, their life-styles and beliefs.

Abner Zook and his three-dimensional painting "The Village Blacksmith," which was sold in 1990 for $6,250.

To make one of his 3-D creations, such as the one entitled "*Amish Barn Raising*" that he donated to the BDRA in 1987 (and was sold for $8,800), Abner first makes sketches, then prepares the background. Next he makes the timbers out of wood for the barn structure and carves the figures from the proper perspective, down to the minutest detail, whether it be a tool carelessly cast aside or catching the twinkle in the eye of a carpenter. Each little detail is important in telling the history and story of the occasion.

When a Zook painting is finished, it is not looked at with just a single glance. Instead, each little detail is studied and admired as the impact of history and an earlier lifestyle is felt and absorbed.

Born and raised in an Old Order Amish home in Lancaster County, Abner began adulthood as a farmer, walking behind a plow and working the rich soil. He was a typical Amish dairyman and had no formal training in art. Interestingly enough, he had an identical twin brother, Aaron, who also had the same gifts in making 3-D art. They called themselves "mirror twins," because when they looked in the mir-

ror, each saw his brother! According to Anna Buckwalter, a long-time friend of the Amish, one little quirk that each brother practiced in his art was that somewhere in each painting he included a figure representing himself. Eventually, what had once been a hobby became their vocation. Most of their compositions were of the realistic genre, such as landscapes, covered bridges, country homes, Amish life and scenes, farm animals, historical landmarks, buildings and architecture.

Ever grateful for the guidance and encouragement others had given him, Abner loved his work, and his motto was "*We are shaped and fashioned by what we love*."

Some of his works and the known sale prices at the BDRA are these:

• 1986 – *An Auction Scene* – sold for $10,200
• 1987 – *Amish Barn Raising* – sold for $8,800

Meredith Miller, White Oak COB, is the familiar announcer of each item as it comes up for sale.

- 1988 – *An Old-Fashioned Public Auction* – sold for $8,500
- 1989 – *A Harvest Scene*
- 1990 – *The Village Blacksmith* – sold for $6,250
- 1991 – *A Harvest Scene*
- 1993 – Unknown subject – sold for $7,000
- 1995 – Nature and Wildlife Scene
- 1996 – Nature and Wildlife Scene
- 1997 – *House with Waterwheel*
- 1998 – *Mill with Waterwheel and small stone bridge* – sold for $6,700

Often before a Zook painting was to be sold, Abner would stand on the BDRA platform and explain the story of that painting and explain that he wanted to use his God-given gift to God's honor and glory and to do his part in helping others who had been struck by a disaster.

Another of the famous sayings quoted by this humble artist was: *"I am only one, but I am one. I cannot do everything, but I can do something. What I can do, I ought to do, and by the grace of God, I will do. May God grant me the ability to continue to portray beauty and truth."*

(1987 SB, p. 17, 1988 SB, p. 37)

C. Auctioneers and Clerks

If you are planning to have a sale, do not plan it for the fourth Saturday of September! Some of the best auctioneers in the Lebanon, Lancaster, and York County areas set aside that day to use their skills to honor God by rais-

Duane Ness, the BDRA Coordinator, enjoys a moment of rest with the Witman auctioneers and brothers, Luke (left) and Jay (right).

ing funds at the BDRA to help those who have been hit by natural or manmade disasters.

Although some of the auctioneers and clerks from the early years have died, we have listed most of them who have served at one time or another. Any omissions are not intentional.

AUCTIONEERS

Harry Bachman – Annville
William Bering – Lebanon
Jeff Bollinger – Lancaster
Stan Bucher – Lebanon
Dave Buckwalter – Lititz
Keith Chronister – York
Allen Diffenbach – New Holland
Carl Diller – Lampeter
Doug Ebersole – Mount Joy
Nelson Ebersole – Annville
Rufus Geib – Manheim
Elvin Gingrich – Lebanon
Roy E. Good, Jr. – Denver
Donald Groff – Manheim
Ben Habecker – Newmanstown
Enos Heisey – Mount Gretna
Joel Heisey – Newmanstown

Dave Jenkins, Ambler COB, is the person who heads the Information Booth and has an answer to every question!

William Hoover – Spring Grove
Wilbur H. Hosler – Manheim
Kenneth Keeny – Stewartstown
Randal V. Kline – Stevens
J. Everett Kreider – Quarryville
Lloyd H. Kreider – New Providence
Jim Landis – Lancaster
Mike Martin – Manheim
Patrick Morgan – New Holland
Clarence Moyer – Manheim
Jeff Moyer – Manheim
Richard Murry – Mechanicsburg
Phil Nissley – Manheim
Aaron Nolt – New Holland
Michele Price – Lewistown
Alfred Reist – Lancaster
Arthur Reist – Lancaster
Jacob Ruhl – Manheim
Steve Schuler – Marietta
Wayne Scott – Harrisburg
Curtis Shenk – Manheim
Matt Shenk – Manheim
Roy Shirk – Lebanon
Keith Snyder – Lebanon
Mike Snyder – Lancaster
John Stauffer – Manheim
Raymond Stump – Tower City

Suzanne J. Stump – Tower City
Harvey Weik – Schaefferstown
Lou Weiler –Lititz
Glenn Wenger – Myerstown
Dave White – Manheim
Keith Witman – Bernville
Clarke Witman – Manheim
Jay M. Witman – Manheim
Luke Witman – Manheim
Matt Witmer – Stevens
Sylvan Witmer – Womelsdorf
Larry Wittig – Bridgewater, VA
Russel Wolf, Jr. – Cleona
Robert Wolgemuth – Manheim

CLERKS

Cindy Bucher – Lebanon
Betty Sue Byler – Ephrata
Jim Gibbel – Lititz
Barbara Hoover – Elizabethtown
Jim Kreider – Quarryville
Linda Kreider – Quarryville
Mike Longenecker – Manheim
Cassel Mummau – Mount Joy
Larry Rutt – Farmersville
Burnell Shenk – Manheim
Harriet Spayd – Manheim
Cathy Stauffer – Manheim
Joyce Wagner -- Manheim
Kris Wagner – Lititz

ANNOUNCER
Meredith Miller

INFORMATION BOOTH
Dave Jenkins

CHAPTER FIVE

"Two of people's most pressing problems seem to be how to keep half the population from starving and the other half from being overweight!"

\- James Alexander Thom

D. Baked Goods, Donuts and Candy

WALKING BY THE Baked Goods stand is difficult. Enticed by the aromas of freshly-baked breads, and the sight of still-warm cinnamon buns sitting beside pies of all kinds and other baked goodies, auction-goers usually succumb. Consequently, baked goods are popular and profitable selling items for the BDRA.

In addition to the foods already mentioned, there are always tempting apple dumplings, cakes, cookies, dinner buns, sticky buns, brownies, Shuey's pretzels and whoopie pies. Most of

Smiling clerks, Keri Cassel (left) and Amy Rohrer (right), await cookie customers.

Left to right: Marian Longenecker, Linda Fahnestock, and Amy Rohrer ask customers, "What kind of pie would you like?"

these mouth-watering breads and pastries are made in private homes by excellent cooks from the many churches involved with the Auction. Although all kinds of pies are available, the all-time favorites are pecan, black raspberry, lemon sponge and apricot.

For several years, the Oehme's Bakery in Lititz donated a humongous 20 lb. cherry pie which usually was displayed and then at an appointed hour on Saturday was sold by individual servings topped with a dip of vanilla ice cream.

In 2006, on the 30th Anniversary of the BDRA, a huge three-tiered cake, honoring the occasion and looking like a tiered wedding cake with smaller layer cakes around it, was on display in the Main Exhibition Hall. Tickets @ $2.50 each were sold, entitling the bearer to one piece of the Anniversary cake with one dip of ice cream, served on Saturday between 11 a.m. and 12 noon.

A TV SPOT IN 1987

At the BDRA, a "variety of food items will be available, from homemade pies (700 are being baked) and ice cream to soups and sandwiches. Incidentally, during this morning's broadcast of the Today Show, NBC's Willard Scott and Bryant Gumbel sampled some delicious shoo-fly pie sent to them by organizers of the auction."   *(1987 SB, p. 22)*

Those who have studied church history know that an early nickname for COB members was "Dunkers" because of their three-dip baptism tradition. In 1989, when women from the Chiques COB were already famous for their delicious apple dumplings, Don Fitzkee wrote an article referring to them as "Dunker Dumplings."

Making dumplings for the BDRA began in 1979 when the Chiques women made and donated 250 of them. Ten years later, in 1988, they made and donated more than 2,600, including 1,000 that were baked. (The others were sold unbaked, as the rotating oven at the Mastersonville Fire Hall couldn't handle more in the allotted time.)

To make this many apple dumplings, the women have the process down to a science, beginning Friday afternoon with the counting and sorting of about twenty bushels of apples. Some are donated and others are purchased at discount prices from area fruit growers sympathetic to the cause. Beginning about 5:30 p.m., between 30 and 40 men and women meet at the Mastersonville Fire Hall to peel, core, wash and dry the apples.

After a short night's rest, several return

The apple dumplings are often still warm, fresh from the oven.

at 4:30 Saturday morning to mix the dough. Others arrive about a half hour later, and there are usually about 45 people engaged in rolling dough, inserting apples, baking the dumplings, sorting orders and delivering the oven-fresh, still-warm doughy treats to the BDRA by 7 a.m. By 9:30, their job is finished, the ovens are empty, and everything is spotless, and the "Dunker Dumplings" are on their sweet mission of raising funds to help others–to the honor and glory of God. *(From the Don Fitzkee article, SB 1989, pp. 22,23)*

We might add that this isn't quite the whole apple dumpling story, as "due to public demand," other congregations now make homemade apple dumplings for the BDRA as well.

Although some Amish attended the BDRA and a few even hosted Share-A-Meals before the tragedy at the Nickel Mines school, they have increased their support tremendously since then. Today Amish come and make soft pretzels and "melt-in-your-mouth" donuts from scratch, "while you watch them," and even donate most of the ingredients so that most monies made from those sales go directly to disaster relief.

If you have a sweet tooth–a passion for chocolate–or you want to make a donation–or all three, then you MUST make a stop at the candy stand at the BDRA.

In the late 1980s, the Truthseeker's Sunday school class of the Ephrata COB, was looking for a project that would bring in money for the BDRA. Since Ken and Bonnie Hosler, who were class members, happened to have a candy stand at the Green Dragon Farmer's Market near Ephrata and were buying candy in bulk each week anyway, it was suggested that perhaps a candy stand at the auction would work.

In 1989, Raymond and Martha Miller, then members of the Truthseeker's class, bought the stand at Green Dragon and along with it, automatically became the managers of the BDRA candy stand. Today it is a joint effort between the Millers, and members of the East Cocalico COB, and the Truthseeker's class of the Ephrata COB.

Each September, on the Tuesday of BDRA week, the Millers go to Smith's Candies in Myerstown to buy a variety of candies in bulk amounts, from licorice strips to caramels, salt water taffy to crème-filled chocolates, and more. That night, a group of 20 to 25 volunteers gather at the East Cocalico COB in Reamstown for about two hours to divvy up, weigh and pack the candy, putting it into

1,500 to 1,800 plastic bags which are then sold at the auction that weekend for $1 per bag. In the 18+ years that the Millers have been managing the stand, the annual profits, which are donated to the BDRA, have averaged between $850 and $900. Their total sales for those years amount to an impressive $14,883.

In referring to their candy project, Martha says: "It's a fun way to bring glory to God AND help people—and it's all done in one week!"

(Personal Interview)

*"Some women have a recipe
That never will be told.
They guard it quite as jealously
As misers guard their gold.*

*They have a way to make a sauce,
A gravy, or a dressing,
That keeps their neighbors at a loss,
Despite their clever guessing.*

*The secret furrows up their brow,
It's kept so closely masked.
They will not tell a soul, but how
It thrills them to be asked!"*

*(Poet Unknown. From Our Daily Bread II,
published by Mechanic Grove
COB women, 1962)*

"AUNT ELLEN'S" CARAMEL CORN

At the annual BDRA, the smell of cooking caramel is as familiar a sensation as the sound of the auctioneer! Since Ellen Longenecker Young received the recipe for delicious caramel pop-

corn from her mother, Barbara (Mrs. William) Longenecker, it has helped to make thousands of dollars for the BDRA.

When the BDRA first started, Ellen was in charge of all the food and told her husband, "As soon as I get out of this, I am going to try to make popcorn to sell."

She thought that perhaps she could make two or three hundred dollars, but her estimate was much too modest. In 1988, the caramel popcorn stand, run by Ellen and her husband, Robert Young, made a profit of $1,900. The Youngs, from the Bachmansville COB, brought their motor home to the Fairground so Ellen could begin preparations and be there early the morning of the sale. Volunteers who helped her with the caramel corn were rewarded with one of her own-baked home-grown raspberry pies along with tomatoes grown in her large garden.

In their tenth year of making caramel popcorn at the BDRA, in 1989, Ellen said, "We're just glad we have the health to do it and that we can give all the proceeds to relief." Those proceeds were increased because the corn was donated by Cope's Canned Corn Company in Rheems; the Youngs donated everything else.

Making the popcorn is a team effort and the Youngs depended on about 40 volunteers each year to make the stand function successfully. It was a simple process with two popcorn poppers and eight caramel kettles preparing the ingredients. Ellen prepared the caramel mixture with her niece, Janice Longenecker Holsinger, helping her stir the caramel to a temperature of 280 degrees.

"Aunt Ellen's" Caramel Corn Recipe"
2 ½ to 3 ½ gallons of popcorn
2 cups of light brown sugar

½ cup of molasses (King or Turkey)
2 sticks of margarine
2 tablespoons of vinegar
2 teaspoons of salt
¼ cup water

Some volunteers popped the corn in poppers fueled by propane and originally given to Ellen by her father-in-law, David Young. On several occasions, there was real excitement when the popped corn inside caught fire and they would have to rush to take the popper out of the building and extinguish the fire. Ellen's son, Rod Young, stirred the popcorn/caramel mixture on Fridays, and Janice's husband, John Holsinger did that backbreaking task on Saturdays. The rest of the folks bagged and sold the tasty treat.

In 1988, almost 250 pounds of popcorn was used. After the caramel and popped corn were mixed in an apple butter copper kettle (donated by Cassel Mummau), the sticky mixture was put on trays to cool. Then it was bagged in $1 and $2 sized bags and sold. Dave Koser, Bachmansville COB, made and donated a wooden stand to stabilize the copper kettle and a wooden paddle to stir the caramel/popcorn. Much of the other equipment was borrowed from the Milton Hershey School, Lebanon Valley Brethren Home, and many heavy cooking kettles from various COB churches.

"It would be much more expensive to buy it at a popcorn stand," Ellen claimed, who said the smallest bags contained at least a quart. She received many compliments, with some saying it was the best caramel corn they had ever eaten. When asked why she didn't put peanuts in the mix, she explained, "If we sell that much without the peanuts, we'll just keep sticking to the plain caramel." (No pun intended!)

When the project became too much for Bob and Ellen's aging bodies to endure, John and Janice Holsinger approached Ken and Carroll Krieder from the Elizabethtown COB to join them in continuing the caramel corn project. In honor of Janice's Aunt, Ellen Young, the originator of the project, they decided to call it "Aunt Ellen's Caramel Corn."

In dividing their tasks, they agreed that the Holsingers, from the Palmyra COB, would purchase/rent the supplies/equipment and cook the caramel syrup and the Krieders would organize the personnel work schedules and sell the popcorn. All four reserved several days each year from their professional vocations to give honor and glory to God by providing this service to a wider community to give help to those affected by disasters. Ken and Carroll were Professors of History and Business respectively at Elizabethtown College, Janice was the owner of U-GRO Learning Centres, Inc., while John was employed by Rayovac as their National Sales Manager.

This foursome began with the 1991 BDRA, making 300 lbs. of popcorn along with 65 batches of caramel syrup into "Aunt Ellen's Caramel Popcorn." On every fourth weekend of September after that, their activities began on Thursday evening by hauling in and setting up the equipment in the Fairground building in preparation for an early start on Friday morning. John and Ken would duct tape 40 squares of cardboard on the floor surface first to assist with the cleanup process later. The popcorn poppers are rented each year from Tents & Events, Annville, and in 2008, the popcorn and oil were donated by Reist's Popcorn Company of Mount Joy whose owners are members of the Elizabethtown COB.

On Friday, after an early start from home, they began working at 7 a.m. and only returned home about 10:15 p.m. With a starting time of 7 a.m. again on Saturday, they all better understood why the Youngs would come and stay on the premises in their motor home. Usually, the popcorn was sold out by 2 p.m. and the cleanup began. This meant scrubbing pots/pans, packing, hauling home, storing the equipment, and breathing a deep sigh of relief because "that chore was completed for another year."

Teamwork goes into making Aunt Ellen's Caramel Corn.

The work crew totaled approximately 75 persons who would volunteer a minimum of two hours each in a pre-assigned work schedule. Besides family members, there were volunteers from COB churches in Elizabethtown, Mechanic Grove, Palmyra, Middle Creek, Florin, Little Swatara, Spring Creek, Lititz, Harrisburg First, Mountville, Lancaster, Annville, Conewago, Hempfield, Lebanon and Mount Wilson who assisted in the project. Besides COB, volunteers were also from Jewish, Catholic, Lutheran, Mennonite and Baptist denominations.

In that first year, their profit was $1,850. For the first three years, their expenses were approximately $300 per year; however, from that point forward, everything was donated. Eventually, they decided to streamline their work process by filling only one-size bag for two dollars.

Their best year was 1995 with a profit of $3,108. During that year, they popped 400 lbs. of popcorn and cooked 96 batches of caramel

syrup! In the year 2006, they raised the price to $3 per bag and that year's sales amounted to a close second with a profit of $3,102. Total contributions to the BDRA as a result of the Caramel Popcorn sales from 1991 through 2008 have amounted to $42,458.75.

Since the Krieders have helped with this project for nineteen years and the Holsingers even longer, both couples have notified the BDRA Board that 2009 will be their last year. However, they are willing to "provide any operational information, advice, or recommendations to any church or anyone expressing interest in continuing this operation."

Be sure not to leave the Fairgrounds without Aunt Ellen's Caramel Corn!

(Excerpted from an article by Judd Mellinger-Blouch, 1989 SB, pp. 58, 59 and updates from John and Janice Holsinger and Carroll Kreider)

MY WORST MEMORY OF THE BDRA!

We were serving on the Baked Goods Stand Committee during 1990-1992 when the Main Hall Auction was held in the West Hall where the Baked Goods Stand and Farmer's Market are located now. At that time, the Baked Goods Stand was in a tent on the grass outside the West Hall.

For at least three years in a row, it rained on the Friday night of the BDRA. And I don't mean just a little drizzle; I mean it rained and rained and rained. Sometimes, it poured! Everything and everyone got wet. We had tables set up inside the tent for the baked items, and we would keep moving them closer to the middle trying to protect them because all the tent's corners seemed to leak or at least, dripped water. Of course, the ground on which we stood was saturated, and before we knew it, we were standing in a couple inches of water. It was a mess!

When the sale was over on Friday evening, we would load all the pies and other baked items into the back of a truck parked nearby to keep them safe and dry.

We were never sure what we would find when we arrived at the BDRA on Saturday morning. The baked items we put in the truck were always safe, but the ground was rather "mushy" where we walked. Thankfully, it usually did not rain on Saturdays, and by the time the day was over, the inside of the tent would begin to dry, especially if it got warm enough, so we could open the sides of the tent.

No one ever complained about working in the tent, because that was just the way it was, but we were OH, SO HAPPY to be placed *inside* the West Hall (after the North Hall Build-

ing was completed and the Main Hall Auction moved over there). It was so nice to be in the dry when it rained, and also to be able to let all of our baked goods on the tables instead of having to move them in and out of the truck on Friday night.

(By Charlene Fahnestock)

The selling of the "special pie" is always a high point of the BDRA as the auctioneer is told over and over to "Sell it Again!"

AND THEN THERE IS THE GREATEST PIE STORY OF ALL!

In 1995, when the Grow Money envelopes containing $10 were distributed, one woman accepted one, thinking that she would bake and sell pies and donate the monies to the BDRA the following September.

Then, in 1996, an unknown man brought an empty pie plate to the Baked Goods stand. Attached to the pie plate was a $20 bill with a note that his wife had received the Grow Money, but had died unexpectedly during that year. Because he was not a baker but wanted to honor her wishes and help her Grow Money double, he was presenting the plate to the sales staff there–and walked away. No one knew him and to this day, no one has admitted that he was that person, so some have surmised it may have been an angel. Only God knows.

When Jay Witman heard the story that same day, he saw an opportunity. Bringing the pie plate with him into the main auction area, he told the story and suggested that the buyer should bring back the plate the following year filled with a pie–and it would be sold again. After he asked, "What am I bid?" he sold the empty pie plate, with the $20 bill attached, for $90. Amazingly, the buyer said, "Sell it again!" It was sold again, and again–and again. That first year that empty pie plate brought in $1,300[5] and started a tradition. In the ensuing years, the pie-*filled* plate has sometimes brought as much as $1,500 to $2,920 by being sold 10 or 12 times. What an emotional high point it is to hear one buyer after another say, "Sell it again."

One year the final buyer was Kay Weaver, who had only baked about three pies in her life—25 years earlier! After her friends had finished laughing at her predicament of having to make a pie for the next year, they took pity on her, and several offered to bake a pie for her to donate. That gave her an idea. She enlisted the help of others in her church, the Lampeter

COB, to make and donate pies to hold a "pie auction" there. When she donated the special pie-filled plate that next September, she also contributed all monies received from Lampeter's mini-pie auction, adding significantly to the returns gained that year from the "Miracle Pie."

In the year 2000, the final buyer of the "Miracle Pie" was Earl Ziegler who immediately proceeded to the front of the room, obtained a mike and with a brief speech of appreciation presented the pie to Jay Witman, the auctioneer who had just sold the pie.

Most people knew Jay was single and was not a pie baker, but he could think fast! Because the next sale, in 2001, would be the 25th Anniversary of the BDRA, he declared he would have 25 pies made and donated to be auctioned, plus one designated to be the ongoing "Pie with a Purpose."

Keep watching at future sales whenever the "special pie" is being auctioned, and be prepared to bid—and say, "Sell it again!" The saga of the miracle pie is not ended!

AND THE PIE STORY GOES ON …

The story of the gentleman who returned the empty pie plate with $20 touched us deeply, and we felt honored to be a part of keeping his contribution growing. God truly blessed us during 1998 as we promoted our "Pies With A Purpose."

We began in January of 1998 by going to a Hanoverdale COB Board meeting armed with two lemon sponge pies. (Mary Lynn was the Church Clerk and thus the secretary for the Board.) That night the Board unanimously

---

[5] According to an article in the 2001 SB, p. 9, by Charles M. Bieber.

supported our project and gave a free will offering of $70.

Our next step was to inform the congregation of our project. Any group or individual could request their choice of pie(s) to be made by Mary Lynn, and Gregg made ice cream to go with it. We promised to deliver the order to the church or a home in exchange for a donation.

Originally, we had set a goal for ourselves of raising $500, but by the end of April, we raised that to $1,000. By the middle of August we were on the way to $1,500.

God truly had His hand in this project, for we never dreamed we would more than triple our initial goal! Some fun facts about what we did:

- Our Church Board had pie at five meetings.
- Pie was served to each Commission, the Deacon Committee, a Bible Study Group, and a Sunday school class picnic
- One pie traveled to New Jersey
- Six persons celebrated their birthdays with pie
- 10 ½ gallons of ice cream were enjoyed
- 54 pies were made
- A total of $1,550 was made and donated to the BDRA

Thank you to Jay Witman for challenging us to "find a creative way to raise money."

We had lots of fun since January and are still getting requests for pies from members of our church. Our prayer was that God would use the proceeds of "Pies With A Purpose" to relieve the suffering and devastation of those involved in disasters, and that His love would be shown to them.

(Gregg and Mary Lynn Kautz, Hanoverdale, Big Swatara COB. 1999 SB, p. 10)

E. Baseball Cards and Memorabilia

During the 1980s and 1990s, baseball cards and memorabilia were hot items and highly collectible. After a Tom Herr signed baseball brought $150 and his bat $350 in 1986, his autographed bat sold for $425 in 1987. In that same year, a Mike Schmidt personally autographed baseball sold for $500 and his baseball bat for $700. In 1993, the BDRA sold a baseball and baseball cards personally autographed by Dave Dravecky, as well as a limited edition of Fleer 1993 uncut baseball cards.

In 2000, baseball cards were combined with other collectibles at an auction in the East Hall. That year there were 20,000 cards for sale, including a Topps complete set 1980 thru 1992, and rookie cards for Cal Ripkin and Mike Schmidt.

F. Building Houses

The first house built to raise funds for the BDRA was constructed along Fruitville Pike in Milton Estates at 1153 Suffolk Drive, Lititz, completed in 1995 and sold for $240,000. Participating builders were: Harold Diffenderfer, White Oak COB, Chairperson, Landis Myer, Conestoga COB, and Marty Witman, Florin COB.

In 1997, the second house was built at 104 Pleasant View Court, in East Berlin, SOPA Dis-

Four of the busy modular home builders taking a brief "time-out" for a photo (left to right): Elvin Wagner, Myerstown COB; Bob Wolgemuth, Chiques COB; Marty Witman, Florin COB; and John Zimmerman, White Oak COB.

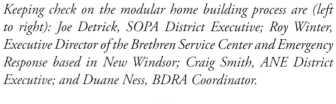

Keeping check on the modular home building process are (left to right): Joe Detrick, SOPA District Executive; Roy Winter, Executive Director of the Brethren Service Center and Emergency Response based in New Windsor; Craig Smith, ANE District Executive; and Duane Ness, BDRA Coordinator.

Groundbreaking in 1996 for the Manheim charity home. Those participating (left to right): Marion Brubaker, Landis Myer, Mel Burkholder, Jay Witman, J. Wilbur Brubaker, Allen Hansell, Harold Diffenderfer, and Marty Witman.

trict. Serving on the Building Committee were: Galen Yeater, Chambersburg COB, Chairperson, William Replogle, Brethren Home Faith Community, Ed Nace, Black Rock COB, Jim Boyer, Upper Conewago COB, Vice-Chairperson, and Nelson Wenger, Chambersburg COB, secretary. It was sold (at a loss) for $146,000.

The third BDRA house was built in Pleasant View Estates, Manheim, on land donated by J. Wilbur and Marion Brubaker, Florin COB. It was sold in 1997 for $179,000.

Ground-breaking for the fourth BDRA charity house occurred in April 1999. That house was built at 1015 Huntington Lane, Elizabethtown, and was sold in September 2000. M. Rodney Young served as Building Committee chairperson.

The first time that a modular home was built on the premises of the Lebanon Fairground was in September, 2004. Serving on the planning committee for that project were: Elvin Wagner, Marty Witman, and Bob Wolgemuth. A second one, 1300 square feet, was built the following year. In 2006, a three-bedroom modular home was built on the auction grounds in four days!

What impressed me the most about the idea of building a house was to have the support of the *total* Auction Committee. Also, the unity of the Building Committee made it a real pleasure to serve on that Committee. The overwhelming involvement of the people giving of their time, talents, materials and financial support was most impressive. To God be the Glory!

(Melvin S. Burkholder,
White Oak COB, 1995 SB, p. 3)

The Building Committee met every two or three weeks and always we started our meetings with prayer asking God to direct us. We soon bought a building lot, and in a few weeks decided on a blueprint, approving the plans and specifications. At the ground-breaking ceremony, I was impressed with the prayer of Dedication by Brother Earl Ziegler as he gave it in God's hands, and truly it was in God's hands. People watched when the sign was erected along the road, and kept watching it. I was amazed.

It was remarkable how many workmen who helped to build the house donated their time, how many building materials were donated, and how many businesses gave discounts. We know it was God working through His children that this all happened.

I really enjoyed working with the Building Committee and also enjoyed helping to build the house. We never heard anything negative or unkind from anyone throughout the year, and again, we want to thank you all for helping to build the house. I was also impressed with the good neighborhood where the house was built and how they helped and kept watch over the house. I am thankful that I was part of this project, and my desire would be that God would get all the Honor and Glory.

(Harold W. Diffenderfer, Building Committee
Chairman, White Oak COB, 1995 SB, p. 3)

When we began this project (first BDRA home) from the word "go," people were eager to

The completed modular home built on the Lebanon Fairgrounds in four days and ready to be moved to its permanent site.

help build a house to raise money for Disaster Relief projects. God has given us people with all kinds of gifts, such as digging, pouring concrete, masonry, framing, roofing, siding, spouting, electrical, plumbing, heating, laying tile, cabinets, trimming, deck building, painting, landscaping and cleaning. When I think of the amount of time it took to complete a project of this size, I would say it was a job well done. A project like this gives people the opportunity to give of their time, talents and money to help others in disaster areas.

Praise God for willing workers.
(Marty Witman, Florin COB, 1995 SB, p. 3)

When I was asked to serve on the Building Committee, I could have said, "No," because I was involved with other phases of the BDRA. Having been taught to work and help others, how could I say, "No"? New friends were made as we labored together for nine months, and the goal was accomplished. Surely God's hand

was at work. It has been a rewarding experience from start to finish.
(Landis Myer, Building Committee Vice Chairman, Conestoga COB, 1995 SB, p. 3)

I was so impressed with the involvement of people, churches and the community in building our first BDRA house. There was such a sense of closeness and fellowship among all who served and got involved. Truly the Spirit of the Lord blessed us! May the profit be used to Honor and Glorify God!
(Jay M. Witman, Building Committee Secretary, White Oak COB, 1995 SB, p. 3)

G. Children's Auction

Since the first Children's Auction in 2005, the children run the show at their own Auction for about an hour and fifteen minutes. They register for a bidding number and check-in to the Auction. Then, with their parents sitting beside them and counseling them, the children bid for their merchandise. Only bidding from children is allowed. Bids from adults will not be accepted–and the kids love it! Having an Auction just for children is a way to involve them in the auction process, giving them a positive, exciting experience and an identity with it.

Sale items which have appeal to children between ages five and twelve are mostly donat-

At their own auction, children learn to bid and the joys of winning as well as the disappointments of losing.

ed by businesses or individuals and are brand new, still in the box. Sometimes those skilled in woodworking and/or crafts will create things especially for this sale. The result is a nice mixture that includes dolls, toy tractors and equipment, footballs, games, toy barns, musical instruments, etc.

Even the auctioneers slow down their fast sales spiel to a more leisurely pace for the kids. In the heat of the low-speed bidding, some children never put their numbers down if they really want the item!

In order to make this an enjoyable experience, and guarantee that no child leaves the Auction without something, any child who has not bid on and received an item by the time the Children's Auction has ended, is invited to stay and receive a free gift.

Other children's attractions which have been offered at the BDRA include strolling clowns, making balloon animals, train rides, face painting, one-dollar-donation pony rides, a Children's Store, and puppet shows.

All of this has been planned to encourage parents to attend the BDRA and bring their

whole family. Free child care is also provided, so it can be a fun day for all ages.

(From an article by Carol Farmer in the 2007 SB, p. 24)

H. Coin Auction and Change Collection

The first Coin Auction, held as part of the BDRA, occurred in 2008 and operated with some pros and cons. The pros were that it had a good location with a lot of traffic, and because of that people noticed its display. The cons were that it had to be finished in an hour, and that it had poor publicity. The only pre-sale announcement was in the 2008 SB. As people walked past the coin display, several commented on their surprise at seeing a Coin Auction.

The idea of holding a Coin Auction as part of the BDRA began in 2007 when someone donated a roll of 20 silver dollars. That raised the question: Why not hold a special one-hour auction just for coins?

The Director of the Coin Auction is Dale Fahnestock. Although he is a long-time coin collector, the 2008 auction was a learning experience for him, as it was the first he had ever solely managed.

For its first year, the Coin Auction had 83 lots of coins, ranging from one coin to perhaps 25 wheat-headed pennies, foreign coins, Canadian coins, etc., and they managed to sell all 83 within their one-hour limited time frame. For information-sharing and time-saving, each lot had been listed and described on a printed list that was available to bidders. The best-priced lot was a set of 24 coins on the life of Christ made in sterling silver with a 24-carat gold coating which sold for $150. The total amount brought in was $3,895, of which $2,700 was profit and donated to Disaster Relief.

In 2009 and future sales, Dale is hoping for more publicity and that there IS a Coin Auction, so that with more awareness, there will be more donations and more bidders. Of course, he is hoping someone will show up to donate a special gold coin to make things really interesting. As Dale sees it, "Greater awareness means greater donations, which means greater profit, which means greater glory to God and a greater capacity to help those in distress."

(Personal Interview)

"A poor widow came and put in two very small copper coins, worth only a fraction of a penny…. 'This poor widow…out of her poverty, put in everything–all she had to live on.' " (Mark 12:42-44 NIV)

In the 2008 SB, an advertisement urged the readers, "Bring Your Loose Change to the Auction! Your bank doesn't want your change. However, this year we are equipped to handle all the loose change you can find. Just bring your jars, boxes, or bags of loose coins, and we'll help you unload it. It will be counted on the premises. Our goal is to have two tons of coins by Saturday afternoon."

(2008 SB, p. 27)

Consequently, for the first time in the history of the BDRA, young boys went through the auction buildings pulling a wagon with a container in which people were to throw any excess change they had. Since pennies add up to dollars, this is an idea that will be repeated—to increase the total amount of funds received to help those less fortunate.

I. Collectible Pottery and Longaberger Baskets

Because collecting quality pottery is a popular hobby, in 1992 the BDRA offered a one-quart pitcher in a series entitled, "Fruits of the Spirit," manufactured in Edgerton, WI, by Rockdale Union Stoneware. Of the two hundred sold, 50 pitchers were numbered and auctioned with #1 selling for $350 while the other numbered pieces brought $75 to $100 each, and unnumbered pieces sold for $45 each.

In 1993, the second "Fruits of the Spirit" offering was a two-quart crock with the inscription, *"This is the day the Lord hath made…rejoice and be glad in it."* Of the 150 sold, 50 were numbered consecutively. The unnumbered were sold for $50 each.

A one gallon pottery bowl with the inscription, *"In Everything Give Thanks,"* was sold in 1994. Out of 200 bowls, 50 were numbered. The unnumbered sold for $60 each.

The fourth piece of pottery was a one gallon crock with the inscription, " *'Tis a gift to be simple, 'tis a gift to be free."* inscribed on front. Two hundred crocks were sold in 1995, with the first 50 numbered. The remaining sold for $65 each.

The special collectible pieces of pottery usually are numbered and display the name of the Brethren Disaster Relief Auction and the year.

For the 20th Anniversary of the BDRA, the pottery was a one gallon jar with a lid and inscribed on the front with the words, "To God Be the Glory" and "20th Anniversary, 1976-1996." Again, 200 were ordered with the first fifty numbered, and 150 jars sold for $70 apiece.

In 1998, the BDRA began selling a new pottery series made by Eldreth Pottery in Oxford, PA. Each piece was handmade, salt glazed, hand-decorated, marked and dated, making each one unique. The one sold that year was shaped like a basket and had written on it, "Church of the Brethren Disaster Relief Auction, 1998." Once again, 200 pottery pieces were made with the first 50 numbered. Five unnumbered, but signed by the owner of Eldreth Pottery, David Eldreth, were also auctioned. The remaining 145 were sold for $75 each.

For the 26th Anniversary in 2002, the collectible pottery offered was a redware plate made by C. Ned Foltz. It featured the words, "Welcome, 2002" written on it in yellow slip along with a pineapple, the symbol of hospitality.

In 2004, 50 numbered pottery pie plates, cream-colored and with a blue daisy design,

were made by the Nola Watkins Collection in Virginia. The following year, 2005, 50 numbered buttermilk pitchers were made to match the pie plates. Each of these items sold for approximately $75 each.

A 1 ½ quart kitchen utensil jar made by Rowe Pottery was sold in 2007. Only 25 numbered jars were made and auctioned. They were inscribed with a heart pattern in the middle of the jar surrounded by the words, "Brethren Relief Auction, 2007."

In 2008, a second piece of Rowe Pottery, a one-quart crock was sold. Again, 25 numbered crocks were sold, featuring a heart pattern with the words, "Brethren Relief Auction, 2008," surrounding it.

Longaberger baskets, made in Dresden, OH, have been sold at the BDRA for many years. From 1990 to 1999, several baskets were donated each year and sold very well.

Beginning in 1999, the BDRA began selling the Generations Baskets, a series of six baskets. They were made in graduated sizes, hexagon-shaped, and were topped with lids donated by Basket Accessories in Akron, PA. Decorated with different hand-painted designs, on the inside of each lid were the words, "Church of the Brethren Disaster Relief Auction" and the year. Having these individually hand-painted lids made each basket unique. During the first five years, 25 baskets were sold each year and the lids were numbered inside from 1 to 25. The last of the series was the exclusive 5" booking basket, and since they were hard to get, only 12 of those were sold.

The first Generation basket we sold was the 8" one in 1999, followed by the 10" in 2000, the 12" in 2001, the 7" in 2002, the 14" and largest in 2003, and the 5" and smallest in 2004.

Since they were a popular collector's item, these baskets often sold for $350 to $400 each.

In 2005 and 2006, we again had 25 Longaberger baskets to sell, but they were different from in the previous years. While we had a 9" bowl basket and liner in 2005, the next year we had an 11" bowl basket and liner. The words, "Brethren Disaster Relief Auction" and the year were embroidered on each liner, and these baskets sold for about $175 to $200 each.

To commemorate the BDRA's 30th anniversary in 2006, we had 15 specially designed baskets made. They were white-washed medium Market Baskets with red and black trim strips around the band of the basket, fastened with Maple Leaf tacks. On the top of their lids were engraved the words, "Church of the Brethren Disaster Relief Auction 30th Anniversary." Each of these basket and lid sets was auctioned at $300 to $400.

In 2007, we had 25 Medium Crocus Baskets with "Brethren Disaster Relief Auction 2007" embroidered on the liners. These sold for $150 to $200 each.

Featured in 2008 were 15 oval Spring Baskets with painted lids, again donated by Basket Accessories in Akron, PA. With their beautifully painted lids, these baskets sold at $150 to $200 each. We also had five very special Collector's Club J.W. Heritage smaller cake-basket sized baskets made by Longaberger in honor of J.W. Longaberger, the founder of the company. An engraved lid topped each basket, and they sold for about $250 each.

The baskets to be sold in 2009 at the Main Hall Auction will be 15 Medium Chore Baskets with hand-painted lids.

❖ ❖ ❖

One of my fondest memories occurred in 1997 when we arranged for a basket weaver from the Longaberger company to come to the BDRA. We planned that she would weave 9 baskets on Saturday while people watched and were given the opportunity to help weave baskets, which were then auctioned. Having woven baskets for over fifteen years for the Longaberger Company, Amy McCullough, a native of Hartville, OH, enjoyed working with those people who stopped by to watch her work.

When her first finished basket was auctioned, it brought $425. Poor Amy was so astonished, she could hardly weave baskets anymore! She said she had never woven a $425 basket before, and it brought a big smile to her face. As the rest of the baskets were woven and sold, they continued to bring $375 to $400 each time. It was so much fun to watch Amy and see her expression whenever someone came to her stand and told her how much the previous basket had brought. She had a great time, but every once in a while said she had to "sit down and recover" because she could not believe a basket that she made was selling so well.

Finally, near the end of the day, her last basket was sold. For this event, Amy was at the Main Hall Auction to watch. After she was introduced to everyone at the BDRA, her last basket was sold for $1,200, and Amy was ecstatic! She could not wait to go back to the Longaberger Company and tell her friends about the BDRA and how much her baskets brought.

I still see her at Longaberger events today (12 years later), and she still talks about the time she came to the BDRA, and we sold her baskets. Having her as our Basket-Weaver at the BDRA has forged a wonderful friendship between us and we share a lot of good memories."

(Charlene Fahnestock, White Oak COB, 2009)

J. Crafts

The African boy listened carefully as the teacher explained why it is that Christians give presents to each other on Christmas day. "The gift is an expression of our joy over the birth of Jesus and our friendship for each other," she said.

When Christmas day came, the boy brought the teacher a sea shell of lustrous beauty. "Where did you ever find such a beautiful shell?" the teacher asked as she gently fingered the gift.

The youth told her there was only one spot where such extraordinary shells could be found. When he named the place, a certain bay many miles away, the teacher was left speechless.

"Why—why, it's gorgeous—wonderful, but you shouldn't have gone all that way to get a gift for me."

His eyes brightened and the boy answered, "Long walk part of gift."

Just as the African boy in the story, crafters work for hours, days, months, and even years at creating various objects of beauty and usefulness. A sampling of crafted items for sale in our main tent as well as those being sold by 50 local artists and crafts persons in the 200-foot tent includes: stained glass, dolls and doll clothes, children's clothing, decorated shirts, needle-work, baskets, handcrafted and custom made wooden furniture and toys, oil and watercolor paintings, lithographed mirrors, photography, Christmas ornaments, handcrafted jewelry, lampshades and lighting, pottery, candles, silk floral arrangements, table runners, placemats, tea towels, handbags, potpourri, pillows and more. Third world crafts sold through SERRV (Sales Exchange for Refugee Rehabilitation Vocation), such as baskets, wood carvings, needle-work, jewelry, toys and musical instruments are also available, and purchasing them helps not only the BDRA but also the poverty-ridden crafts persons who made them. In addition, you will find books sold by their authors, tapes and/ or CD's by musicians, African violets, games, and wreaths made from fresh greens and/or pine cones.

Including the stories of all the gifted people who have shared so generously of their skills and their creations through the years would be impossible in a single book, but we will share a few as illustrative of the many persons God has used to bring honor to Himself.

CHARLES BIEBER – CANING CHAIRS

My dad never knew he was going to be contributing to the BDRA of the ANE and SOPA Districts of the COB. In the first place, there was no such Auction in his lifetime. In the second place, Dad was a Methodist, not a Dunker. Nevertheless, Dad made a contribution.

Dad ran a laundry in Williamsport, PA, which had been purchased by its owner from an industrial home. Above the laundry was a third floor which was used for storage. When Dad visited up there, he found a man, formerly a resident of the industrial home, who was caning chairs. To keep him company, Dad often took his lunch to the third floor and—eventually, learned to cane. As soon as convenient, he taught his two sons, and later his grandson, how to cane chairs.

So, when I decided in 1995 to contribute to the BDRA by caning chairs, Dad was making a contribution. My plan is to provide the material and the skill to cane chairs for persons willing to make their payment to the Auction. The contribution feels good, but beyond that, it feels good for a retired pastor to be doing a task which gets finished. As much as I loved pastoral work, I would have to say that it was often difficult to see the progress. When I cane a chair, I can see the progress.

(Charles Bieber. 1997 SB, p. 34)

GARRY AND CINDY BLEVINS— SHAKER BOXES

In 1 Kings 17:2-6, God told Elijah to wait by the Brook Cherith, where he sent ravens to feed him until it was time for him to go into the city. When the idea of crafting Shaker boxes came to Garry and Cindy Blevins, it came in much the same way. God sustained them by providing what they needed to make quality boxes.

A little bit of history is built into each of the graduated sized boxes. The top box is made from wormy chestnut wood from the Miller House built in 1840 on Tannery Road in York County, PA. Its bottom is yellow pine from the

original Shrewsbury (PA) Lumber Company. Wood from a cherry tree that stood on a farm in Winemiller's Mill, MD, for over two hundred years has been used for another box. Approximately forty-five years ago, Valley Taylor, the farmer, cut down the tree and took it to the local sawmill to have it cut into boards. The owner of the sawmill "happened" to be Arthur Blevins, Garry's father.

Each box is handcrafted in authentic Shaker style, secured only by custom, hand-tooled copper tacks and wooden pegs. Two coats of hand-rubbed finish give the boxes a beauty to enjoy for generations to come.

(2000 SB, pp. 34,35)

BEN BRUBAKER—DOLL HOUSES

A retired farmer and member of Calvary Church in Lancaster, Ben Brubaker at age 75 was busier than ever making–doll houses! From June 1982, when he made his first one, until 1990, he had made 39 houses, of which 7 were sold and the others were donated to charity auctions for Lancaster Bible College, Lancaster Mennonite High School, Lancaster Christian School, Philadelphia College of the Bible and the BDRA.

His doll houses are distinctive because of the meticulous detail he puts into them. Bricks are individually painted, shingles are hand split, windows slide up and down, lights turn off and on, floors are parquet, and the banisters are hand turned with a lathe.

Enjoying creating houses in a variety of styles, he has made some that are Victorian, "The Scarborough"—a handcrafted English style, and Early American, similar to a Lancaster County farm house.

In 1989 he donated one in the Early American style with a large, wrap-around front porch and 6,500 individual pieces. Requiring 230 hours of labor and love in its construction, this child's dream house was complete with a date stone on the end. *(1989 SB, p. 41)*

A Vermont-style farmhouse with workable windows, 12-volt lights, parquet floors, cedar shingle roof, a 7" wrap-around porch, and a bay window with a copper roof, was his donation to the BDRA in 1990. The dimensions of this house were 33" x 29" with a height of 36" to the top of its chimney. Constructed from approximately 7,000 pieces and taking 250 hours to be built by this skilled craftsman, it brought $1,250 for the BDRA that year.

(1990 SB, p. 55)

DON DIBERT AND THE TALE OF THE TRIVETS

Those attending the BDRA in past years may recall auctioneers calling for bids for wooden hand-crafted trivets that resembled a "waffle with holes," cut from one piece of wood.

Making trivets became a constructive way for Don Dibert of Everett (Bedford County), Middle COB District of PA, to spend his days after being diagnosed with multiple sclerosis in 1990. Because of the disease, Don and his wife, Doris, discontinued dairy farming after nearly thirty years, the

Although disabled by multiple schlerosis, Don Dibert, Snake Spring Valley COB (left), made trivets in his shop. His son (right) sometimes gave him an extra hand.

third generation on the family farm.

While visiting former Brethren Volunteer Service (BVS) friends in Delaware, Don noticed a trivet on their kitchen table. Intrigued with how it was cut to look like two pieces of wood glued together, he carefully examined it to see how it was made. In 1991, with Doris back in the teaching profession and time to tinker in his workshop, Don decided to try his hand at making one.

The trivets started out as trees on the family farm—oak, cherry, walnut, locust, wormy chestnut and sassafras. A local sawmill cut the timber into one-inch boards. In an upstairs workshop, the boards were planed down to exactly 3/4th of an inch, then cut into sections for each trivet. Cuts were made on a table saw by a dado blade that moved back and forth to cut out each strip of the waffle pattern.

Dimensions had to be very precise so that

each strip left and the open spaces were exactly half an inch. By working from the outside in toward the center, and turning it over after each two cuts on opposite corners, the last strip of wood remaining measured one-half inch–if all went well! Two-color trivets were made by gluing together long strips of different kinds of wood, which provided a nice contrast. It took several hours to do all the same cuts in a stack of trivets that were all the same size. The next step was sanding with a belt sander and then by hand until all was smooth, and finally spraying it with several coats of mineral oil as a preservative.

As Don's multiple sclerosis progressed, it became more difficult for him to get to his upstairs workshop, so a chair lift was donated by the MS Society. In 1999, the farmhouse was remodeled to make a downstairs handicapped-accessible bedroom and bathroom. A new workshop was created in an adjoining summer house so that he could drive there in his motorized scooter without going outside, then helped to transfer to a chair at the table saw to work.

Don began making trivets in 1991 and found that he enjoyed giving them away as gifts or donations instead of selling them at craft booths or fairs. A record book was begun, listing the name of each person that received one, or where it was donated. The last count in his record book showed 1,104 were given away, and over 100 of them had been donated to auctions or for various causes. Another 220 were sold for $5 each, which helped to pay for the costs of sawing the boards and other supplies.

While traveling with Ken and Carol Kreider (from Elizabethtown) several years on bus tours to Annual Conferences, the Diberts met Hershey and Anna Mary Myer, who invited them to attend the BDRA in 1995 and

stay overnight in their home. Hershey's sister, Mildred, had been a teacher at Lybrook Navajo Mission in New Mexico while the Diberts were there as BVS'ers, and began a lasting friendship.

That was the first of six visits to the BDRA between 1995 and 2003, and the donations of trivets began. The Diberts looked forward to attending the BDRA as long as possible in order to greet old friends, enjoy the good food, craft booths, and be a part of the wonderful spirit of giving demonstrated there. They are proud owners of several quilts and other special items, each one a reminder of enjoyable times at the Auction.

A total of twenty trivets were sold at these auctions during those years with prices ranging from $15 to $40 each, and a total of around $425 was raised. In addition, the Diberts twice attended the SDDA in VA with nine donated trivets bringing in $322 there.

Several years ago, as Don's MS progressed and he lost the use of his left hand, it became more dangerous for him to use the saw, and sadly, he had to give up making his beloved trivets. Since April 2006, Don has been in a nursing home, but he still has his pleasant smile and love of life.

Because of his severe, progressive MS and being confined to a scooter, Don always regretted not being able to go on disaster relief trips as a volunteer. Instead, he used his talents at home with a saw and sandpaper to make trivets to help support the cause. This was his way of volunteering, giving thanks and glory to God and doing what he could to raise money to help others in need.

(Written by Don's wife, Doris Dibert)

❖ ❖ ❖

VERDA FAHNESTOCK—BASKETS

When she was a young married woman, Verda Fahnestock, now 88, saw some baskets and thought, "If others can make baskets like those, I can too!" She found a book on basket-making and, using it as a guide, taught herself the skill. Since then, she has made literally hundreds of baskets and continues to do so.

She has made Easter baskets for her five children and fifteen grandchildren and the arrival of great-grandchildren keeps her family numbers growing. As a member of the White Oak congregation, she lives in Manheim and doesn't regard her basket-making as an extraordinary skill. It's just something she has enjoyed doing for many years.

However, others truly value her work, and small baskets she has donated to the BDRA have sold for between $300 and $400 and are prized collector's items. What a blessing it is to see her using her gifts to raise money to help those in need! *(Personal Interview)*

❖ ❖ ❖

C. NED AND GWEN FOLTZ—POTTERY

Growing up in Lititz, PA, Ned Foltz graduated from the Philadelphia College of Art with a degree in graphic art. Upon graduation, at the age of 21, he began teaching art at Schuylkill Valley High School. During that time, he taught himself to make redware, the oldest form of pottery made by the early German settlers in Lancaster County, and has continued working in this traditional art form for over forty years. After 18 years of teaching, he

decided to devote his career to making pottery full-time.

Using red clay found locally, often digging it himself, he makes the pottery using many different techniques such as forming over molds, casting, hand-turning and sculpting. His decorating styles also are varied.

Today he is renowned internationally as one of the finest redware pottery artists, and his pieces have been exhibited in museums throughout the world. *Country Living* magazine, in its October 1998, issue, mentions Foltz pottery as one of the next collectibles.

Living locally, in Reinholds, PA, Ned made fine loaf slip decorated platters exclusively for the BDRA's 25th Anniversary year in 2001 with numbered pieces sold by auction and unnum-

Norman Gingrich is well known as a maker of quality baskets.

bered pieces sold at the information tables. We are so fortunate that he has such a giving spirit, for the BDRA has sold a number of his creations through the years, and in 2008, he donated a pottery birdhouse and a small pitcher.

(2001 SB, p. 65 and the website: www.foltzpottery.com)

NORMAN GINGRICH—BASKETS

For the last 20 years, Norman Gingrich, a retired farmer, has donated his distinctively tightly woven baskets to the BDRA. Having been married for 65 years, he is now a widower with six children and four grandchildren. He is a member of the Annville COB and says basket making is his main hobby. Today he lives at the Lebanon Valley Brethren Home, and although he is in his nineties, he still enjoys making baskets and thanks God that he is still able to participate and contribute to the BDRA.

FORREST AND VERA GORDON— APPLE BASKETS

"Let him labour, working with his hands the thing which is good, that he may have to give to him that needeth." Ephesians 4:28 (KJV)

After Forrest Gordon retired in May, 1991, from being a rural letter carrier, he and his wife, Vera, attended the BDRA in Lebanon. Although they had been to the BDRA before, and knew what the Grow Money challenge was all about, they never had plans to get involved. However, this time Forrest felt motivated to ac-

Forrest and Vera Gordon

cept an envelope containing the $10 because he felt sure there would be some way he could produce additional funds. When he took one, it was an on-the-spot decision.

A few days later, as he and Vera were considering money-making possibilities, Vera suggested, "Why don't you try making apple baskets?"

On their way to the 1990 COB Annual Conference in Milwaukee, WI, the Gordons had visited relatives in Eau Claire who took them to see the Paul Bunyan Logging Camp Museum. Some handcraft items were displayed there, including an apple-shaped basket, cut from a flat board, that telescoped into a basket with a handle on it. Forrest says, "Since my father was a sawyer and I had spent my earlier years as a lumberjack, I examined it and considered buying it. In attempting to open it, the handle broke, so then I felt *compelled* to buy it."

A cane and some of the wooden duck and apple collapsible baskets that were created by Forrest Gordon and sold in the BDRA crafts tent.

Sometime later, he showed it to a friend who was a real genius at making things. He asked to borrow it to make a pattern, and ended up making a few and had no trouble selling them. After Vera's suggestion of making apple-baskets, Forrest bought the woodworking machinery needed, set up a small shop in his basement and began production in October 1991.

Later a friend said, "If you ever make duck baskets, I would like one." So Forrest bought a duck basket at a craft show and a cane with a novel handsaw handle, designed patterns for them and began making them also.

To date, the Gordons have made 1800 apple baskets in oak, walnut and cherry wood, nearly 200 duck baskets, and 250 canes, and their sales from 1992 until after the BDRA in 2007 have totaled an astounding $47,361. What a return from a $10 Grow Money investment! From the beginning, they decided to give their total sales to the BDRA and have funded the expenses of purchasing needed materials themselves (about $6,000). The time

required in making these items was about 3 hours each or around 6,750 hours in all.

Forrest likes to ask, "Do you think God had something to do with that handle breaking on that basket at Eau Claire?"

But the Gordon story doesn't stop there.

Fresh out of military service in World War II, Forrest wanted to "do something of service to people." He operated a small excavation business in Bedford County for 12 years and then was called into the ministry. For almost 20 years, he served as pastor of the Bunkertown COB and Free Spring COB in Juniata County.

Forrest and Vera were both widowed as a result of auto accidents within a few months of each other. At the time of their marriage 42 years ago, two families were merged. At that time, Forrest was serving as pastor of the Bunkertown COB, and Vera says, "Taking on the role of a pastor's wife was quite an adjustment."

Forrest quickly adds, "She's done a great job," and they are still members at Bunkertown. Together they have four children, nine grandchildren and six great-grandchildren.

Both the Gordons are "people persons." With a quick wit, Forrest has enjoyed the hobby of performing over 800 magic shows since 1972 with the one most distant from his home being done in the Atlas Hotel in Cairo, Egypt. (They were on a Holy Land Tour, and Forrest "just happened to" have had some of his "magic equipment" along in his luggage. Others in the tour group kept urging him to do a show for them, so in Egypt he complied.) If you ask Forrest for one of his business cards, he will gladly share one with you and you can see his "show name" is *Flash* Gordon!

Since 1959, Forrest has donated 24 gallons of blood which he figures would weigh 40 pounds more than his present body weight. Meanwhile, Vera has been a volunteer cook for Meals on Wheels since the 1970s.

About 1978, an acquaintance from NJ, Robert Cryan, approached Forrest and told him of his dream to build an altar on some land he owned on Shade Mountain in Snyder County. Since he was "not too good with words," and wanted some way to express his belief in God and to share his faith with others, he had designed a place of worship that would be inspiring to people. Would Forrest consent to oversee the construction of it? After giving it prayer and thought and seeing the potential of a worship area on the mountain, Forrest agreed.

Thus it was that the Mt. Pisgah Altare ("high altar") was built and dedicated in June, 1980. Facing a view which, on a clear day, consists of eight counties, and constructed from mountain stone, the 10-foot high Altare is dominated by a 9-foot high rugged wooden cross mounted on its top. From the air, one can see that the concrete sidewalks that lead away from the Altare form a large cross, 104 feet x 62 feet, with the Altare in its center. Around it is a cleared area where 700 people can gather and worship.

Although the Altare has been promoted only by word of mouth and a notation in the Snyder County travel brochure, during the last thirty years it has been the site of over 600 weddings, plus church and Easter sunrise services, vespers, and other events. People are welcome to worship God there, regardless of denomina-

tion, free of charge and at any time. A small sign at the entrance indicates a phone number to call to make reservations for a wedding to avoid two groups arriving at once, and to help Vera keep a record of the services held there.

In his 90s, Forrest continues to preach frequently in other churches holding revival services or as guest speaker. Since 1981, he has been a volunteer speaker for the PA Council on Alcohol Problems at many Sunday morning church services throughout the year.

In a letter to the Gordons written in March, 2004, Rachel Good commented: "What a blessing you have been (and still are) to the Auction. Your age makes it all the more amazing and should be a challenge to older people that *retirement is never mentioned in the Bible!*"

In tallying up all his accomplishments, Forrest says, "Some people might call this 'boasting', and I would not argue with them. However, I believe it is witnessing for the cause of the Kingdom of God and our way of giving thanks to God for a great life."

(1997 SB, p. 45, 2004 SB, p. 29, and updates from Forrest & Vera Gordon)

CLARENCE GROFF —TROLLEYS

Trolleys from the Hershey Transit Company once ran along the main street of Palmyra, PA, carrying workers and milk to the Hershey Chocolate factory. It was the Palmyra-Hummelstown line, and it cost five cents to ride from Palmyra to Hershey. The last time a trolley traveled that route was on December 22, 1946.

There are still trolleys in Palmyra, although they would get crushed traveling the main drag. They are smaller models from various companies and they transport miniature people on tiny tracks. The chief executive officer of this transportation empire is none other than Clarence Groff.

Clarence is 84 now,[6] but his collection of trolleys started when he was seven. His mother bought him a tin toy trolley, which Clarence held on to, despite raising a house full of kids. It was that trolley that Clarence turned into his first electrical model when he was 65 or 70. "After I had that one built, I became trolley happy," Clarence said.

He's helped the BDRA to become "trolley happy" too. This is the fourth year in a row he will donate a handmade trolley to be auctioned. The previous donations brought $1,000, $2,000, and $900.

"I felt I'd like to do something different for the auction," Clarence said. "I was surprised the first one went so high."

Clarence's trolley company is housed in a long room in his basement. A long table in the middle of the room has seven tracks where trolleys can run back and forth. The room is also ringed by tracks, two of which go the whole way around the room. The section of the track that runs across the doorway is hinged so it can be dropped when the track is not in use. "I paid Edith (his late wife) $5 for the right-of-way across the door," Clarence said.

Clarence once ran a trolley off the track because he had this hinged portion down. He rigged it with lights and bells that warn him if the section is down when the power is turned on.

Clarence's trolleys are as ingenious as his hinged track. One could say Clarence "recycles" his cars, because each one is a collection of discarded items. The wheels are made from the lids of Plastic Wood cans. The bodies of the trolleys are fashioned from heavy gauge tin while the cow catchers on some of the cars are raised and lowered with delicate chain Clarence was given by Edith.

When he first started, Clarence painstakingly cut, drilled, and filed the windows and other details of the trolleys. Now a fabricator punches out windows and doors. A tinsmith rolls out the rounded roofs. Clarence handles the electrical work on his own. He has plenty of experience after founding and operating the C.L. Groff Electrical Contractor and Appliance Dealership (now called C.L. Groff Sons) in Palmyra.

The most amazing thing about Clarence's trolleys is their detail and accuracy. Tiny people ride the cars, while the freight models carry milk cans tended by uniformed workers. Windows have just the right shape, and each trolley has the correct number of windows. At one convention of trolley buffs a man told Clarence the windows on one of his cars should be straight at the top and not curved. Clarence made sure the next such model was accurate.

Clarence says that building and collecting trolleys "is what I did when I couldn't climb the Rock Pile (at Camp Swatara) anymore." This hobby has done more than replace a physical activity; it has preserved a piece of history and benefited the COB disaster relief effort.

(Judd Mellinger-Blouch. 1990 SB, p. 53)

Although the above article is a good introduction to Clarence and his trolleys, his life included many other interests. As a member

---

[6] Article was written in 1990.

of the Palmyra COB, he was a Sunday school teacher for 41 years, having a total of 586 students. He was elected a deacon, served as a delegate to Annual Conference five times, was chairman of the building committee for the Christian Education Building, helped in Youth Club, was a counselor for youth trips and assisted the pastors in hospital visitations and anointings. Not only that, but he served as head usher at the Ocean Grove Annual Conference and as Bible teacher and director at Camp Swatara who named him "Volunteer of the Year" in 1987. As part of the Palmyra COB Gospel Male Quartet, he traveled to many states.

Each year he faithfully continued to contribute his latest trolley creation to the BDRA, and although they always brought nice amounts, his trolley in 1988 brought the hefty sum of $2,000.

The widower of Edith M. (Boyd) Groff, he was the father of three children (one deceased), nine grandchildren, 20 great grandchildren, and one great-great-grandson at the time of his death on February 4, 2009 at the age of 102 after a long and productive life of serving the God he loved.

RUTH KNISS—DOLLS

When John N. Kniss died in 1983 after 52 years of marriage, his widow, Ruth, felt lonely and isolated. Locking the door to her home of 47 years in Bird-in-Hand, she opened the door to her new apartment at Brethren Village saying, "*You know, when God closes one door, He always opens another.*"

Ruth Kniss in 1989 with one of the bride dolls she dressed.

After a happy childhood on a farm in Mascot, Lancaster County, and growing up in a home rich in Brethren heritage, at age 16 she was asked to teach a junior class in Sunday school. Although she was apprehensive at first, this began 35 years of teaching various Sunday school classes at her home church, the Conestoga COB.

A graduate of Lancaster Business College, Ruth did office work until her marriage to John, a builder and cabinetmaker with an interest in collecting antique china and glassware. In his retirement years, he built over 300 grandfather clocks that were shipped throughout the U.S.

As the mother of three sons, Ruth was busy mothering, being a homemaker, fulfilling church commitments, and keeping account books for her husband's business. Upon request, she also made gowns for weddings, from the bride's dress to those of those of the flower girls. Because of her husband's hobbies, Ruth learned the art of repairing chips in china, a skill which became a springboard later into the world of dolls.

Years later, when an antique dealer asked her to replace a lost finger on a bisque doll, she obliged. The word spread, and soon others were coming to her with their damaged china and broken dolls, and she became known as "The Doll Lady."

Working on dolls for others kindled childhood memories of the first bisque-headed doll she had ever owned, one with beautiful blue eyes and long blonde curls, a Christmas gift at age six. She remembered well the heartbreak she felt when that doll was accidentally broken by her younger brother. These thoughts motivated her to begin a long, obsessive search for one exactly like her. Ruth was 63 before she successfully found and purchased that doll.

Her love of dolls sparked the decision to begin her own collection, and she accumulated quite a large one. Before she moved to the Brethren Village, most of them (about 250) were sold at auctions. She continued repairing dolls along with designing bodies for china-head dolls and dressing them. As she got older, she created her own dolls on a limited basis and donated them to the Brethren Village Auxiliary and various benefit auctions, including the BDRA, generating substantial funds.

During these years she said, "I am grateful that at this time in my life I am able to help others. The Lord has blessed me way beyond what I deserve. Not only do I find a special joy for myself in working with my dolls, but I also receive a great deal of satisfaction in being able to help others too. Giving to others is something which was passed on to me from both of my parents."

Among the quality dolls she donated to the BDRA was a Jumeau bride doll reproduction wearing a Gibson style gown, headpiece and bouquet which she made at age 81. With a bisque head atop a fully-jointed composition body, this 20-inch doll had earrings dangling from pierced ears, a lace-trimmed train, with every pearl and bead precisely in place. (Selling price was $775.)

She also made the clothing for a baby doll reproduction of the A.M. Dream Baby and it was sold resting in a replica of an 1885 cradle handcrafted by her son, Gerald. It was sold at the 1989 BDRA for $600.

One of her most popular and unusual creations was a doll donated in 1992 which she called, *"As I Remember Mother."* Dressed in the plain garb worn by Brethren women in the late 19th and early 20th centuries, the clothing style was copied from a photograph of her own mother.

The God-given combination of creative imagination and skilled needlework of Ruth Kniss will long be remembered, as well as her generosity in sharing what her nimble fingers accomplished so that others who were less fortunate could receive help.

(Excerpted from an article in the 1994 SB by Florence G. Mellinger, p. 47, and an article by Grace Joanou in the Intelligencer Journal, Lancaster, PA on Monday, September 18, 1989).

Olen Landes, Virginia, often made a little speech before Jay Witman would sell the wagon he had constructed and donated that year.

OLEN LANDES — WAGONS

The Rev. Olen B. Landes, 86, operates the deafening saw with steady, skilled hands, and a driving purpose. Landes cuts trees from his farm to build handcrafted wagons. He has been working in his woodshop for over 20 years.

"I don't know how many I've made. I never kept track of them," Landes said. He also has never kept one of his wagons and has never sold one for his own profit. After spending over 100 hours to build a cart, he will donate it to the BDRA or the SDDA.

Landes learned woodworking skills 69 years ago on his first job in a cooper's shop where he made barrels for apples, flour and produce. After gaining metalworking skills on his second job with a heating company, he started his own heating and air conditioning business in 1948. At 65, he retired and built a woodworking shop behind his house.

A leaf-covered rock path leads from the house to the cottage-like building among trees. The entrance to the shop is marked with a sign in the shape of a handsaw that says, "Dad's Shop." Inside the shop, there is a stack of oak, white ash and other grained wood. The smell of fresh sawdust lingers in the air.

The woodshop is not the typical shop. There is a lathe, table saw, jointer, band saw, planer, edge trimmer, mortiser and drill press. Obviously, building wagons is more than just a hobby for this craftsman.

To start the process, Landes selects an oak tree from his farm. He cuts it down and runs it through his own one-man sawmill to make it the right dimensions. The oak is then stripped and stacked outside for six weeks. Cutting trees and moving heavy wood requires strenuous labor and careful coordination, especially for a man in his 80's.

"The Lord gives me the ability and physical strength," Landes explained.

The wood is placed in his solar kiln, a triangular building with one side made of wood and the other clear plastic. It uses solar energy to dry the wood to prevent cracking. Wood stays in the kiln for another six weeks.

It requires 90 to 100 hours to make one wagon, not including the time it takes to prepare the wood. When it is time to make the wagon, Landes' mind's eye conjures the pattern. Each cart is made without a blueprint.

"They are not built to scale, but from memory," Landes said. He builds miniature replicas of a one-horse wagon from his childhood farm on West Mosby.

The crafter starts by turning the hub (center of the wheel) in the lathe. The spokes are made the same way. The router shapes the outside rims of the wheel, called "fellers." Spokes fit into the rims. The wheel is dipped into warm linseed oil to preserve it. Landes then stains and varnishes it.

"Each spoke has been turned out separately on the lathe. That's time consuming. There's 48 spokes to a wagon. After you get the wheels finished, you're about halfway through," Landes explained.

He then cuts the boards, sands and finishes them. The assembled boards form the body of the wagon. The wood is transformed from the rough, splintered texture to a smooth, flawless finish. Steel tires, footrests, and braces are welded and drilled. Inserting two sections of steel into the wood makes the axles. Steel springs are added by hand. The steel is cut and drilled to give it curves and then bolted with clamps to secure it to the wagon.

Landes donated a cart to the Bridgewater Home Auction, bought it at the auction for $3,100, and gave it back to the charity Auction. It sold a second time for $2,100. This is his typical contribution.

He makes five wagons a year. Each one is donated to a charity organized to help with disaster relief or social issues. His hard work and dedication to helping others touches many lives. The proceeds from his craft benefit the Mennonite Relief Auction, the Bridgewater Home Auction, the Weekday Religious Education Auction, The BDRA in PA and the SDDA held at the Rockingham County (Va.) Fairground.

Landes' handmade wagon is much more than a toy: It is a way for one man to make a difference. He has said, "This is something constructive I can do to help relieve the suffering in the world for the good of mankind because Jesus said that it is better to give than to receive."

Among the crafts persons are those who sell books they have written. Typical of these are Amos and Miriam Cassel selling the book We Called Him Papa *about Elder Charles D. Cassel, Amos' father.*

(From an article by Cynthia Norris, originally printed in The Shenandoah Journal. 2004 SB, p. 6)

❖ ❖ ❖

MARVIN ZIMMERMAN — WALL CLOCKS

Known for donating handmade wood items to the BDRA, Marvin Zimmerman, a member of the Reading COB, has also created beautiful colonial-style wall clocks with faces cross-stitched by the ladies of the Coffee, Crafts and Chatter group. Using a variety of woods including walnut, cherry, oak, maple and poplar, Marvin has been practicing his craft for over twenty years, but since his retirement, has become much more serious about it. He works on projects as time permits and can make and assemble an entire clock in about five hours.

(2000 SB, p. 34)

CHAPTER SIX

*"Love is a lot of little things that add up to caring. It doesn't always add up
to three little words. Sometimes it adds up to six: "I got your tank filled today."
"May I help you with that?"* Erma Bombeck

K. Endowment Fund

THE ENDOWMENT FUND of the BDRA was established in 1994 when Robert Young approached Mary Grace Martin about her interest in a Fund guaranteeing the continued existence of the Auction. Interest from this Fund is used to underwrite expenses of the BDRA, including rental of the fairground buildings and facilities and equipment such as tents, chairs, etc. When Mary Grace passed away in 2001, she left the Endowment Fund $131,000, bringing the total of her gifts to the Fund to $249,000.

Other donors giving significant amounts include the Wenger Foundation, which gave a gift of $100,000 in 1996 and three additional contributions since, bringing its total to $175,000, and the Marvin D. Messick estate, which has given three gifts bringing its total to over $108,000. Among the others who have given are: Carlos and Georgiana Leffler, F. Paul and Anna Ruth Shenk, Sale of Mohler COB Artifacts, Harry Gibble Estate, Landis and Audrey Myer, Raymond and Phyllis Zimmerman, Martha Bachman, Florence May Kreider, and anonymous donors bringing the total amount in the Fund at the time of the 2009 BDRA to $707,000.

The Endowment Committee does not actively solicit funds, but they do accept financial gifts from individual foundations or organizations who wish to designate monetary gifts for endowment purposes. Persons, organizations or foundations considering a gift to the Endowment Fund should phone or speak with a member of the Endowment Committee. Dennis Ginder serves as Chairman.

(2009 SB, p. 73)

A GIFT THAT KEEPS ON GIVING!

Gifts received for the 50th Wedding Anniversaries of Landis and Audrey Myer ($2,550) and Raymond and Phyllis Zimmerman ($1,940) were added to the BDRA Endowment Fund helping to guarantee its continued existence. *(2006 SB, p. 9)*

This is an idea other families could emulate.

L. Farmer's Market and Flowers

CLARENCE A. AND ANNA KEENER

In the early days of the BDRA, when the sale was still held at Root's Country Market, the original Produce Committee consisted of Claude Hess, Chairperson, C.B. Horst, Blue Ball COB, and Clarence Keener Jr., East Fairview COB, and they continued to serve for many years after the sale moved to the Lebanon Fairgrounds.

As a farmer, Clarence enjoyed working in the soil and watching things grow.

Today he and his wife, Anna, are retired and living at Brethren Village, but they still have green thumbs, and enjoy taking care of plants and shrubbery. In fact, they often do special plantings of pansies, geraniums, or other annuals in the inner courtyard area of the Lititz COB, where they now attend.

Married for 56 years and the parents of three children and having two grandchildren,

Clarence and Anna helped the BDRA in other ways. They enjoyed choosing colors, materials, and a pattern for quilts and then having others piece them and do the quilting. When a quilt was completed, the Keeners would donate it to the BDRA. They also made many contacts, collecting items to be sold, and helped in transporting them to the Auction.

Besides their gardening hobby, the Keeners enjoy travel, and Anna plays the accordion in a musical instrumental trio with Ken and Polly Graybill. Clarence says: "I praise God for giving me continued good health and the ability to have been a successful farmer."

(Personal Interview)

Ken Heisey (left) and Ed Kegerreis are ready to sell the top-quality, freshly-picked donated green beans and cider in the produce area. Ron and Wendy Copenhaver have been donating 35 bushels of greens beans to the BDRA annually.

FERN KING

In the early years of the BDRA, the farm produce, consisting mostly of sweet potatoes grown on the Lord's Acre of the Middle Creek COB, was on a wagon and auctioned along with used lawn and garden items. In 1987, Fern King came by and wondered why the sweet potatoes were not displayed. "People can't see what they're buying," she commented to the committee of Claude Hess, Clarence Keener and C.B. Horst.

When that sale concluded, Fern came back and said if Eugene Miller would help her, they would plan the Farm Market arrangement for 1988. Without knowing what they would be selling besides sweet potatoes, potatoes and eggs, they combined excitement with hard work and put up a tent just for the produce. When people brought in donations of vegetables and fruits, Fern arranged them in colorful sections.

On the first day, inquisitive people started coming in to see and to buy what was in the tent. Since it was early and the displays were not completed, a rope was placed across the entrance with a sign that clearly announced the time the market would be open for business. However, that didn't deter buyers, and they kept climbing over or stooping under the rope line to get in! That first year, the Farmer's Market sales were $3,132, and they have grown since to over $12,000.

The produce tent survived not only untimely visitors, but also storms. One year the tent was being lifted by heavy winds, and various men on the Committee had to literally hold onto the poles. Even though Eugene Miller was tall, he was almost lifted also! In fact, when a pole snapped in his hands, all welcomed the help of men with sledge hammers who secured the pins.

On another occasion, a "peppermint pussy" (skunk) came to investigate the produce,

"All the flowers of tomorrow are in the seeds of today."

Unknown

but wisely chose neither to eat nor to leave new scents there!

Fern kept a journal beginning in 1988 of the amount and kinds of produce offered in the Farmer's Market. For starters, you could see green beans, peppers, potatoes, cabbages, eggplants, zucchinis, cucumbers, onions, apples, peaches, plums, grapes, berries, celery, lima beans (even shelled), jams, jellies, pickles, chow-chow, apple butter, and endless other items. For example, one year's totals included 70 bushels of green beans and 500 quarts of chow-chow.

Today, when BDRA attendees enter the Farmer's Market area and view the abundance of homegrown produce that has been donated for the glory of the Lord and in thanks to Him, their thankful thoughts should include the late Fern King, (a wife, mother and grandmother), and Eugene Miller who had the vision and dedication to bring this vital feature to the Auction.

(From an article by C.B.Horst. 2003 SB, p. 4)

One year a farmer brought a wagon-load of watermelons, which looked beautiful from the outside. However, when Eugene Miller picked one up, he heard and felt sloshing inside. When he cut one in half, he discovered it was rotten. Immediately, he concluded, "I am not offering these for sale. These are only fit for pigs."

The farmer returned and wondered why his watermelons were not on display to be sold. When Eugene explained that they were rotten inside, and he only wanted to sell first quality produce in the BDRA's Farmer's Market, the farmer became angry and said, "When you get something given to you, you should be grateful. I am never going to donate anything to this auction again."

(Personal interview with C.B. Horst)

Dwight Markey loves growing beautiful flowers which his wife, Treva (above), enjoys arranging in bunches to be sold at the BDRA.

DWIGHT AND TREVA MARKEY

Treva Markey, a former member of the Board, can usually be found at the BDRA sitting behind a table of bright-colored floral arrangements, smiling and ready to sell you a bouquet of flowers grown in the huge field behind their home along Joppa Road in York by her husband of 57 years, Dwight. With their own greenhouses, the Markeys are semi-retired from the floral business, but Dwight still grows flowers to cut and arrange in bunches to sell at the Leola wholesale auction bringing in $3,000 last year, which he donated to various charities. In 2008 their flower sales at the BDRA amounted to $800.

At the BDRA, Dwight is usually nearby, helping at one of the produce stands. When he is not working in his flower garden, Dwight enjoys taking apart, repairing and repainting old farm machinery. Because both Markeys enjoy travel, they have toured extensively from Iceland to Australia, from Alaska to the Panama Canal, Scandinavia and Europe, taking thousands of photos of the wonders of God's creation and especially, the flowers.

Treva, a nurse, also has gone on mission trips to orphanages in Moldova and has been a member of the COB Disaster Childcare Services for about ten years. In LA, she remembers especially a little 3-year-old boy who couldn't get interested in playing until he shared his story. Having been rescued from the roof of his house by a man hanging from a helicopter, he lifted his shirt to get sympathy for his "boo-boos" which he got in the process.

When the children did painting or coloring, Treva noted that they always chose dark colors such as dark greens, dark blues, browns and blacks as that was how the hurricane looked to them, and that experience was still prominent in their thoughts.

One black couple with four children were so traumatized that they didn't trust to leave their children with the childcare team. Refusing to leave in the car, the father kept sneaking back to check on his children. Finally the caretakers took some Polaroid pictures of the parents with their children and gave orders to everyone: "Only give these children back to these people on the photo." When they would come back for the children, the photo would be returned to them. When they returned, the mother apologized because the children didn't want to leave with them—they wanted to stay!

Even though both are in their eighties, the Markeys host several Share-A-Meals each year, not only for the BDRA, but also the Brethren Home at New Oxford and other York County charities. They explain, "We do it because we want to do it, not to receive praise for it. We praise God for life, health, strength and the ability to continue to use our abilities and skills to serve Him and our fellow man."

(Personal Interview)

EUGENE AND MIRIAM MILLER

"Coming together is a beginning. Keeping together is progress. Working together is success." This statement, often repeated by Eugene Miller, also describes his philosophy of life.

When Eugene was selling a head of cabbage for a nickel at various markets for his father, Graybill Miller, in the 1930's, little did he know that he was in training to be a truck farmer with expertise in fruits and vegetables. Or that God was going to some day use that knowledge in starting a produce stand at the BDRA.

Members of the White Oak COB, where he taught Sunday School for 58 years, Eugene and his wife, the former Miriam Dagen, have

Eugene Miller (left) shares his years of marketing experience by attractively arranging the fruits and vegetables.

five children, 15 grandchildren, and several great-grandchildren.

Eugene and Miriam farmed many years at Washington Boro near the Susquehanna River. In addition to selling his produce seasonally at stands at Root's Market and year-round at Green Dragon, Eugene built a roadside stand near his home. The Millers grew acres of strawberries, raspberries, endive, lima beans, and were well known for their tomatoes and sweet corn. During dry spells, they would irrigate out of the Susquehanna. In addition to experimenting with new varieties of produce, Eugene developed methods of storing tomatoes and endive for Thanksgiving and even for Christmas, but he always said, "The Lord gave me the ideas."

Together with Fern King, who worked with him at his Green Dragon produce stand, Eugene took on the challenge of starting the Produce Stand at the BDRA—in a tent. He vividly remembers one year of winds and heavy rain, hanging on to the ropes holding the tent down, with streams running through the tent, causing wet feet. He continues to work tirelessly to have a bigger and better Farmer's Market display each year. Many times he goes without sleep during the Friday night of the BDRA, driving to various places overnight to pick up more fresh produce for Saturday.

Although Fern King has passed away and Eugene has had two hip and one knee replacement surgeries, he continues to make contacts, seek and pick up donations, display and sell produce for the glory of the Lord. He feels that God has been faithful in healing him and he has been very dedicated to his niche in the BDRA ministry—so much so that sometimes he even celebrates his birthday there!

(2007 SB, p. 4)

The Blue Ball COB is famous for its chow-chow. Here Thelma Kline (left), Jane Weaver (center), and Linda Brubaker (right) are ready to sell it.

CHOW-CHOW TIME AT BLUE BALL

In 1990, Doris Horst from the Blue Ball COB helped to sell canned goods at the BDRA and observed that chow-chow was something that sold very well. After talking to several ladies, we

decided to can chow-chow for the 1991 BDRA. Here's a short history of how we did it.

We used the recipe of the late Eva Wanner, who canned chow-chow and sold it at her market stand. Her daughter, Jane Weaver, shared it with us.

In March, we put a note in our church bulletin reminding everyone, before they plant their gardens, that we would be needing vegetables in September.

In August, there was a list prepared as to the amount of things we would be needing. This was passed in our adult Sunday school classes for several Sundays, and we always had people willing to donate the vegetables, jar tops, sugar and vinegar. The following is an approximate list of vegetables we used: 24 qt. diced red peppers, 32 qt. diced celery, 60 lbs. diced carrots, 32 qt. cut green beans, 24 qt. cut yellow beans, 20 lb. small onions, 24 large heads cauliflower, 80 lb. sugar, 8 #10 cans kidney beans, 3 gal. vinegar, and 44 qt. pickles.

On the second Tuesday of September, we met at 7 a.m. in the Blue Ball COB kitchen to process and can the chow-chow. We invited whoever was able to come Monday evening to help chop the vegetables. Tuesday morning each vegetable had to be cooked separately and lightly salted. Jane Weaver usually oversees this part of it, as they may not be cooked too long or they will be mushy. After they were cooked, we drained them and poured them into a large washtub where the syrup was added and all was mixed well. We then returned it to the stove in large kettles and it was brought to a full boil. We all got involved in filling and sealing the jars. It sure smelled good, and the jars looked beautiful when they were finished. Usually, six to ten ladies were helping, and by noon we were finished and ready to go home to wash our sticky hands and clothing.

The amount made each year varied between 102 qts. and 26 pts. in 1991 to 149 qts. and 156 pts. in 1997. The reason it varied so much is because sometimes folks have a little extra of something, and that makes the final count different.

We hope each of you who bought the chow-chow enjoyed eating it as much as we enjoyed making it for you and for the honor and glory of God.

(By Polly Good and Doris Horst. 1998 SB, p. 49)

M. Foods

WHAT DO THE WOMEN DO IN THE BDRA KITCHEN?

Changes are taking place--more food, more people, more work. Just imagine, our breakfasts went from serving 600 in 1984 to 1,000 in 1993 and 1,150 in 1996. We served 70 gallons of soup thirteen years ago and now[7] we prepare 160 gallons. Pot pie, one of the favorites, sells out fast. We will have 15 roasters serving 600 people at $2 a bowl. Hamburgers and turkey burgers have gone well, selling 1,000 of each. Fries, fries, and more fries! We sold 2,000 lbs. of them in 1993, but we now sell 3,000 lbs.! Pork sausage sandwiches numbering 450 are obviously popular, and we can't forget another favorite: the hot dog with sauerkraut. In 1984 we sold 1,000; in 1996 that number was 2,500, sold at the reasonable price

---

[7] In 1997.

of $1 each. In 1993, meals using 3 roasted pigs were consumed and we also sold 1,000 pies and 95 dozen sticky buns. Refreshing drinks from Wengert's have reached a high of 4,000, and we sell the same amount of sodas. Pork sandwiches and pork dinners at $7 are Saturday's big-time eating choices.

New menu items during the last two years have been 500 chicken barbecue suppers, cheese steaks and chicken sandwiches, serving about 1,000 of each. Food, yes, we served food–and LOTS of it!

Speaking about change, a big one for us happened when we went from a very small 2 x 4 kitchen to a "mansion" where everyone feels we can work together. However, when the BDRA is over, it's hard to believe how we did it all, but we do want to give God the glory and honor.

(By T. Grace Ziegler for the Food Committee: Lois Witman.(Co-chair), Richard & June Blouch, Verna Kline, Grace Cox, Leah Ritter, Martha Hackman, Darel Seibert, Anna Mary Hess, Ruth Henry and Darlene Godfrey. 1997 SB, p.49)

Hungry auction-goers can enjoy a hearty breakfast of either pancakes and sausage or ham and scrambled eggs. Homemade soups are served at lunch.

Aspects of the role of the cooks that few of us think about are the fact that these women work through the entire auction and never get to participate in the buying and selling–even as spectators. Lois Witman pointed out, "In the last few years I finally got to hear the Auction in the main hall."

And their work is not over when the BDRA ends on Saturday afternoon. Lois added: "We always went back to the Expo kitchen on Monday to sort things and pack them away."

(Personal Interview)

❖   ❖   ❖

HAROLD AND MIRIAM HORST

Ever wonder how the chicken barbecue dinners got started at the BDRA? At a Share-A-Meal hosted by Landis and Audrey Myer, among the guests were Jay Witman and Harold and Miriam Horst. During their dinner conversation, the subject came up that having a "Sit-Down Meal" on Friday night at the Auction might be a good idea.

Since Harold had done barbecued chicken (using his dad's secret recipe) as a part-time income for many years and had earned the reputation as being one of the best, all eyes turned to him. After some coaxing and persuasion, Harold said he would present the idea to the Pathfinder's Sunday School class at the Conestoga COB, and they agreed to give it a try. Harold prepared the chicken and baked the potatoes while Miriam, with the help of a committee, organized the rest of the menu and servers. Because it was such a success, they continued

preparing the dinners each year from 1996 through 2004. After those nine years, other members of the Conestoga COB stepped up to the grill under the direction of Irvin and Joyce Groff and Donna Riehl and have continued serving the chicken barbecue dinners on Friday nights at the BDRA ever since.

The dinners are truly a group effort, requiring as many as 65 pairs of hands and feet and most of the month of September to get everything accomplished. Among the tasks required to prepare this important segment of the BDRA are these:

- Gathering 7 ½ bushels of apples, cooking them, sieving them through a colander to make applesauce for the BIG DAY
- Ordering paper supplies to serve 1,000 meals
- Ordering 12 gallons of Wegman's pepper cabbage
- Ordering 1,000 drinks from Graybill's Dairy through Sharp Shopper
- Ordering 85 dozen rolls from Achenbach's Bakery
- Ordering enough chicken to make 650 halves and 350 legs & thighs
- Getting the best price on 1,000 Russet potatoes
- Baking 97 dozen cupcakes
- Ordering 16 lbs. of butter pads, 40 lb. of sour cream
- Soliciting workers to make the applesauce, package the plastic ware, fill 1 oz. containers with sour cream, fill over 1,000 4 oz. cups with pepper cabbage or applesauce, wash-dry-&-wrap the 1,000 potatoes, and load the truck with all the supplies.
- Pick up the rolls at Achenbach's Bakery

- Pick up the truck and keep the perishable goods cold until the next morning
- Load and unload the equipment for the chicken to be grilled
- Set up the pits, light the fires, rack the chicken, then spray and turn it at the right times, get those potatoes baking and taken off when finished
- Pack in insulated containers and transport to the serving site
- Give service with a smile to all the wonderful customers—and then—
- CLEAN UP!!

During the nine years that the Horsts were in charge, 7,688 chicken dinners were consumed consisting of 33 bushels of apples, 88 gallons of pepper cabbage, 618 dozen potato rolls, and 7,450 drinks plus cold water, resulting in a profit of over $25,000 for disaster relief. In the years since then, over 3,500 more meals have been served, bringing in $20,000 more.

Since their "retirement" from making chicken dinners, Harold and Miriam, who have been married 48 years and have two children and four grandchildren, are still very active in their church. They continue serving as deacons, choir members, on the Witness Ministry team, National Bible Bee Planning, as well as counseling part-time at COBYS and going on Disaster Relief Projects in Va., Fla., Mich., and La. Their only comment: "We thank God for good health to serve Him wherever and whatever He leads us to do."

(Information sheet from Harold and Miriam Horst, BlueBall COB)

T. GRACE ZIEGLER

"What a fellowship! What a joy divine!" T. Grace Ziegler from the Richland COB uses these words by hymn writer, Elisha A. Hoffman, to describe her experience of serving as co-chairperson of the BDRA Food Committee (along with Lois Witman) for fifteen years before transferring that role to Darel and Jan Seibert in 2000. During those years, she and her committee literally prepared and served thousands of meals at the Lebanon Fairgrounds.

Without any education beyond high school but strongly motivated by having lived in foster homes as a child, having a deep love for all hurting people, and a strong religious faith, T. Grace Ziegler has made a difference, not only in the BDRA's kitchen, but also by:

- Serving as a teacher's aide with Special Ed children in the Eastern Lebanon County School District for one day a week for nine years.
- Having a nursing home for senior citizens in her own home from 1965-1972 with a maximum of eleven people at one time between the ages of 65 and 88, nine women and two men.
- Co-sponsoring (with her husband) fifteen international refugee families and helping them get acclimated and started in their new life in the United States.
- Opening her basement as temporary living quarters to ten of the above refugee families, other foreign visitors, prisoners released from jail, families whose homes have burned, and others in crisis situations.
- Helping to begin the Lighthouse Ministry in 1980 in Richland for pregnant girls and

unwed mothers. Ten years later it combined with the Susquehanna Valley Pregnancy Center and Grace served on their board from 1996 to 2007.

- Participating in numerous short-term work camps in Nicaragua, Honduras, Nigeria, Mexico and MS.
- Always being active in her local church's women's organizations, a church deaconess for 20 years, teaching children from third through twelfth grades in Sunday school, doing volunteer work in the kitchen, etc.
- Serving 4 years on the board of the Alpha and Omega Church of the Brethren, a Hispanic congregation located in Lancaster.
- Promoting natural health products to help people live fuller, drug-free lives.
- Always being available to drive someone to the doctor, comfort the ill, care for children, etc.
- Being the mother of five children, the grandmother of 20, and the great-grandmother of eight, plus "mothering" ten foster children.
- Saying, "Whatever I can do for them, I do." No wonder her husband called her his "Amazing Grace," and her son says, "Mother is always willing to help anyone, anywhere, anytime."

Grace was married for 52 years until her husband, Victor, a Lebanon County dairy farmer who also served his church and community well, died in December, 2004. Because she has reached out to people in her community and in the world in all of these ways, she was a recipient of WGAL-TV's Jefferson Award in April, 2006.

Along with Grace Ziegler and Lois Witman, women who have served in the BDRA

kitchen for many years are Verna Kline, Anna Mary Hess, Helen Patches, Ruth Henry and others. Since we all love to eat, the food committee is an important one! We are grateful for the commitment of these ladies who have worked hard behind the scenes for many years and served us all graciously, providing us with plenty of delicious food.

AT THE BDRA, ANYTHING GOES!

On Saturday, September 27, 1997, an unidentified woman attending the BDRA with some friends stood in a food line for herself and for those in her party. After a long wait, the woman finally got to the front of the line and her food of choice–several bowls of chicken pot pie–was handed to her on a tray.

As she returned to her seat in the Main Hall, Dave Buckwalter, who was auctioning on stage at the time, saw the steaming bowls of pot pie pass by on their way to being devoured. In front of everyone, he abruptly stopped auctioning, and addressed the woman, "Could I have a little–one bowl–of that chicken pot pie?"

"You wouldn't ask that if you knew how long I stood in line for this pot pie," she quickly retorted.

"If you stood in line that long," Buckwalter reasoned, "then they must be worth something."

To the amazement of the crowd, without hesitation, he began auctioning off the bowl of pot pie. The audience entered into the fun of giving and $280 later, Dave was relieved from auctioning for a few minutes to enjoy *his* bowl of pot pie. Undoubtedly, the woman returned to standing in line once again, happy with the knowledge that she had unintentionally helped the cause of the BDRA that day.

N. Gift of the Heart Kits

In 2005, Hurricane Katrina, one of the strongest hurricanes on record, hit the southern shores of the United States less than three weeks before our BDRA was to begin. Although we wanted to get involved, there was little time to plan and less time to organize. Sometimes, however, this forces us to depend upon God to supply the answers and solutions.

The answer seemed to come rather clearly and quickly. The idea of building 10,000 Gift of the Heart health kits was conceived and plans began to be finalized. The support for the project seemed to grow rather quickly, and, as a result, we (Duane Ness, Jay Witman, and Larry Hollingshead) increased the goal to 20,000

kits. On the Tuesday morning before the auction, I authorized the purchase of items that would be required to assemble approximately 30,000 kits, with an estimated cost of goods well over $100,000.

Then we waited and prayed. The items necessary for 30,000 kits were on their way, but would anyone show up to assemble them? By Saturday morning, Larry Hollingshead, who had volunteered to supervise the project, had briefed his core group of leaders of the task ahead, and the challenge was begun sharply at 8 a.m. When the onslaught of 450 volunteers arrived, the leaders provided directions to the group. The spirit of camaraderie and service to those in need was apparent to all, including the very young, the middle-aged, and the young at heart.

Before 11 a.m., the kits were completed and loaded on waiting trucks ready to take them to disaster relief. What had never been done before had been accomplished in grand style and at a record-breaking pace of completing one kit about every three seconds. There was a dedication of the kits later in the day to acknowledge that God had blessed our work, so that our efforts would bring honor and glory to Him. By the time the accounting for auction year 2005 was complete, individuals and churches had contributed funds greater than what was spent to purchase the items for the kits. The vendor who provided the goods proved to be very generous. Normally, the estimated cost for assembling these kits is about $12, but our cost per kit was slightly more than $3 each.

(Excerpted from an article by Duane Ness in the 2006 SB, p. 7)

By working together, it is amazing how many "Gift of the Heart" kits can be packed in several hours!

"Many hands make light work" in packing "Gift of the Heart" kits.

In 2006, because it was the 30th Anniversary of the BDRA, we decided to prepare for 30,000 health kits which were then assembled by more than 300 volunteers. Again, every 3 seconds a kit was completed and over $80,000 was donated for supplies.

More than 200 volunteers assembled 12,000 school kits in 2007, 12,000 school kits in 2008, and plans are in the making for 12,000 more to be completed at the September, 2009, BDRA.

(Larry Hollingshead, Codorus COB)

O. Golf Tournaments

The idea of holding a Golf Tournament to raise funds for the BDRA began in 1995. The following are some of the facts in brief showing the contributions made by those who enjoy this sport:

1995 August 17 – First BDRA Golf Tournament was held with 124 golfers on Par-Line Golf Course in Elizabethtown. Raised $4,771.

Beginning in 1995 and including 2009, the Mechanic Grove COB sponsored an annual Golf Tournament, raising a total of $150,049 or an average of $10,003 per year for those 15 years. See below for more data on those tournaments for 2007-2009.

2007 July 28 – BDRA Golf Tournament at Cool Creek Golf Club, Wrightsville. Cost: $75 pp.

2007 August 3 – BDRA Golf Tournament at Pilgrim's Oak Golf Course. Sponsored by Mechanic Grove COB. Cost: $60 pp. Raised $12,100.

2008 July 26 – BDRA Golf Tournament at Cool Creek Golf Club, Wrightsville. Cost: $75 pp.

2008 August 6 – BDRA Golf Tournament at Pilgrim's Oak Golf Course. Sponsored by Mechanic Grove COB. Cost: $60 pp. Raised $13,050.

2009 August 7 – BDRA Golf Tournament at Tanglewood Manor Golf Club, Quarryville. Sponsored by Mechanic Grove COB. Cost: $65 pp. Raised $12,500.

2010 August 6–Northeast Golf Tournament. Sponsored by Mechanic Grove COB. Cost $65 pp.

P. Grow Money

Introduced at the 1989 Auction, GROW MONEY has become an important part of the proceeds of our annual sale. Every year 220 envelopes, each containing $10, are distributed to any interested individuals. Using the principles taught by Jesus in the parable of the talents in Matthew 25: 14-30, the challenge is to use this money and make it grow for the BDRA the following year.

When the envelopes were returned last year, $14,000 was received. Some of the completed projects and the amounts raised were:

$ 74 raised – knitted and sold caps
$100 raised – planted and sold sweet corn
$100 raised – made and sold crib quilt
$125 raised – car wash
$154 raised – made and sold Easter lollipops
$250 raised – crocheted images of various fruits and sold them
$320 raised – baked and sold shoo-fly pies
$336 raised – baked and sold sugar cookies
$350 raised – sold miniature Indian corn
$372 raised – baked and sold Christmas cookies
$500 raised – housecleaning
$556 raised – lemonade and tea stand at craft show
$810 raised – yard and bake sale

You, too, can participate. *Just use your imagination!* *(By Ken & Deb Weaver. 1991 SB, p. 15)*

I was called into the home of an elderly lady, and all these envelopes are alike; they say GROW MONEY. The inside of her house was pretty crude. I saw a bed, I saw a chair, I saw a table, I saw a dish on the table and I saw a kettle on the stove. The room temperature was sort of cold.

The woman said, "Mr. Witman, between Lizzie Longenecker (an elderly lady) wanting to do something and the little children (we have a lot of children's stuff being incorporated into the Disaster Relief Auction), I wanted to do something also. But, you see, I couldn't do anything with my $20."

I said, "That's okay. It's all right."

Then she pulled out the GROW MONEY envelope and gave it to me. It was thick, very thick.

She continued, "Every time I thought of the Disaster Relief Auction and I would pray for the Executive Committee, I would try and put fifty cents or one dollar in, and this is what I am giving back."

I walked out of that house, and I'll never forget it. I hopped in my car and went home. I counted the money and it was over $500. This woman must have been in prayer all the time!"

(Jay M. Witman, 1994 SB, p. 56)

"Plant a seed for those in need."

Breanna Kreider proudly holds one of the five zucchini breads she made from "scratch" with Grow Money. To her amazement and joy, they sold for $125 each at the 2002 BDRA!

At the BDRA in 2007, I watched the auctioneers pass out Grow Money and wondered how I would be able to make that money grow. Then I got an idea: Why not invest it in my hobby/retirement business? I buy toy 1/16 scale trucks which need repairs and recondition them, returning them to what they were back in the 1950s, specializing in Smith-Miller L Model Macks, and also American Needle Nose Kenworths.

So I accepted $20 of Grow Money, and when I invested in my very next transaction, the Grow Money grew by 51%. Then came an order for a very specialized piece of equipment, an all-

stainless tanker, and that deal grew the money by 30%. After 36 more deals, the Grow Money grew enough for a 1952 L. J. Smith-Miller Mack Northwestern Lumber Hauler for me to repair and customize to its heyday condition.

It was surely wonderful to be able to donate this beautiful toy truck to the 2008 BDRA with 100% funding from Grow Money.

(By Irwin L. Groff, Conestoga COB, 2008 SB, p. 19)

BREANNA KREIDER

What can a twelve-year-old do for the hungry of the world? Ask Breanna Kreider of Quarryville, PA. She has an answer!

"Oh, my goodness! I'm in shock!" Those words flowed from excited twelve-year-old Breanna Kreider as she met her parents after the first of her five donated 6 ½" zucchini breads brought $125 at the BDRA in September 2001. By the time all five had been sold, Breanna's contribution had raised $650.

Auctioneer Jay Witman invited her on stage to display her zucchini bread and this Mechanic Grove COB lassie beamed brighter as the bids went higher. Given $10 as "grow money" from the BDRA last year, Breanna turned $10 into $650 for hunger and disaster victims around the world.

Having always loved her grandma's zucchini bread, she had asked for her recipe to try her baking skills to make several loaves for her church auction to benefit the building fund. The response to that experience inspired her to bake loaves for the BDRA. Hearing that her grandfather, Russel Kreider, bought the first loaf, she said to him, "I could have made one for you for nothing!"

Her challenge continues. Reflectively, Breanna exclaimed, "Thank you to the bidders for being so generous. I'll be back!"

(From an article by Earl K. Ziegler, 2002 SB, p. 11)

WHEN THE SEED OF AN IDEA IS PLANTED…IT GROWS!

Landis, Audrey, Candy and Randy Myer, members of the Conestoga COB, had a crazy idea about how to use their $40 of GROW MONEY: to host people in their home each month and donate the proceeds to the BDRA. At first, the idea was daunting, but after an-

nouncing their plan at the wrap-up meeting for the 1990 Auction, they were committed. Beginning in November, 1990, on the second Friday of each month, from 6-8 p.m., they would provide a soup and salad meal for whoever would come to their home. Publicity was by word of mouth, with a special invitation to members of their home church.

When they designed and built their home, Landis and Audrey planned their spacious and attractive basement to handle large family gatherings, so they could accommodate up to ninety persons.

Each family member was involved. Landis prepared and served the soup. Audrey baked the cakes and served as hostess. With all helping to prepare the salad, daughter Candy was in charge of setting up and coordinating the dining area, while their son, Randy, handled clean-up. Thirty persons showed up the first month, and on the final month, they served 130 persons!

Those interested were asked to call each month to make reservations for their simple, but ample, meal. The soup of the day was always a surprise! Guests could count on a varied salad bar, cake and homemade ice cream for dessert. Prayer was offered at the beginning of each evening. After that, folks could come and go as they pleased, going past a crock for donations as they left.

The result? From the "seed" of their $40 of GROW MONEY, the Myer family were able to contribute $5,859 to the BDRA, and the benefits didn't stop there! In addition to extending disaster relief work and honoring God, the Myers family discovered other rewards.

Landis felt that "fellowship—meeting all the different people—was the most fulfilling for him. The meal was good, but I think the fellowship was the highlight of the whole thing. We met people that we never would have met otherwise."

Audrey agreed, adding: "Meeting different folks—as they experienced fellowship with each other. I think we all felt that, and just having people who hadn't seen each other for years meet once again. That just surprised us. Folks told us, 'It's so nice that we can come into a home and enjoy the evening.' "

When asked to identify the toughest part of this project, Landis replied: "Keeping Audrey calm! But over all, things went smoothly."

Audrey added, "It was a great year, a trying year sometimes, but very rewarding. It was an opportunity for us to share our Christian witness and at the same time to give God the glory for the tremendous results."

(Excerpted from an article by Del Keeney, pastor of the Conestoga COB. 1992 SB, p. 10)

With the seed of ten dollars each for nine persons ($90), members of the Pathfinder's Sunday School class at the Conestoga church continued the project that the Landis Myer family had started–of using grow money to serve a meal once a month. Headed by sisters Miriam Horst and Ruth Shirk and their husbands, Harold and Glenn respectively, the same basic menu was served, only more persons became involved in the preparations and serving and the location was changed from a home to the church's fellowship hall. Mim Horst explained, "We have tried to provide decorations to make it appealing, with a friendly, homey atmosphere to encourage folks to come back." For example, a special touch for February was a huge heart-shaped cake topped with the Disaster Relief Auction logo made by Gloria Burkhart.

At the end of four months, their contribution had grown to $1,321 and they were serving an average of 81 guests per month. Ruth summarized, "It is a very fulfilling venture for God's glory."

(Excerpted from an article by Del Keeney. 1992 SB, p. 10)

CHAPTER SEVEN

"It is true that ignorance and poverty abound in some places; but are the souls of the poor less dear to the Lord than the souls of the rich?"
- John Kline, 1797-1864, 1994 SB, p. 48

Q. The Heifer/Livestock Sale

As chairperson for the Heifer Auction Committee, Bob Lentz has been a strong encourager. Every year he says, "We're going to have a *good* sale."
And the Committee always believes him!

During drought years, many dairy farmers were discouraged because of not knowing where the feed was going to come from for their animals to eat. How would it be possible to buy new ones at the sale? Even then, Bob's faith for a great sale was contagious and victorious.

(2004 SB, p. 50)

On the day of the very first Heifer auction in 1982, when the BDRA was in session in the Main Hall, Harold Kettering suddenly came in the door carrying a very young calf on his shoulders. He walked to the front and the auctioneers invited him to come up on the platform. After some questioning, he said he had come there to remind everyone that at a certain time a Heifer Auction would be beginning at a certain place. Since it was so unexpected, it was a scene that some attendees never forgot!

HAROLD AND RACHEL GOOD

With their strong faith and generous spirit, Harold and Rachel Good exemplified by their lives, *"I can do all things through Christ Who gives me strength!" (Philippians 4:13).* For over ten years, they gave countless hours to the BDRA as they served on both the SB and heifer committees for almost 20 years.

After losing his first wife, Jane (Kreider), by drowning in her attempt to rescue one of their children from drowning, Harold and his second wife, Rachel (Zug), endured many more times of tragedy in their personal lives. During their 38-year marriage, they operated a large dairy farm in York County, PA, and raised eight children.

In their home church, the Pleasant View COB, they served as deacons. Known for their friendliness, smiles, sense of humor, hard work and compassionate spirits, they served their church and the BDRA faithfully through the years. Harold was affectionately known by his twinkling eyes and jolly, wheezing laugh and Rachel as a strong supporter, skilled needleworker and wonderful cook.

With their hard work and generous giving, they were not ones who stood by saying, *"Lord, when did we see you hungry and feed you, a stranger and invite you in, or needing clothes and clothe you?" (Matt. 25:37, 38 NIV).* Harold and Rachel were always there, praying, feeding, welcoming, sharing and serving.

After Harold's death on January 18, 1999, the BDRA SB of that year was dedicated to him and to Rachel in appreciation for all they had done in sharing of their time, money, and talent to the glory of God.   *(1999 SB, p. 4)*

Since then, Rachel has continued to serve on the BDRA Publication Committee another ten years to date and donated at least one quilted wall hanging each year with $385 the highest amount bid for one. Active in her church's women's fellowship group, she also continues to help others by volunteering at the York Rescue Mission Economy Store and babysitting her twenty-one grandchildren and twenty-eight great-grandchildren.

"I thank God for the many friends Harold and I made working on BDRA committees. I can't think of any church activity in either of the two Districts that bring people working together (both liberals and conservatives) like the BDRA does–and for such a worthy cause!"

(Rachel Good)

ROBERT AND RUTH HENRY

"Whatever your hand finds to do, do it with all your might." Ecclesiastes 9:10 (NIV)   This verse exemplifies so well the spirit that motivates Bob and Ruth Henry in every aspect of their lives.

In 1989, when the SOPA District became full participants in the BDRA, the Henrys, who were already involved, became one of the first coordinators from that district. Since then, Bob and Ruth have been familiar faces at the auction. Bob may be found in the Pole Barn area, unloading items he has hauled from the SOPA District. He has also served for years on the Heifer Committee, raising small calves at his home to be sold at the auction. Two sons, Wayne and Mark, have also caught the spirit and help to clean and show the heifers.

Ruth has been a member of the Food Committee and helps to feed the volunteers on

Wednesday and Thursday of Auction week, and both serve on the Publications Committee. During winter months, Bob delivers many pick-up truck-loads of blankets and other needed items to the York Rescue Mission, Access of York, New Life for Children, soup kitchens and other agencies which serve the York area needy.

Although Bob has retired from employment in a furniture factory and more recently as a security guard, and despite a heart operation several years ago, he is still busier than ever. Besides mowing lawns with his sons during the summer and working at seasonal jobs with Brown's Orchards in Loganville, he still has time for such hobbies as gardening and showing his collection of miniature cows on display in their sun porch.

The Henrys have been just as busy in their home congregation, the Pleasant View COB, where they have served as deacons for more than thirty years and have participated in Men's and Women's Fellowship and various committees. In recent years, they joined Gideon's International and give Bible presentations at churches and other locations. Through it all, these faithful servants continue to work quietly behind the scenes, seeking no recognition but serving willingly and prayerfully to "Honor and Glorify God."

In appreciation for all their efforts, the 2002 SB was dedicated to them.

(By Rachel Z. Good. 2002 SB, p. 4)

ONE COW'S TALE

Question: What's black and white and increases the participation of a congregation in the BDRA?

Answer: A heifer named Megan

In 2003, the Madison Avenue COB, located in the city of York, was challenged to buy a heifer for the BDRA. They had never done this before and were not sure at first if there would be enough support for this project. An experienced farmer from the congregation was helpful in answering questions about the project, and the decision was made to raise the money to buy one. Megan, a bred heifer, was purchased and when September arrived, was off to the Auction. The congregation had been kept informed regularly of the project's developments.

When Auction day arrived, several members from Madison Avenue COB went to Lebanon to see how much money Megan raised and to say goodbye to this honorary four-legged member of the church family.

Following the Auction, the congregation was pleased to hear Megan had been purchased by a Lancaster County farmer for $1,500, turning their contributions into funds enabling them through the BDRA to give glory to God by helping others. When the church heard that Megan had given birth to a bull calf in January, they were happy again.

Throughout the project, the congregation learned more about the BDRA, and as a result became more active participants. Perhaps your church could do this also.

(From an article by Elizabeth Kauffman and Deanna Crawford. 2004, SB, p. 50)

CLARENCE L. KEENER, SR.

When he was baptized into the East Fairview COB following a revival by Elder

Henry King, did Clarence L. Keener realize how he would be led to service?

When he was welcomed into the church by a kiss of fellowship from Jacob Ruhl, did Clarence L. Keener realize how that might lead him to being excited about the BDRA?

Basic to it was Clarence's own statement: "I was happy to be a farmer!" And that is what he did until back problems at the age of 57 made it necessary to leave most of it. With a special interest in celery farming and with five acres of it, his Keener celery became well-known in the Lebanon/Manheim area. Another love was dairy cattle and his well-respected herd of registered Holsteins. As if that wasn't enough to do, he also raised hundreds of pounds of potatoes from Maine and Nova Scotia seeds.

However, his friendship with Ruhl and his commitment to service are what got him involved with the BDRA from its very beginning. For 22 years, until he "retired" in 1998 at the age of 89, he made personal visits and telephone calls to solicit advertisements for the annual BDRA sale booklets. He followed up his work by distributing the booklets to the advertising businesses and churches.

Recognizing that helping often begets more helpers, he became involved for twelve years with HPI. He provided supervision in Lancaster, Lebanon and Chester counties for 600 heifers to be sent overseas. When he was almost seventy, he planned to travel along to take heifers to Tanzania, and had actually boarded the plane. However, at literally the last minute, to his great disappointment, he was prevented from going because of FFA regulations on the number of human passengers allowed. However, Tanzania remembered, and on Clarence's ninetieth birthday in 1999, the

farmers there sent him an internet letter of gratitude.

For 56 years, Clarence's partner in his work were his wife, Ruth (Arnold) and their three children: Clarence A. Keener, (husband of Anna M. Gantz), Barbara, (wife of Fred Longenecker), and Nancy, (wife of Christian Landis), seven grandchildren, seven great-grandchildren, and for his last eleven years, his second wife, Thelma (Haldeman).

In appreciation for his honoring God through a life of service, the 1999 BDRA SB was dedicated to Clarence L. Keener.

(1999 SB, p. 4 and updates from
Clarence A. Keener)

Clair and Betty Kreider

CLAIR AND BETTY KREIDER

As a dairy farmer, Clair Kreider, from the Mechanic Grove COB, had a keen interest in the Heifer Sale, and even after he retired, that interest continued. According to Clair, the Heifer Sale began when Olive Peters asked if he would serve on the Communications Committee of the BDRA. In checking to see what the churches of the ANE District were doing for the sale, he discovered that women were baking, making doilies, comforts, and quilts. He decided the men should be contributing more than money!

One day, while sharing this concern with Stan Bucher, Stan suggested that one answer might be to have a Heifer Sale. Since Clair thought that sounded like a good idea, he invited these five men to a meeting: Cliff Gibble, Henry Kettering, Amos Balsbaugh, Cassel Mummau and Glenn Shenk. Together, they formed the first Heifer Committee.

Their meetings were always held at the Kettering's home, and Clair remembers fondly that Maybelle always served delicious refreshments.

After contacting the churches of the ANE District, the first Heifer Sale was held in 1982 with 42 head selling for $42,565. At that first sale, Carlos Leffler bought $3,300 worth of heifers and resold each one.

One year a man from the Palmyra COB donated an Angus. Although the committee had never had a beef animal donated before, they decided to try it. She was sold and resold seven times and brought $3,000. The next year she was brought back with a calf.

Clair served as president of the Heifer committee for thirteen years, and was succeeded by Robert and Sandy Lentz. The SOPA District churches joined in 1988.

The Kreiders like to sing, and Clair is no exception! Each year, on the Sunday after the BDRA, during the sharing of "Joys and Concerns," the Lampeter COB congregation, where Clair and Betty are members, can expect Clair to stand up quickly singing with zest the spiritual, "Sit Down, Brother, I Can't Sit Down, I've got good news and I can't sit down!" Then he shares

the financial results of the BDRA, especially emphasizing what the Heifer Sale amounted to and also the selling prices of the quilts, wall hangings, theme baskets, or craft projects that anyone in the congregation had donated.

An idea for celebrating birthdays and/or anniversaries: A donated heifer, which had been purchased with monies collected by the family and friends of Clair and Betty Kreider in honor of their 60th Wedding Anniversary, was sold at the 2005 BDRA and brought in $5,800 for disaster relief.

(2006 SB, p. 31 and Clair and Betty Kreider)

A black heifer, donated to the 1992 BDRA by the Harvey T. Bomgardner family, was sold at the heifer auction on Friday evening. Purchased by a Palmyra COB Sunday school class,

Clair Kreider introduces the Sunday School children of the Lampeter COB to the heifer they have bought with their offerings so it can be donated and sold at the 1991 Heifer and Livestock Sale.

this heifer was then donated to HPI to become one of 105 head that were donated to the Jessor organization in Jordan.

The first week of October, the heifers were flown by plane from Middletown, PA, to Amman, Jordan, where they were given to needy families to produce milk for them. The family receiving a heifer must agree that her first female offspring will be passed on to another needy family. In that manner, the gift goes on. Praise God!

Founded in 1944 by Dan West, a midwestern COB member, HPI is a *help-up* rather than a *hand-out* program.   *(1993 SB, p. 30)*

LITTLE CHILDREN
SHALL LEAD THEM

Without the benefit of *Isaiah 11:6, "… and a little child shall lead them" (KJV)*, but with the same spirit, the children in the third and fourth grade Sunday school class of the Palmyra COB decided in 1999 to purchase a heifer calf for the BDRA. Beginning in February, they saved and contributed their money each week and decided to buy their heifer locally so it could come to visit their Sunday school class before going to the BDRA.

One Sunday in May their dreams came true. By that time, they had collected enough money so that they were able to buy a black and white heifer calf, which they named "Oreo" when she actually visited their class. It wasn't clear how much Oreo learned that day in Sunday school, but the children were very excited! Just as the animals given away by HPI eventually provide for many people, the chil-

dren wanted *their* heifer to help others. With the help of George and Michael Ungemach, who fed and cared for her until the time for the sale in September, the children hoped to attend the BDRA and see Oreo once again. In doing this project, they gave glory to God, helped the needy, and–perhaps led others.

(George Ungemach. 1999 SB, p. 45)

When Warren Eshbach was serving as Moderator of the SOPA District of the COB, he and his wife, Theresa, lived on a small farm near East Berlin in York County, PA. At the BDRA, they bought a small heifer calf but had no way to get it to their farm.

Harold and Rachel Good had come to the BDRA in a van, so they offered to take out the middle seats. They put the calf in the van, and Rachel sat on the floor holding it for the entire 90 minute ride to its new home. Rachel's comment afterwards: "It was worth it."

In the Spring of 1990 the Lancaster COB Daily Vacation Bible School Committee was presented with a challenge: to use Bible School offerings to purchase a heifer calf for the BDRA. The committee and staff were excited about the idea, and the children who came to Bible School that first night were thrilled with the challenge. The following night, the calf we were buying visited our Bible School. The children instantly fell in love with "Joanna," a darling black and white spotted 3-month-old heifer. As they petted her, they learned that it would take $300 to buy her. Therein lay the real challenge! Our Bible School offerings had never totaled that much.

On the next to last night of Bible School, we had only raised a total of $160. The amount collected was posted on a thermometer chart so the children knew exactly where we stood. At that point, everyone's faith became a little shaky. "We'll never get enough money in just one more night," and "How are we going to handle the children's disappointment?" These were just a few of the many thoughts racing through our minds.

On the last night of Bible School, the offerings came in. Children had raided their piggy banks, and parents had dug deep into their pockets to go that extra mile. The final result was well over the required $300. The expressions on the children's faces when they learned of their success were sights that most of us will never forget. Smiles went from ear to ear, and shouts of joy could be heard all over the church.

On the night of the Heifer Auction, several children from Bible School traveled to the Lebanon Fairgrounds to escort Joanna to the ring for bidding. They beamed with pride as they stood in the ring with "their" calf and observed the auction process, eagerly waiting to see how much Joanna would raise for disaster relief. Joanna was sold for $2,600. As if that weren't enough, the gentleman who bought her donated her back to be sold again, so Joanna was sold a second time for $1,900. That buyer also donated her to be

resold. In the end, Joanna was sold a total of five times and raised $5,450 for disaster relief!

What a fabulous experience for all those involved! The children learned that even though they are young, they can still play an important role in showing God's love to the hungry and displaced persons in our world.

(By Becky Fuchs. 1991 SB, p. 38)

❖ ❖ ❖

A young black goat that was sold again and again.

ELVIN AND IRENE MOLISON

Wherever there are people with needs, Elvin and Irene Molison feel compassion, so they are always ready to volunteer in many areas of the BDRA.

Being dairy farmers, they've been active in the Livestock and Heifer Sale for many years, raising, donating and helping provide for numerous heifers. Elvin can tell interesting stories of spending nights in the cattle barn caring for the animals prior to the Auction. For example, sometimes they took the back seats out of their van, curled up somewhat, and managed to get a little sleep. Other BDRA sleeping quarters for them were the back of their pickup truck, a camper, and also on hay bales. Fortunately, the cattle were usually well-behaved and quiet at night.

Their participation in the BDRA began when Cliff Gibble, a semen salesman for Select Sires, who regularly came to their farm, asked if they would be willing to donate a heifer. That year they had been blessed with more heifer calves than bull calves, so they were "happy to donate to this worthy cause." Later, their church, the Hanover COB, also got involved in buying calves from the Molisons and donating them to the Heifer Auction.

In 1993, when they were Disaster Relief Work Camp volunteers, they prayed that since they were farmers, they would get to work on a farm, and their prayers were answered. They were assigned to Hull, IL, where the Mississippi River had flooded the area. Elvin and his 16-year-old daughter did wallboarding, Irene helped with cooking and spackling, and they all shoveled debris from one home. All agreed it was a very rewarding week. In fact, Elvin recalls it as "the best week of our lives."

As SOPA District Coordinators, they attended Board meetings, arranged for Kick-Off Dinners, assisted with TURF disbursements of funds, shared as hosts and as guests in Share-A-Meals, and worked on Disaster Response teams. Not only that, but Irene has coordinated tractor trailer truck trips to Winchester, VA, to pick up Rubbermaid items and assisted in selling them as well as promoting the sale of flower bulbs.

They are not only heavily involved with the BDRA each year, but also support and attend the Mid Atlantic District DRA in Westminster, MD, the SDDA in Harrisonburg, VA, and the Mennonite DRA in the Harrisburg Farm Show building.

In their church, they serve as deacons, church board members, and are active in Sunday school, and Elvin is the contact person for The Decade to Overcome Violence emphasis. In their community, Elvin volunteers at the Inclement Weather Shelter sponsored by the Hanover Council of Churches, and Irene assists with Meals on Wheels.

Married while serving as conscientious objectors in alternative service on the Norristown Hospital farms, they continue to give On Earth Peace, another COB emphasis, priority in their lives.

Since Elvin and Irene are the parents of two children and two grandchildren, they especially enjoy having family and friends gather and sing together around the piano while Irene plays. In her "spare time," Irene enjoys reading, tropical fish, caring for children, entertaining, and exercising her "green thumb" by working in her rose garden and sharing beautiful home-grown bouquets, while Elvin enjoys carpentry.

Because the Molison's serve their Lord so gladly, prayerfully, humbly and faithfully, the 2003 SB was dedicated to them. Today they are grateful to God for their salvation, their family, their church family, and their good health.

(From an article by Doris Fogelsanger.
2003 SB, p. 4 and updating questionnaire)

In 1982, at the first Heifer Sale, 42 head were sold for $42,565.

In 2008, 60 head brought in $102,000.

To God be the glory!

Left to right: Jean, Doran, and Cassel Mummau.

CASSEL AND JEAN MUMMAU

For almost two decades, Cassel Mummau was a faithful member of the BDRA's Heifer Committee. Having worked as a salesman for 39 years, Cassell worked for Florin Farms for 20 of those years selling baby chicks to poultrymen and selling for Young's Inc. the other 19 years. And he isn't finished selling yet! On most Saturdays he goes to flea markets and garage sales to buy farm and garden-related items and on Mondays he goes to sell them at the New Holland Flea Market and Horse Sales.

Having retired from working at the Manheim Auto Auction, Cassel and his wife, Jean, retired from seamstress work, both enjoyed square dancing for many years. They are the parents of two sons, Jeff and Doran, and are members of the Florin COB. Because they also enjoy traveling, for years Cassel planned and directed numerous short trips for senior citizens of the ANE district and beyond. Jean's favorite travel destination is the Grand Canyon, and they have hiked down into it at least twelve times. In fact, they celebrated their 64th wedding anniversary in 2009 by going down into that beautiful canyon one more time!

Snowmobiling is another favorite hobby, and Cassel organized 18 snowmobile trips in 17 years through Yellowstone National Park. One year he had a group of 64 people with him, but he really feels 12 is enough!

With a compassionate heart, Cassel has been a part of several disaster response teams. In addition, Jean, an excellent seamstress, and Cassel have donated quilts and many feed bags to the BDRA. Most of the feedbags were from local companies, many with logos of Florin Farms/Wolgemuth Brothers and other farm suppliers. After being quilted by members of the Florin COB or by Ann Diller from the Lampeter COB, the feed bags brought between $175 and $350 each toward disaster relief.

Although Cassel has retired from serving on the BDRA Heifer Committee and organizing tours for seniors, he still enjoys traveling and can be counted on to have a few good stories to share. About his retirement, he simply explains, "I thought it was time to sit back and let the next generation take over."

When he counts his blessings, he has his "good life partner, Jean, and my two sons" at the top of the list, followed by the good health which has enabled him to enjoy a long and fulfilling life.   *(Personal Interview)*

At the beginning, only dairy heifers were to be sold. Several years ago, a family from the Palmyra Church gave a Black Angus, and the committee decided to accept it. It was sold and resold eight times bringing a total of $1700. Last year one of the heifers on the sale had a bull calf a day or so before the sale. "To sell or not to sell," that was the question. The calf was sold and resold for $885.

(Clair E. Krieder, Chairperson of
Heifer Committee. 1987 SB, p.14)

As a family in 1987, we donated a heifer to the BDRA. The Lewiston, ME, COB also gave $100 toward the expenses of the heifer. Marlin's cousin, J. Hershey Myer, Jr., and family came to Maine to truck the heifer to PA, and when the heifer was sold, Marlin's brother, Paul, who is a farmer in Lancaster County made the highest bid. We were delighted to see our animal go to a familiar home and again felt blessed to be able to give to the BDRA in ways far exceeding our expectations.

(Lois Ann Minnich, 1997 SB, p. 29)

At the 2008 BDRA Heifer and Livestock Auction, students of the New Covenant Christian School in Lebanon donated a lamb named "Midnight" which brought $1,100 after being sold several times.

We would like to pay a special tribute to Roy Miller and Stanley Kleinfelter who were faithful through all the years of the heifer auctions in helping to prepare the animals for the auction. We know the Lord will bless their families for their service. Stan's son, Randy (Whitey) has been helping for several years and when his father passed away on the morning of last year's auction, he came to Bob after the auction and told him that he will continue to help in preparing animals because this is what his father would have wanted him to do."

(Sandra Lentz. 2000 SB, p. 28)

GERALDINE AND DANIELLE— GOOD BRETHREN HEIFERS!

A really good heifer has a way of staying in one's thoughts. At least, that is what happened to Don and Lois Brandt from the Mechanicsburg COB after Geraldine and Danielle were sold at the BDRA.

Although Don had helped with the produce stand several years, in 1998, he volunteered to help with the heifer sale, as he was then retired and had time on his hands. Some heifers were hard to manage and didn't want to go where they were being led.

That's when Don decided to buy one and give her a "proper training." In fact, he did this two years in a row and states, "I raised two good Brethren heifers!"

Since Don isn't a farmer but does love working with animals, he built a small pen under roof and enclosed an area as a pasture of sorts so that these heifers could feel at home, sort of. Both Don and Lois could be found on any given day holding talks with these heifers! Not surprisingly, it was difficult to part with each of them, but knowing the proceeds went to help others made the parting a bit easier.

"Anyone with a couple of acres can do this," Don reasons, admitting that his age was a factor in discontinuing the process after the second heifer, Danielle, went to Auction. By the way, Geraldine was named in honor of Don and Lois' pastor, J. Gerald Greiner, and Danielle was named in honor of Dan West, founder of HPI.

(From an article written by Lois Brandt and Sara Wilson in the 2002 SB, p. 44)

R. Hymn Sings

Hailed as "The Celebration of a Decade," the first BDRA Hymn Sing entitled Sing unto the Lord—"An Evening with a Treasury of Great Hymns" was held on Sunday evening, September 29, 2002, at the Lebanon Area Fairgrounds. With a 400-voice choir and a full or-

Music directors of the 2006 Hymn Sing with Jay Witman and Duane Ness (left to right): Jay Witman, Ben Detrick (violin soloist), Thomas Diehl, Arlene Keller, Martha Shaak, Michael Shelly, Bob Kettering, Thomas Wise, and Duane Ness.

chestra, the choral and orchestra directors were: David Diehl, Tom Ford, Arlene Keller, Robert Kettering, Deryl R. Lutz, T. Michael Shelly, and Tom Wise. Total congregations participating were 115.

Two years later, on September 26, 2004, "Sing to the Lord," the second evening with "A Treasury of Great Hymns" with a 400-voice choir was held again at the Lebanon Area Fairgrounds. The third Hymn Sing occurred on Sunday evening, September 24, 2006, and celebrated the 30th Anniversary of the BDRA.

In 2008, some changes were made. "An Afternoon of Favorite Hymns" was held on Sunday, October 19, at the Sight and Sound Millennium Theatre near Strasburg, PA.

Featured on the program was a 300-member choir with orchestra, and Dr. Myron Augsberger was the speaker. Music directors were

In June 1995, those at the "special table" at the Kick-Off Dinner under the white tent on the Jay Witman lawn (seated left to right): Betty and Merville Messick, Earl and Vivian Ziegler, Ken and Marion Messick, and Bob and Marie Messick, were treated to extra perks such as shrimp cocktail appetizers, cloth napkins, and were to be served by Jay Witman. However, Jay was hospitalized at that time, so the servers at the "special table" were Laura Stoltzfus and Nancy Wenger.

Robert K. Kettering, Don V. Mitchell, and David Diehl. During orchestral numbers, Venona (Bomberger) Detrick and her son, Ben Detrick, each had a violin solo. The offering received that day was $9,360. This program was rebroadcast on AM radio on November 2, 2008, on WLBR 1270.

❖   ❖   ❖

S. Kick-Off, Praise and Faith Dinners and Concerts

In 1993, Jay Witman developed the idea of a Kick-Off/Fund Raiser dinner to both bring honor and glory to God and also to raise funds to defray the expenses connected with the annual BDRA. Consequently, on June 12, 1993, the first dinner was held under a huge tent on the spacious lawn at Jay's home near Manheim and sponsored solely by Jay himself. After those attending (close to 300), had enjoyed a sumptuous meal with dinner music provided by the Hand Bell Choir of the Palmyra COB, Jeryl Metzler, from the White Oak COB, along with Bob and Libby Kettering, provided a vocal program.

At this first Kick-Off dinner, a tradition was begun when Jay Witman asked the audience to suggest the names of aged, sick or shut-in persons to receive the lovely centerpieces which had been created and donated by Carl and Millie Bomberger. When the reservation money and the offering were combined, the event raised $5,700 for the honor and glory of God and disaster relief.   *(1993 SB, p. 30)*

Since then, at following Kick-Off dinners, early arrivals could socialize with friends and enjoy punch and crackers under a small tent in the Witman front yard. By the time the dinner hour arrived, 400 to 500 persons were ready to move into the large dining tent, where tables were attractively set with linens, beautiful floral centerpieces donated by Carl and Millie Bomberger, china dishes, and silverware by volunteer helpers. The menu, prepared by Landis and Audrey Myers, Marty and Lois Witman, and other volunteers, was usually fruit cup, steak, chicken, baked potatoes, angel food cake with fresh strawberries and all the fixin's that go with a meal like that.

When all the guests had been seated, Jay regularly welcomed them warmly. An opening prayer usually expressed gratitude for God's many blessings and for the privilege of ministering in God's name to those who suffered disaster, as well as for the meal. Entertainment during the evening was provided by soloists or musical groups from within the two church districts sponsoring the BDRA.

In 1994, a special table seating eight was sold (for fun—and to add to the proceeds for that evening) with the understanding that only Jay would be the server for that table and that they would have some special "perks" throughout the evening.

After hosting the dinner in the tent for five years, at mid-morning on Saturday, June 13, 1998, it was decided to move the Kick-Off Dinner to the Hempfield COB due to the predictions of an approaching violent storm. Although it was held there again in 1999, it was moved in 2000 to Yoder's Restaurant near New Holland, and has been held there ever since.

As a result of the meal tickets sold, the "special table" sale, and an offering received at the dinner, the annual proceeds raised by the Kick-Off dinner usually amount to $10,000 to $15,000. To God be the glory!

CARL AND MILLIE BOMBERGER

While working with and for Millie's dad, Paul D. Wenger in his flower shop, Carl and Millie were influenced in their faith, spiritual growth and in reaching out to help others. Several years after Paul, a minister and moderator of the Conestoga COB, died in 1981, and the Wenger's Flower Shop closed, Carl and Millie found themselves free to follow God's leading. Beginning at home, they became mentors and encouragers of their three children and nine grandchildren: daughter Carlene, and sons Ken and Larry and their families.

As members of the Lancaster COB, Millie became involved as a bridal coordinator, while Carl took on the nursery as his calling. In these roles, they saw opportunities to share the love of Jesus in practical ways with younger generations.

Carl saw the nursery as the church's first line of defense in inviting and keeping young couples participating in the church's worship and fellowship. What he would do is stand in the background ready to serve if a volunteer arrived late or not at all, or if more children showed up than were expected. Soon Carl became known to these little people as the "man with the big bear hug" or "Grandpa."

To increase the involvement of younger people as leaders of small groups doing together prayer, study, support and helping one another develop and grow their faith, the Bombergers offered scholarships to those willing to participate in continuing education aimed at equipping them for this new style of ministry. This new movement of worship and fellowship, Morning Psalm, has now met in Lancaster's Family Life Center for over eleven years, reaching a generation once far from God and introducing them to the gospel.

When the Lancaster COB began its twice-a-year Dinner Theater productions, Carl and Millie contributed by providing the ingredients for the meal and organizing church members to serve the meals. That ministry is now in its eighth year.

Both Bombergers have been deeply involved with the BDRA. Milly's spiritual gift of craftsmanship is utilized for kickoff dinners and hymn sings by providing beautiful floral arrangements which are afterwards shared with those who are hospitalized, shut-in, elderly or disabled. The years spent delivering floral arrangements prepared Carl for locating, delivering and distributing BDRA Sale Booklets to local churches and businesses.

At the Auction, Millie is known as a relentless and ruthless bidder. Sometimes Millie misjudges other folks' willingness to bid and an item ends up going home with her, providing inventory for the next year's auction. By participating in the Grow Money and Share-A-Meal projects, they have made many new friends.

One year, as they were helping to make apple and pecan pies for the Auction, they finished and then noticed that an ingredient was left over. They all shrugged their shoulders and consoled one another reminding themselves that what they were doing wasn't so much about making great pies as it was about faithfully serving God.

The 30th Anniversary BDRA Sale Booklet was dedicated to this remarkable couple.

(From an article by their son,
Ken Bomberger. 2006 SB, p. 4)

RENEE A. LAYSER
September 9, 1974 – August 13, 1994

Renee was the middle child of three born to John and Nancy Layser, the granddaughter of Carl and Margaret Wenger and Joseph Earl Layser and his deceased wife, Doris, all of Myerstown, PA. Her siblings were an older sister, Greta, married to Michael Koppenhaver, and a younger brother, Eric, who still lived at home.

The intermingling of hardships and joys, common to most families, strengthened the bonds of love within the Layser family during Renee's growing-up years. Since both her parents came from large families, and many of them also lived in the Myerstown area, Renee and her siblings were surrounded by an extended family of supportive and loving aunts, uncles and cousins.

By age thirteen, Renee was a happy, bubbly, teenager with sparkling eyes. However, sensing her need for the forgiveness of her sins and wanting the assurance of eternal life, she accepted Jesus Christ as her Lord and Savior and was then baptized into the fellowship of the Myerstown COB where she and her parents attended regularly.

Outgoing and vivacious, she frequently made spur-of-the-moment visits with her grandparents and extended family, borrowing shoes or a handbag, going for a walk with someone, babysitting cousins, telling stories, and even accompanying her grandmother to the nearby diner for a late night snack. In caring for children, she had the gift of being able to relate to them and being especially sensitive to their needs. Wherever she went, her helpfulness, smiles and laughter brought joy.

After her graduation from ELCO, (Eastern Lebanon County High School) in 1992, she worked part-time for Wenger's Farm Machinery, Inc. as a secretary-receptionist, where she always answered the six ringing telephones with a friendly voice and accommodating spirit.

Spreading her wings in many directions, she began working as a bank teller at the Lebanon Valley National Bank in Womelsdorf. After a short time there, she was transferred to their branch office in Ephrata, making new friends wherever she went. On the side, she was a successful sales consultant for the Longaberger Basket Company and always carried a catalog in her car.

Although she enjoyed having her teenage friends gather at her home for swimming or a game of volleyball, Renee always had a special concern for her peers who were less fortunate. Empathizing with them, she would reach out to listen and help them whenever she could.

In early 1994, a young man gained Renee's attention and affection, and a few months later, she reluctantly and sadly shared the news with her parents that she was pregnant. Emotionally on a roller coaster, they experienced the sorrow that most parents would feel on hearing that news from an unmarried daughter but also were joyful that she had chosen life for her unborn child.

However, on August 13, 1994, the lives of the Layser family were changed forever when 19-year-old Renee and her unborn child were murdered by the child's father, Renee's former boyfriend. In coping with this unthinkable tragedy, her parents, grandparents and extended family learned the truth of Jesus' statement to the Apostle Paul in *2 Corinthians 12:9: "My grace is sufficient for thee."*

THE BEGINNING OF THE RENEE LAYSER MEMORIAL DINNERS

In January 1996, the Wenger family established the Wenger Foundation, Inc. and on May 2, 1996, a Renee A. Layser Memorial Dinner was the first event organized through the foundation. With Melvin and Gloria Burkholder, the BDRA's coordinators at that time, serving as co-sponsors, all funds raised that evening were donated to the BDRA. Approximately 800 people attended this $100 per person gala evening at the Lebanon Valley Exposition Center where they enjoyed a delicious dinner and top-notch Southern gospel music by The Anchormen, a Christian comedy ventriloquist act by Geraldine and Rickey, and soloist Kirk Talley. Glenn Wenger emceed the event and also served as auctioneer during a "mini auction" that brought in an additional $16,000 when he sold a peacock quilt made by the women of the Myerstown COB, two artworks by Abner Zook, and several Longaberger baskets. The total amount raised for the BDRA that evening was $110,000 – showing not only love for Renee but how the Lord can receive glory and bring positive things from times of deep human sorrow.

(Excerpted from an article in the 1996 SB, p. 34)

Because of the success of that first Memorial Dinner, the Wenger Foundation and the Burkholders co-sponsored a second one the following year on April 24, 1997—at the same location and at the same cost per person. With a program featuring David Ring from Orlando, FL, as speaker and the Canaan Land Boys as Southern Gospel singers,   450 people attended and $45,000 was raised for the BDRA.

❖ ❖ ❖

OTHER FUNDRAISING SUPPERS

In addition to the Soup 'N' Salad suppers held at the Landis and Audrey Myer home (described in the Grow Money section), other families held BDRA fund-raising meals in their homes. Two of those, both from the Mechanic Grove COB, are Jim and Eleanor Kreider who did it for 22 years, from 1982 through 2003 and Alan and Barb Platt who succeeded them as hosts in 2004. Their method was to sponsor a free picnic supper with a free-will offering basket available. All contributions went to the BDRA. At first, the Krieders prepared everything themselves, but then hired the Hess's Barbecue caterers to prepare the food. To give you an idea of what a project like this, (which other families could emulate), might contribute each year, we are listing their results:

1982 – $1,210	1996 – $4,000
1983 – $2,408	1997 – $4,600
1984 – $3,064	1998 – $4,200
1985 – $4,382	1999 – $4,400
1986 – $4,640	2000 – $5,100
1987 – $6,000	2001 – $6,000
1988 – $6,100	2002 – $6,606
1989 – $7,000	2003 – $5,200
1990 – $6,500	2004 – $5,300
1991 – $6,100	2005 – $5,600
1992 – $5,250	2006 – $6,200
1993 – $6,500	2007 – $6,200

1994 – $5,000	2008 – $6,700
1995 – $5,000	

To this date, the combined total of this continuing effort is $139,260.00—all given to honor and glorify God and to help those stricken by disaster.   *(Personal Interview)*

MARTY AND LOIS WITMAN'S CORN ROASTS

Marty and Lois Witman participated for years in the Share-A-Meal programs, entertaining a variety of people in their home each year. Then they began having corn roasts for small groups of their neighbors and friends—just for fun!

Eight years ago, in 2001, they decided to sell tickets for their corn roast and give all the money received to the BDRA, and that first year they served twenty people.

Each year since, the corn roast has grown. At first, they held the corn roast in their back yard, but by 2008, it had grown so much that it was held at the Florin COB and friends from the church volunteered to help to prepare and serve the food. Last year (2008) the tickets cost $25 each, and as a result, the corn roast raised $2,400 for the BDRA. Because of the current depressed economy, the Witmans lowered the ticket price for 2009 to $20 per person and are planning to serve 200 on August 1st. To God be the glory!

T. Miscellaneous

FACE PAINTING

A colorful clown captivates the attention of small auction attendees with his balloon-twisting antics.

After working with her parents, Ken and Carroll Kreider, at Aunt Ellen's Caramel Popcorn stand, Brenda Kreider Barlet approached the BDRA Board with the idea of allowing her to set up a Face-Painting table as an attraction for children. In 1994, a card table, draped with a bright pink cover, two chairs, a brush, an assortment of colored face paints and a stand-up vanity mirror were all that were needed. Painting a few faces provided all the advertisement necessary, for as soon as a child saw a beautiful butterfly, flower, or rainbow on another child's cheek, he or she found the source.

That first year, Brenda charged 50 cents, and the demand was extremely high. Being a one-woman show, she painted cheek after cheek with very few breaks during both days. Since her expenses were minimal, Brenda decided to donate all money received from the children (and some adults), who had their faces painted, to the BDRA.

The second year brought two changes. The first was to increase the price to one dollar,

and the second was to add sparkles. Brenda continued to paint every year through 2009, doing her best to paint what the children requested: hearts, stars, balloons, horses, unicorns, dogs, cats, fish, dragons, spiders, bats, snakes, mice, dinosaurs, pumpkins, soccer balls, footballs, baseballs, cars, trains, trucks, and tractors (green, of course!). She was eventually assisted by her own two daughters, Laura and Sonia, as they grew old enough to not only be their mother's canvases but also to create beautiful designs themselves.

Each year, one dollar at a time, the children attending the BDRA contributed an average of $150 toward helping needy children by eagerly watching and then smiling at their own reflections as they brightly and colorfully proclaimed that they had been to the BDRA.

(By Carroll Kreider)

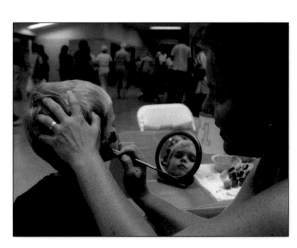

Brenda Kreider Barlet paints one boy's face as he watches the process in a mirror.

*Jasmine Minnich is one satisfied
face-painted customer!*

David Kline takes a smiling girl for a pony ride.

*David Keller, Midway COB, was the "engineer" of
the Ideal Express train that took children for rides
around the Fairgrounds.*

In this miscellaneous category are included other children's activities, such as the Petting Zoo, Clowns, Pony Rides, Balloons, Train Rides and more. In each case, dedicated individuals were willing to "go the extra mile" to entertain the children, make them smile, and encourage them to bring their parents to the BDRA.

Other unusual family activities included the tethered balloon rides (for a fee), Hoop Day, round name buttons, and "I Gave 1 Hour Buttons."

The BDRA Committee is always looking for new ideas for fund raising and making the two-day experience memorable and fun for all ages.

U. Quilts and Needlework

QUILTER'S BEATITUDES

Blessed are the quilters,
*   for they are piece makers.*
Blessed are the quilters,
*   for they make ends meet.*
Blessed are the quilters,
*   for they know how to cut corners.*

Blessed are the quilters,
for they make great comforters.
Blessed are the quilters,
for they patch things up.
Blessed are the quilters,
for they cover you with warmth.
Blessed are the quilters,
for they pick up the pieces.
Blessed are the quilters,
for they save you energy.
Blessed are the quilters,
for they put color in your life.

by Ina R. Jacobs

Quilts have been a primary attraction at the BDRA since its beginning, growing to include over 150 quilts and wall hangings. Traditional pieced quilts, such as the Log Cabin and Irish Chain, look beautiful beside the new contemporary Color Wash and Bargello quilts.

Some of the quilt tops are bought at local quilt shops and auctions and then hand quilted by women of the contributing churches. Other quilts are pieced, appliquéd, and quilted by the church women and a few are made solely by individuals.

The quilting group at the Elizabethtown COB is typical of the many church quilting groups in this area. Nine women, ranging in age from their 30s to their 80s, meet every Wednesday morning in the 2nd floor quilt room in the church. Along with their needles and thimbles, they bring an enthusiasm for an ancient craft, a wealth of creativity, and many interesting topics of conversation. Since meeting regularly for several years, the women have

developed a closeness that is common among small groups. As they have become more proficient, they have pieced a quilt top in a day or two. Together they cut, sew, and iron the hundreds of small pieces that slowly become a quilt.

Wherever this scenario takes place, there is one thing in common: Quilters of the ANE and SOPA Districts of the COB are grateful that by working together at a hobby they enjoy, they can honor and glorify God and serve their neighbors. *(2000 SB, p. 14)*

IVY ALWINE, 1900-2000

Ivy Alwine from the Annville COB had a large crocheted doily auctioned at the 2000 BDRA, even though she was not able to be present to enjoy seeing what it would bring. She planned ahead and got her doily finished and ready to sell, just as she had done in 1998 and 1999, even though she was going to be 100 years old in September.

However, she missed her birthday also, as she went to be with her Lord on April 2, 2000. *(2000 SB, p. 35)*

ANN DILLER

It was about 1994 when Cassel Mummau came and cleaned out our barn. In that process, he found a feed bag with a nice big red rooster head with a comb on it and he said, "Oh, somebody should quilt this for the Disaster Relief Sale."

I said, "Well, I have grow money. I could use my grow money to quilt that bag."

"You'll have to dry clean it first," he advised.

So I got it dry cleaned, quilted it, and took it to the BDRA, and it brought $300! I could hardly believe it.

After that I probably quilted about thirty feed bags, making one almost every year. They usually brought from $250 to $1,000. The one that sold for $1,000 was a Quail Company bag with the picture of two quails facing one another on the front of it. Usually, the bags I quilted were Eshleman Red Rose, Florin Feeds, or Quail Company bags. Most were sold for around $300.

(Ann Diller, Lampeter COB, personal interview)

JIM AND EFFIE ESHELMAN AND JULIA LONGENECKER

When over 3,500 people attended the Town Fair in downtown Lancaster, PA, in

One of the feed bags quilted by Julia Longenecker. Note the egg shapes designed by Julia in the quilting patterns.

1989, they voted for the best quilt and needlework on display there. The winner for quilts was Effie Eshelman, member of the Florin COB, whose quilt of peach and green tulips got the most votes. Known for her creativity and tiny, precise stitches, Effie, along with Julia Longenecker, co-chaired the BDRA Quilt Committee for many years.

Married for 63 years and currently living in the Brethren Village, Effie and her husband, Jim Eshelman, have three children, six grandchildren and one great-grandchild.

After being a farmer, a lay minister, and a mail carrier for many

Left to right: Julia Longenecker, Effie and Jim Eshelman. Julia and Effie co-chaired the BDRA Quilt Committee for many years.

Four Florin COB quilters (left to right): Julia Longenecker, Effie Eshelman, Connie Kline, and Ardeth Wolgemuth proudly hold a "Heart of Roses" 92"x108" quilt which sold for $800 at the September 2000 BDRA.

years, in his retirement Jim keeps busy singing bass in the Village Voices Male Chorus, conducting tours of Lancaster County Amish Country, reciting poetry, teaching adult Sunday school classes, volunteering at Brethren Village and doing latch hook rug making. Besides quilting, Effie enjoys knitting, singing, and is an excellent cook.

Effie's memories of the early days of the quilt auction part of the BDRA include the first year when the quilts were hung in the West Hall with 2x4's donated by Merville Messick. When the main part of the BDRA was moved into the new building, Ken and Joanne Hess joined the Quilt Committee and Ken designed new aluminum racks to replace the wooden racks that were being used by that time. Stanley Earhart printed the cards that were pinned on each quilt describing the quilt name, its size and the quilter/donor.

For several years, on the week before the BDRA, Effie remembers with gratitude the help given by Millie Lutz and Julia Longenecker in setting up a quilt display at Penney's in Lebanon and at the Watt & Shand mall at Park City. Working on a pre-planned schedule, quilters from different

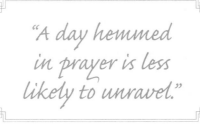

"A day hemmed in prayer is less likely to unravel."

church congregations volunteered to work at the mall demonstrating the technique of quilting. When the display was disassembled, that quilt was donated and called a *District Quilt*.

One outstanding memory for Julia was that she was given a sugar cane bag with the name "Hershey" on it. Being a creative person, she decided to quilt a design of three Hershey kisses on it, patterned after a popular TV advertisement at that time featuring three Hershey kisses. In 1992, when it was finished, she had it on display at the quilting demonstration at Park City. A man walked by and asked her, "Where did you get that bag?"

"Someone gave it to me, and I was the one who quilted it," she responded.

"Do you know where it came from originally?" he persisted, and when she admitted she didn't know, he explained, "It came from the sugar plantation in Cuba that was owned by Milton S. Hershey. He and Fidel Castro were friends. By the numbers on the bag, I can even tell you in what field the sugar was grown."

Julia was amazed.

"What are you going to do with it?" he questioned.

"I'm taking it to Lebanon to the Brethren Disaster Relief Auction in September."

"Oh, I won't be around that long," he said sadly. "I won't be able to get there."

Julia did take that sugar bag she had quilted to the BDRA and to her delight, it brought $500.

Although the bags she quilted were somewhat plain, Julia enjoyed adding a creative touch such as designs of eggs or baby chicks on feed bags, tobacco leaves on fertilizer bags, etc. "I did fun things," she says.

Today, Julia, a resident of Brethren Village, enjoys sewing, reading, writing and her family, consisting of three children, eleven grandchildren, and seven great-grandchildren.

On the other hand, Effie always preferred quilting "pretty things" and set a goal for herself of donating either a quilt or a wall hanging each year. A few of her donations were: *Amish Pansies* 32x32, *Fisherman Freddie* 37x37, *Sunbonnet Sue* 37x47, *Swirling Blocks* 32x42, *Amish Puzzle* 24x28, *Calico Cats* 34x20, *Reversible Pineapple* 96x100, *Baskets of Love* 21x25, and *Christmas Wreath* 33x33. The Florin COB quilters continue to be one of many church groups who have the goal of producing and donating a quilt for the BDRA each year.

Today, Effie is still making quilts and wall hangings and is so thankful for her good health so that she can enjoy this hobby which she loves so much and by doing so, can help others have a better life.

THE SIX TOP FUNDRAISING QUILTS

Although every quilt donated was a work of art and a wonderful witness to the faith, creativity and perseverance of its maker(s), according to the records available to the author, the six quilts which brought in the most during the first 32 years of the BDRA were these:

$10,600   *1989—A Trip Around the World* made by Lizzie Longenecker at age 100, White Oak COB. The buyer was her son, Carl Longenecker.

$10,450   *1994*—A quilt sold in memory of Renee Ann Layser, 19, a bank teller at Ephrata's Lebanon Valley Branch,

The "Woodland Butterfly" quilt made by Joanne Hess and Nancy Erwin sold for a total of $10,000 at the 2008 BDRA.

who was shot and killed in August, 1994, when she was five months pregnant. Carl Wenger, her grandfather, bought the quilt to give to Renee's sister as a wedding gift.

$10,000   *2008—Woodland Butterfly* made by Lititz COB members, Nancy Erwin and Joanne Hess. They were hoping it might bring $1,000 and were pleasantly surprised when it was sold twice, bringing a combined total well beyond their expectations.

$ 7,100   *1986—Around the World* made by Lizzie Longenecker, 97.

$ 6,300   *1990*—Made by Lizzie Longenecker, 101.

$ 5,500   *1987—Lone Star* made in 1904 but never used. Donated by Anna Lutz, Lititz.

❖ ❖ ❖

QUILTING STORY

The quilting group in our church originated in 1986 with a class taught by Donna Baughman in her home with the first project being that each lady would make a wall hanging for herself. By 1989, we had progressed so much that we decided to buy material, cut patches and sew them together, making a 93"x96" *Garden Staircase* quilt and a *Trip Around the World* single bed quilt for the BDRA. The frames were set up at the one end of a Sunday school classroom and on the weekends were covered with bed sheets with a sign on them stating: "Please do not lay anything on this!"

One Saturday afternoon a wedding was held in our church. The next morning, on Sunday, our pastor came to me and said, "Ethel, look at your quilt. Someone spilled punch on your quilt."

When I looked, I exclaimed, "Oh, No! That is not punch; that is red fingernail polish!"

However, thank goodness, it was all on one patch. We pulled the quilting stitches out and also the strip of cloth beside the stain. Fortunately, we still had material that matched it, so we sewed in another strip by hand and quilted the patch again. When we were finished, no one could ever tell it had happened.

The *Garden Staircase* sold for $310 and a matching wall hanging for $150, while the

Piecing together a single "Trip Around the World" quilt for the BDRA in 1989 are these women from the Lampeter COB (left to right): Ethel Meck, Donna Baughman, and Mary Kreider. The finished quilt brought $125 at the sale.

single-sized *Trip Around the World* brought $125.

Unfortunately, because of deaths, people moving away, and old age creeping up on the rest of us, our group has shrunk to two persons, Mary Kreider and myself. Our quilt for the 2009 BDRA will probably be our last."

(Ethel Meck, Lampeter COB)

KATHRYN R. GRIM

Kathryn R. Grim, born on a farm near Abbottstown, PA, on December 19, 1910, was the second of seven children born to Harry Lillich, a farmer and carpenter, and his wife, Velva Fissel Lillich, a homemaker. After attending Abbottstown High School for two years, she quit to work in a sewing factory, a shoe factory, and eventually Middleburg Sewing Factory where she made men's dress suits.

She and her husband, J. Vernon Grim, were married on May 31, 1930. Together they had three children, two of whom died at birth. Through her surviving child, Barbara Grim Rollman, (Mrs. Roy), she had one grandson and three great-grandchildren. In 1950-51, Kathryn and Vernon had an exchange student in their home, Erna Treml Lang, who became like another daughter to them, keeping in contact with them through the years.

Vernon was a "free" minister in the Hanover COB, and with his brothers owned the Grim Brothers' Trucking Company in York. After moving to York in 1954, the Grim's joined the York First COB and kept their membership there the rest of their lives.

Kathryn's grandmother Fissel, who worked for a tailor, taught her how to quilt and sew. When she moved into assisted living at Autumn House at Powder Mill Road in York, one of the things she missed most was her sewing machine. When she got a new portable one for Christmas in 2002, she was delighted. With it, she continued to make numerous doll quilts and wall hangings for charity auctions such as the BDRA, Habitat for Humanity, and the Lehman Center. Kathryn also donated her needlework creations to The Brethren Home in New Oxford where she helped to start their gift shop (now called the Beehive Shop), served as one of the first officers of the Women's Auxiliary, started the monthly display of art work, and made some of the first quilts to be sold at their annual chicken barbecue and auction.

Although she was already a life member of the Quilter's Guild and the Suburban Garden Club, Kathryn realized a lifelong dream in the 1960's by taking art lessons and learning to work with oils and watercolors. Her paintings, which decorate her room at Autumn House, show not only that she is talented as an artist but also her love of flowers and her garden. At the York Art Association, she exhibited her paintings in her own shows.

When she was well into her 90's, she continued to make and donate her quilts and wall hangings to the BDRA and to crochet baby booties for the premature infants at Hershey Medical Center, York Memorial Hospital and York Hospital.

Being a "people person" and wanting to find ways to honor God for his blessings, Kathryn has found that doing things with her hands and sharing the results with others continues to bring her much joy and satisfaction.

(Excerpted from an article by Barbara Grim Rollman. 2004 SB, p. 4)

KEN AND JOANNE HESS

What does a retired industrial electrician have to do with the BDRA Quilt Committee? Ken Hess, from the Lititz COB, has served on the Quilt Committee since 1989 and designed and constructed the aluminum quilt racks where the quilts are displayed prior to their sale. Although he still sets up these racks each

Joanne and Ken Hess with Janet Steffy (right). Both Joanne and her sister, Janet, were members of the Quilt Committee for many years.

year, he has also worked at building maintenance, served on disaster response teams, and driven wheelchair transport with the Warwick Ambulance Association.

The vocation of his wife, Joanne, a member of the BDRA Quilt Committee since 1988 and an expert at quilting and sewing, has been making draperies. In 2008, she and Nancy Erwin, another member of the Golden Needles group from the Lititz COB, took a pattern for a wall hanging and adapted it into making a quilt entitled *Woodland Butterfly*. To their surprise, it was sold twice for a total of $10,000, the third highest amount raised by a quilt in the history of the BDRA.

Other notable quilts Joanne remembers are these:

• In 2008, Harry and June Badorf from the Lititz COB found a quilt in a mall parking lot. After months of futile attempts to find its owner, they donated this *Country Love* quilt to the BDRA where it brought $1,550.

- Elaine Gibbel bought the top, backing and batting for a *Log Cabin Star* quilt at a public auction. Since the Lititz COB was in the middle of an expansion at that time and the Golden Needles quilters had no room to work there, they took their hoops to Jean Bachman's living room where they quilted. The result was a quilt sold at the 2004 BDRA for $500.

- *Millennium Homestead* was an appliqué quilt with a house, trees and flowers on it. Embroidered, displayed and sold in the year 2000, it was made to celebrate the millennium, and it went for $4,700.

Some of the other quilts and wall hangings that Joanne has donated to the BDRA include *Bow Tie* 16x16, *Convergence* 37x37, *Moon's Out Tonight* 27x27. Together with Brenda Stauffer, she helped make and donate these: *Wheat Flowers* 38x43, *Circles* 20x20, and *To AxA & Back* 30x30.

Today, the Hesses praise God for their health which enables them to work for a great cause—the BDRA! They marvel: "It's amazing how it all comes together. God is great!"

(Personal Interview)

FERN HITZ

Some of the exquisite, lacy creations that have been sold at the BDRA through the years

have been made and donated by Fern Hitz, from the Midway COB. Although her trademarks are her doilies, made in all sizes and patterns, and usually sell for $35 to $75 each at the BDRA, she has also made and contributed crazy-quilt patterned comforters, knitted items, and a large, round crocheted tablecloth. She also contributes items to other charities and has knitted sweaters for the "Guidepost Sweater Project."

In addition to sewing, knitting and crocheting, the hobbies of this retired mother of three and grandmother of nine, include reading, traveling and volunteering. At the BDRA, early on Saturday morning, she can often be found helping other Midway members prepare and serve the pancake and sausage breakfast.

When asked about her needlework abilities, she responds: "I just thank God for the time and ability to make things for someone else, to comfort them and keep them warm."

"What you leave behind is not what is engraved in stone monuments, but what is woven into the lives of others."   *(Pericles)*

DAVID, CAROLE AND PATRICK KLINE

Known as the Family Heir-Loom Weavers, the Kline family of Red Lion, York County, PA, began making Jacquard coverlets in 1983 in the tradition of the Pennsylvania German weavers of the mid-19th century. Combining their love of antiques and David's twenty-five years of experience as a loom fixer in area silk mills, they started searching for a Jacquard loom. In an unheated, rented garage with no plumbing of any kind, they set up their first loom, which they had found in Wilkes Barre. A Jacquard attachment, which had been taken out of production at the end of World War II and stored with seven others on the third floor in the loft of a York silk mill, was discovered by the Klines, who bought it in 1982-83.

From November 1982, they hunted sources of yarn and other supplies until October, 1983, when they sold their first coverlet. To make it, they borrowed an 1838 *Bird and Bush with Four Roses* coverlet from a Red Lion antique dealer and took it to a Jacquard card cutter in Philadelphia, where they punched 2,200 cards to create the pattern for the Jacquard loom.

To get a client's name woven into the signature blocks requires 132 punched cards. These cards go to the customer when they pick up their coverlet. If more coverlets of the same design and name in the corner block are ordered, the Klines deduct $100 from the original price. An older couple bought one for themselves, and one year later brought back their Jacquard cards, saving themselves $400, and the Klines wove four more so they could give one to each of their children.

After working by themselves for three years, in 1985 their son, Patrick, joined the company. One of their customers, an employee of the National Park Service, approached them about trying to weave ingrain carpet. A flat-woven carpet with no loops or piles, ingrain carpeting was very popular with middle class wives in the 19th century. To do this, the Klines needed to find a building to set up another Jacquard loom. After a long search, the rural setting of the former Meadowview Dairy, al-

though it was in dire need of a new roof, convinced the Klines to buy it. A few years later, they dug a pond on the property and a pair of swans settled on it.

After they had set up the second Jacquard production plant, the Park Service awarded them with an order for three rooms of wall-to-wall carpet when they were renovating the Abe Lincoln home in Springfield, Ill. Upon receiving the carpet for the first room, they upped the order for another pattern and two more rooms, making a total of five rooms. Today there is carpet woven by the Klines in the homes of seven ex-presidents, including Andrew Jackson's *Hermitage*, Martin Van Buren's *Lindenwald*, James Buchanan's *Wheatland*, James Monroe's and General Ulysses Grant's, plus many other historic homes in America and abroad.

Expanding in 1998 by buying a former cigar factory in Red Lion, their son, Patrick, runs this operation weaving historic fabric for Civil War reenactors. Although he began this type of weaving in his garage, he soon discovered he could not keep up with the demand in that small space. Today they supply fabrics running from Confederate jean cloth, suspender tape, federal jersey, woolen broadcloth and blankets, in addition to doing commission weaving for other mills. Many of their wool and cotton products are reversible and available with a custom name and date woven in, a true heirloom in the making.

The Kline's Heir-Loom Weaving operation has donated coverlets, table runners, and carpets to the BDRA each year for over twenty years so that they can be sold to the glory of God and benefit persons in need. *(2001 SB, p. 38)*

"A quilt is pieces of fabric woven by the hands
and minds of many;
Which becomes an Heirloom, a Masterpiece
or a priceless Treasure.

Quilts express thoughtfulness, love, kindness,
Warmth, comfort—dependent upon the viewer.

Quilts are a form of art which can be appreci-
ated by all,
Regardless of age, profession or position in life.
Everyone can recognize the craftsmanship and
many long hours spent
Completing the Masterpiece.

A quilt is a windowpane through which
One sees the craftsman."

(Jay M. Witman)

Quilts tell us many stories. Although it is an ancient art, quilting always has had special significance for American women. Recently, social historians have studied quilts just as they do diaries and letters, to learn about life among the pioneer families or early America and the western frontier.

Quilts were made to celebrate marriages, to welcome new babies, and to honor friends. Album quilts and "friendship quilts" were embroidered with names. To chronicle their lives, Afro-American quilters created narrative quilts using intricate appliqué. Quilting parties are still important events, and a quilt may be a record of community history or a symbol of personal remembrance.

(Joyce S. Steward, 2001 SB, p. 14)

"Piecin' a quilt's like livin' a life … The Lord sends us the pieces, but we can cut 'em out and put 'em together pretty much to suit ourselves."

(Eliza Calvert Hall—1898, 2001 SB, p. 14)

A quilt with patches from the 67 congregations of the ANE District of the COB was purchased for $1550 in 1987 to be donated to the Rufus P. Bucher Meetinghouse on the campus of Elizabethtown College.

A QUILT FOR JESSICA

I found it last spring while cleaning a downstairs closet. Neatly packed away in a storage box was the unfinished quilt I had started to make for Jessica.

Although I had started the project with much enthusiasm, eagerly choosing the colors and the pattern, I can't pinpoint the moment it came to be Jessica's quilt. One day, for whatever reason, it just was. While she was still in elementary school, I promised her it would be finished in time for her to take to college. I thought I had given myself an ample time frame to complete the task.

Jessica was my niece, the youngest child of my brother and sister-in-law. With the totally biased opinion of an aunt, I can add that she was a beautiful and gifted child, talented in art and with an innate love for animals, so much so that she was determined to become a veterinarian.

Time passed, and during her high school years, Jess would occasionally ask if the quilt was finished. By this time, my enthusiasm had waned. I had finished the top, but it still needed backing, binding and actual quilting to be considered finished. However, when she asked, I would choose my words carefully and continue to promise to have it finished in time for her to take to college.

On February 26, 2003, Jess left school at noon to participate in a work/study program. It was her 18th birthday, and she was ecstatic at the prospect of spending the afternoon with a local veterinarian. However, on her way to his office, she was involved in a car accident, suffering injuries from which she would never recover. She went home to be with the Lord on March 20, 2003.

In the two years following her death, I thought often about the relationship between starting and finishing. Jess never got to finish many things, including high school, and never got to start college. In my view, her life was too young to be finished, but it was God's plan for it to finish that day.

Then I thought of all the projects I have started—but never finished. So many times I have not "followed through" to the end. About that time, I found the unfinished quilt. I had packed it away thinking there was no purpose now in finishing it.

Then it occurred to me that in her short life of eighteen years, Jess had gone on three mission trips with our church, one of which was to NC sponsored by the Disaster Relief Committee. Suddenly, I had an idea for a purpose for Jessica's quilt, and Bonnie Peachy of Belleville, PA, helped me finish the quilt.

When Jessica's earthly life ended, her new eternal life began in heaven. Just as this quilt's original chapter and purpose ended, its new journey began at the 2005 BDRA when it was auctioned to the glory of God and to help those less fortunate.

(Lucy Cascioli, Springfield COB. 2005 SB, p. 49)

BORED? TRY A HOBBY THAT WILL HELP OTHERS

Lebanon County is where Leroy Krall, 76, was born and has lived all his life. With the vocation of farming, he has lived in the Buffalo Springs area where he had cows, pigs, and steers. Because of failing health, this is the first year he has not farmed the crops on his farm and a relative uses his barn and meadow for heifers.

In wanting to be occupied and useful, Leroy tried woodworking, making wooden rakes, basket weaving and even sewing strips of material together for comforters. His wife, Ethel, enjoys quilting and nearly always has a quilt in a frame in their home. Many times Leroy would wash, dry and put away their dishes so that Ethel could get back to her quilting--but not anymore!

In January it was too cold to work outdoors, and he was bored with television, so he looked for another challenge. He asked Ethel if she would give him a needle so he could quilt. In a short time, he had jabbed his finger so often that he declared, "I can't do it." However, he didn't quit. He kept trying again and again, and soon the stitches began to fall into place, and he began quilting almost every day.

From January to April, 1994, Leroy and Ethel quilted and finished four queen sized quilts and one wall hanging. They donated one of the quilts, an off-white one with a bird pattern, to the BDRA. Leroy has taken boredom and turned it into creativity, which in turn is being used to honor and glorify God.

(1994 SB, p. 29)

LIFE IS LIKE A QUILT

Life is like a Patchwork Quilt
And each little patch is a day.
Some patches are rosy, happy and bright
And some are dark and gray.

But each little patch as it is fitted in
And sewn to keep it together,
Makes a finished block in this life of ours
Filled with sunshine and rainy weather.

So, let me work on life's patchwork quilt
Through the rainy days and the sun,
Trusting that when I have finished my block
The Master will say, "Well done."

(Author Unknown. 2000 SB, p. 26)

"Quilt-making puts you between the past and the future, where your grandmother's and your quilts will, hopefully, be joined by your granddaughter's."

(Jennifer Patriarche)

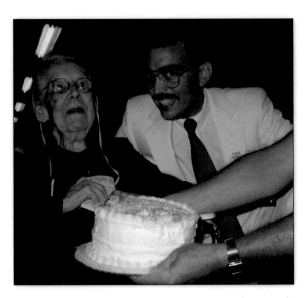

Jay Witman is presenting Lizzie Longenecker a cake in 1989 to honor her 100 years of life. Her quilt that sold for $10,600 that year was the all-time highest fundraising quilt of all time.

I saw a lady, that was, I think, 95 years old, who thought her life was absolutely stopped and she wasn't worth doing much any more. You see, her hands looked like this (crippled), and she sat on a wheelchair when she wasn't in bed (which was 24 hours a day.) She came to be known as Grandma Lizzie. She was an elderly lady, bless her heart; I think she still lives today at 104 or 105. Until her eyes gave out, she would quilt a quilt. It was magnificent to see this lady work. She would take her crippled hands, and I witnessed it so many times, and she would weave and make that quilt called *A Trip Around the World*. It took sometimes 1,500 pieces of material to be sewn together. I think it is absolutely the hardest quilt to produce, but she *did it*! Amazing!

I remember her being on the podium because we lifted her and her wheelchair onto the podium, and she received a standing ovation after her quilt brought $10,600. The quilt was not worth that. We knew the quilt was only fabric, but something happened that day. God walked in and moved in a mysterious way.

I remember standing with Jake Ruhl many times and we would be in deep prayer. Then he'd look out at the crowd and say, "Jay, can you imagine that the monetary goal that we are supposed to achieve today, (something like $100,000)—Can you imagine that we are going to have to sell those quilts to produce that amount?"

We knew there was no way that we could do it, and yet somehow God always blessed it and our goals were reached. He continues to do it to this day.

(Jay M. Witman. 1994 SB, p. 56)

LIZZIE LONGENECKER, ONE OF A KIND

"I hate to sit around and do nothing." (Lizzie Longenecker)

Lizzie Longenecker, (March 26, 1889 - December 20, 1995), whose nimble fingers created quilts even at age 100, was one of God's unique creations. With a keen sense of humor and excellent health, she was the matriarch of a large family whose love and loyalty witnessed to their faith in God and faithfulness to the church of Jesus Christ. Her family was an extension of her fierce commitment to Jesus Christ and traditional family values. Her vision was always a forward one, caring about others.

"Grandma" Lizzie Longenecker

Sitting on the stage in a wheelchair at the BDRA in 1988, "Grandma" Longenecker was about to witness the biggest bid for any quilt ever sold and (she thought) it would be her last quilt, as she was also celebrating her 100th year of life. She was speechless and overwhelmed as the auctioneer's emotional voice shouted, "Who'll give me $10,000 for Lizzie Longenecker's quilt? An unidentified woman on the back bleacher nodded her head. "Who'll give $10,200, $10,400?" When Lizzie's own son, Carl, spit out $10,600," the bidding ceased and the auctioneer yelled, "Sold!" The crowd rose to their feet, breaking into spontaneous applause for five minutes while Lizzie, in her wheelchair with her head bowed, could hardly comprehend what had happened. Yes, she had made possible a gift of $10,600 to feed and clothe the needy of the world. One of her great loves in life, sharing and caring for others, was accomplished again. Lizzie, at 100, was God's special ambassador to those coping with the losses of natural and man-made disasters. Lizzie's quilt brought more than the entire proceeds of the first BDRA, and she did it all "to the glory of God and our neighbor's good."

When the audience returned to their seats with Lizzie still on the throne (stage), Jay Witman, the auctioneer, presented her with a 400-piece birthday cake to celebrate this momentous accomplishment. At $1 a piece, four hundred were only a fraction of those who wished to share in her birthday celebration.

Lizzie defied the odds many times and got to be 106 years old. Even the computer could not deal with her stamina and spirit. When a pacemaker was implanted to assist her heart rhythm at age 102, the computer could not register 102. The hospital staff gasped when the computer told them that a two-year-old was the pacemaker recipient! She had done it again!

Her *Around the World* [8] quilt design had 1800 patches which she sewed by herself in preparation for the quilting. Actually, Lizzie started quilting with the White Oak COB Ladies' Aid Society after she retired from farming in 1949. *"I'm still sticking in needles and going in circles,"* she would quip. She made quilts for her children, her twenty grandchildren, and twenty-nine great grandchildren. The

---

[8] Lizzie's granddaughter, Rachel Copenhaver, spent over 18 years as a missionary in Africa. Grandma Lizzie made dresses, blankets, and other useful items which were sent to Rachel who greatly appreciated them. Grandma Longenecker may never have left the country, but her talents have helped spread God's Word "around the world." (*From a tribute to Grandma Longenecker written by Janice M. Garber.*)

nine great-great grandchildren each received a quilted wall hanging. Often she would embroider the ititials, "LLL", standing for Lizzie Lutz Longenecker, on her quilts. She estimated that she produced around 100 quilts in all.

A special celebration on her 104th birthday was held by her family and close friends at the Mt. Hope Dunkard Brethren Home where her grand-son-in-law, Glen K. Ziegler, was administrator. About fifty people toasted her long life with fun and stories.

Not to be undone by anyone, she was quick to respond when Jay Witman, a close friend and head auctioneer at the BDRA, inquired of her, "Grandma, Lizzie, how does it feel to live to be 104 years old?"

With a twinkle in her eye, she looked straight at him and said, "Oh, Jay, I think the Lord forgot me!"

Mrs. Longenecker was born on March 26, 1889, on the Hershey homestead in Penryn, PA, and was baptized at age 17, joining the White Oak COB where she remained a faithful life-long member. Occasionally, she was able to attend worship in her 106th year! A very outgoing, positive lady with a delightful spirit, Lizzie raised her six children (three boys and three girls) and one foster daughter with her husband, Edwin, who died in 1965. Those children are: Verna Copenhaver, Manheim; Ray Longenecker, Lititz; Elva Miller, Fort Myers, FL; Carl Longenecker, Lititz; Floy Kover, Manheim; Jacob Longenecker, Rothsville; and foster daughter, Elva Martin, Lancaster.

Lizzie, the oldest of ten children born to Jake and Annie Hershey, was the sister of Rev. Milton Hershey. She and her husband lived on what was known as the Longenecker farm for six generations, located next to the Longenecker COB, where her husband served as janitor in addition to his farm work. Cooking for farm workers all her life, she made lots of meals.

In 1965, a big fire on the home farm destroyed all the farm buildings, but firemen were able to save the house. At the time, Lizzie's husband, Edwin, was in the hospital with a severe leg problem that resulted in amputation. The family never told him about the fire, and he died less than a week afterwards. After living in a trailer next to her daughter's house for about 12 years, Lizzie moved to the Mount Hope Dunkard Brethren Home, where she started making quilts.

At age 100, her day began at 6 a.m. and would end around 8 p.m., "when the company goes home," she chuckled, adding, "That's what my brother used to say."

Of course, she napped a few times in between those hours.

Her daily discipline of scripture reading and prayer energized her ministry of loving and caring for others. One of her favorite passages was in Matthew where Jesus told His disciples, *"I was hungry and you fed me, I was sick and you visited me, I was in prison and you came unto me, I was thirsty and you gave me a drink…. Inasmuch as ye have done it unto one of the least of these, my brethren, ye have done it unto me." (Matt. 25:40b KJV)* Lizzie was a woman with a big heart and with fingertips filled with love.

Another glimpse into this "one-of-a-kind" lady came when Susanna Johns, her roommate of ten years, died. Her observation was "She made only one mistake; she forgot to take me along."

She was not a woman with a worldly appetite. In fact, she tasted her first banana split at age 98, and declared it would be her last one! "I could hardly get through that banana split," she explained. "I'm sure I'll not order another one." And she didn't!

Imagine Lizzie's lifetime of change and adjustment: from the feathered chicken in the back yard to the frozen, packaged chicken, from horse and buggy travel to flying around the world in 24 hours, from walking a message to a neighbor to emailing around the world in seconds, from a six cent loaf of bread to paying $1.79 in the supermarket.

At her birth, Grover Cleveland was president of the United States, and a nation recuperating from the Civil War was soon to be plummeted into the Spanish-American War.

Yet, Lizzie's consistent qualities that defied change were her faith and trust in the Lord and her Brethren garb of plain dress and bonnet which witnessed to her solid Christian values and love of life. When she was 100, the word that could have defined her would have been *determination.* She was determined to make her life worthwhile, determined to keep others around her happy with her humor, and determined to keep on quilting as long as she had the eyesight for the delicate work. In addition to being a blessing to those who knew her, her talents and commitment brought help and hope to children and adults in Appalachia, Ecuador, India, Somalia and many other places.

(From an article by Earl K. Ziegler in the 1996 SB, p. 10, an article by Grace Joanou in the Friday, March 24, 1989, Intelligencer Journal *newspaper, and a personal interview with her son, Carl Longenecker).*

CHAPTER EIGHT

"Ingredients for successful entertaining: Always have—
Too many people for the number of chairs you have,
Too much food for the number of people you have,
And everyone will improvise and enjoy themselves."

- Anna Beahm Mow

V. Share-A-Meals and Cookbook

I T IS A pleasure making new friends and renewing old friendships through the dinners we sponsor for the BDRA. Cooking has always been an enjoyable event in our household, with everyone doing their part to make a dinner possible. The added element of not knowing who is going to be sitting at your table provides us with the incentive to do *our best* for God's guests.

In addition to having people in our home for dinner, it is equally as enjoyable to be a guest in other homes throughout the church district. This enables us to learn more about God's work within their local churches and communities. We cannot think of a better way to practice our Christian heritage of giving to those in need and at the same time creating a stronger Christian community at home. *(Abe & Mary Bruckhart, Annville COB, 1994 SB, p. 43)*

I feel it is a way I can help to raise money for the Brethren Disaster Relief Fund. I love having these meals as I enjoy the Christian fellowship and the excitement of not knowing who is coming. Walter and I also enjoy buying several Share-A-Meal tickets, and we always have a wonderful time attending the meals.

I would encourage others to have meals. It is an opportunity to meet new Christian friends and to share your faith. After you try it, I am sure you will enjoy having a Share-A-Meal.
(Esther Hackman, Mohler's COB, 1994 SB, p. 43)

"Share-A-Meal – What a deal!
Good food – Festive mood
Enjoy fellowship – Develop kinship
A meal for guest – Only the best
As host you state – How many,
main course, date
Guests arrive to partake –
What the host will make
Food and laughter abound –
As everyone gathers 'round
What an exciting way to help others –
Sharing a meal with sisters and brothers
Try it and you'll see –
What an experience it can be
Share-A-Meal – Is for real!"
(Audrey and Candy Myer. 1993 SB, p. 20)

Left to right: Candy Myer, Nancy Fahnestock, and Fern Fahnestock are at their table in West Hall to sell Share-A-Meals. Note the charts in the background listing the homes offering meals.

"Let no one ever come to you without leaving better and happier."

- Mother Theresa

FOOD, FELLOWSHIP, AND FUN(DS)

When my husband, Bob, worked for Brethren Village, many retirees there told him that they knew about the BDRA and wanted to contribute in some way but didn't know how, as they were unable to attend. That birthed the idea of having a meal for retirees.

For the last ten years, I have invited eight to ten people from Brethren Village to a charity donation meal in my home, where I prepared and paid for the food. During the evening I asked for donations, clearly explaining that the entire proceeds would go to the BDRA. In a single evening, these meals have raised between $500 and $1,000.

My Proposal:

I would like to see each church in the ANE and SOPA Districts establish a plan by which one or more families within that church hosts at least one charity meal per year. At this meal, either the church or the host family will cover the cost, and the understanding would be that a donation (with a recommendation for the minimum) would be given for the BDRA. Only those who are homebound or living in a nearby retirement home should be invited.

The way I did it was to present the idea to one resident and ask him/her to spread the word. Each year we had more persons desiring to come than we had table space. The invitation could also be given through their intra-community announcements or publications. Just think, if one family in each of the sixty-four churches in our district would do this and the rate of donations would be similar to what we received, this concept would raise between $32,000 and $64,000 for the BDRA. Just as important is the goodwill it would spread between the retirement communities and the participating congregations. If there are no retirement homes close by, there are still retirees and homebound individuals who could be invited.

I would recommend that you disclose what food you will be serving, i.e. soup and/or salad, name the meat you will serve, or if you will serve a no-fat or low-salt meat, low or no sugar, a breakfast, basket lunch or supper, the time of the meal and if any transportation will be provided.

(Ellen Longenecker Young, 1998 SB, p. 31)

Although some Amish attended the BDRA and a few even hosted Share-A-Meals before the tragedy at Nickle Mines school happened, they have increased their support tremendously since then. Today Amish come and make soft pretzels and donuts, "while you watch them," and even donate most of the ingredients so that most monies made from those sales go directly to disaster relief. More and more Amish couples are opening their homes for Share-A-Meals which have proven to be so popular that buyers are now restricted to buying meals at only one Amish home, so that more people can have that unique and enjoyable experience. Some-

times the Amish invite members of the BDRA Board to also be there to be sure that none of their Share-A-Meal guests attempts to take pictures. Although it is very tempting, picture taking is viewed by the Amish as a violation of the 2nd Commandment (Exodus 20:4) and thus it is a belief of theirs that we should all respect–especially when we are in their homes benefiting from their hospitality and generosity.

I have participated in the Share-A-Meal program since it began. For the first several years a friend, who also lives at the Brethren Village, and I helped each other with the meals. Since my friend is no longer able to do this, I now entertain my guests in the Atrium Room of our Village Community Center.

If I were asked to choose my favorite Share-A-Meal experience, I would have to choose my first one. My friend and I were all ready for our guests and excited to know who was coming. Because of the way my car was parked in the driveway to my lower-level apartment, I could only see the bottom half of our guests as they arrived. It was shocking to see them in full length formal skirts, and I said to my friend, "My word, they are in formal attire!"

By that time they were on my front porch, and I saw they were friends from the Village. All were dressed up in fancy long dresses with flowers (artificial) in their hair and jewelry like you wouldn't believe, 3 or 4 strands of long beads and several pairs of earrings (the long, dangling kind). They looked very sober and dignified like strangers until I opened the door and let them in. Then we all collapsed with

laughter at their get-ups. It took quite a while to calm down enough to eat the dinner we had prepared. This was my first Share-A-Meal dinner and my most memorable one.
(Zenobia Bensing, Brethren Village. 1996 SB, p. 56)

*"The most indispensable ingredient
of all good home cooking:
love for those you are cooking for."
(Sophia Loren)*

"We saw another outfit come into being and that is Share-A-Meal. I was blessed many times as I was asked to come into homes to share a meal with somebody. Everybody can get involved, every human being and the fellowship– I remember one time we were at the Smiths, and we were having this beautiful dinner. There was not even one other Brethren person sitting there. They were all from somewhere else, different walks of life. They were Lutheran, Baptist, Episcopalian or whatever you want to call them. But they were there, and they had given, and their main purpose was to honor and glorify God."   *(Jay M. Witman. 1994 SB, p. 56)*

Greetings to you all in Jesus' name. May this be to His Glory and Honor. Wishing God's blessings to all of our friends who may read this. Our friends, Landis and Audrey Myer, have been the reason for our help in the Share-A-

Meal project. They have coached us and helped in many ways. We have made many friends and enjoyed the fellowship and the sharing of those things with which we have been blessed. We have learned how other church members also depend on their friends for love and caring for each other.

The many different churches and beliefs are all working together with the same goal, to meet on that happy golden shore at Jesus' feet. May our home and our Share-A-Meals be a blessing and honor to God as you use the money for the many needy families. May God bless our nation and churches as we face each new day."
(Isaiah and Linda Ebersol 2000 SB, p. 17)

In 1992 over 500 meals were served @ $8.50 each at Share-A-Meals with over 60 hosts and hostesses extending the welcome mat.
(1993 SB, p. 20)

In 2008, a Share-A-Meal ticket cost $15 each, and for a truly outstanding meal, that is still a bargain!

"Our first Share-A-Meal experience convinced me that we will make it a regular happening. But it took a suggestion from Bob and Ruth Henry to make it become a reality.

Bob and Ruth know from past experience that I enjoy hosting dinners, and while being guests at one of my dinners, they told me they thought I would enjoy participating in the

Share-A-Meal project. With five daughters-in-law, my husband long ago agreed to have our family Christmas celebration after the actual holiday, and our children and grandchildren now look forward to another "holiday" after December 25. But what do Wilford and I do on Christmas Day? Surely there must be other couples in this same situation!

So we opted for ten Share-A-Meal guests on Christmas Day, and it was a very rewarding experience! Put us down for ten guests for Christmas Day 1996!

(Wilford and Helen Myers, 1996 SB, p. 56)

On Sunday evening, October 15, 1995, Ken and I hosted our first Share-A-Meal in our house with Minerva Lentz, Lucille Meyer and Mildred Kirst as co-hosts, helping us to plan and prepare the meal. We had six guests and also invited Neville Tomlinson, who is from Jamaica and attends Mt. Zion Road COB.

While we were waiting, it was very exciting to anticipate who our guests would be and if we would know them. The Lancaster, Conestoga and Jennersville COB's were represented and we all had a great evening of fun and fellowship.

(Ken and Hilda Blatt, 1996 SB, p. 56)

"Share-A-Meal has been a highlight for our family. We've met many nice people and enjoyed the Christian fellowship and singing. We also enjoy working with Landis and Audrey Myer and with my two sisters and their hus-

bands that help to cook and serve the meal. It is through their support that we have been having one the last five years."

(Amos and Sally Stoltzfus, Narvon. 2000 SB, p. 17)

A Brethren Disaster Relief Cookbook was published in 2000 and sold for the amazing price of $5 each. Containing over 1,000 recipes submitted by members and friends of the ANE and SOPA Districts of the COB, the cookbook was edited by Audrey Myer and her daughter, Candy. Carl Shull typed all the recipes so that they all would have a similar style and consistent appearance.

Designed with a four-color hard cover and spiral binding, this attractive and useful cookbook of almost 400 pages was the product of several years' work. Recipes were divided into eight different categories with colorful tab dividers for easy reference.

It also contained a brief introduction to the COB written by Don Fitzkee and a foreword written by Jay M. Witman. On the page of acknowledgements is listed this poem:

A Favorite Recipe
Take a cup of kindness,
Mix it well with love
Add a lot of patience,
And faith in God above.

Sprinkle very generously
With joy and thanks and cheer,
And you'll have lots of "Angel Food"
To feast on all the year.
(Poet Unknown—From the BDRA Cookbook)

> *"When God's children
> are in need,
> you be the one to help
> them out.
> And get into the habit
> of inviting guests home
> for dinner or, if they need
> lodging, for the night."*
>
> Romans 12:13 (TLB)

I first heard about Share-A-Meal through my husband's parents, Mr. and Mrs. Earl Minnich, who have participated in the program for many years. It sounded wonderful--too bad we lived 500+ miles away! Then Carol Fahnestock mentioned how they offered meals and lodging. I thought, maybe next year we'll try that too. She saw that I got the application, and our wonderful adventure began.

My initial thoughts were: Maybe some of the folks we know will buy our tickets. We'll get some guests again that way and benefit the BDRA. To date, all our Share-A-Meal guests have been strangers who quickly became friends.

This has far exceeded our expectations! God has such neat ways of meeting our needs. He sent a mason contractor from Maryland. My husband is a mason contractor.

They both enjoy flying. Then we had a couple who had taken a lengthy trip around the United States with their children, and we did that in '87. I could go on and on. This has been such a blessing and helped meet our need for fellowship with new folks plus enable us to contribute to the BDRA in a more personal way."
(Lois Ann Minnich, Lewiston, ME, 1997 SB, p. 29)

WHY NOT "BRETHREN YOUR WAY?"

One of the nicest ways to meet new friends during the BDRA weekend is to be a host/hostess for a traveler attending the big event. Hosts and guests may meet as strangers, but in a very short time they experience a common bond and a sense that they've been friends a long time.

We had a most delightful time with a couple who came approximately eighty miles, along with two more sisters visiting from out of state. Others from the Midway COB have a standing invitation to visitors who return to them each year. The fellowship is rich, and the time passes all too quickly.

Hebrews 13:2 says, *"Do not forget to entertain strangers, for by so doing some people have entertained angels without knowing it."* (NIV) We believe we have met some!
(Earl and Eleanor Hitz, 2001 SB, p. 17)

W. Theme Baskets

Since 1999, theme baskets have become popular attractions at the BDRA because they

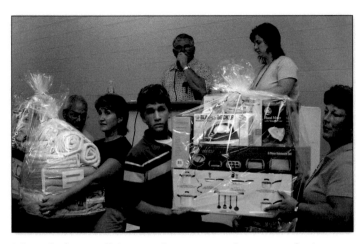

Theme baskets in all shapes and sizes are popular items at the Auction.

information on that form, a numbered listing of all baskets and their contents is prepared and given to persons attending the Theme Basket Auction. The basket preparer will receive a corresponding number to attach to the front of his/her basket. All theme baskets should be brought to the registration table in the Southeast Hall by Friday noon, so they can be lined up and viewed before they are auctioned that evening.

are fun, easy, can be made by anyone, make nice gifts, and consequently bring good prices. To make one, you need a basket or container to stuff full with new or collectible items, pertaining to a certain theme, with a minimum value of $25. Wrap the whole thing with clear cellophane, add a bow and it's done! (Do not use Saran wrap, colored or patterned cellophane as people can't see all you have included. If you add any home- made foods, each item must carry a label listing all the ingredients.)

Theme ideas can be as varied as your imagination can create. To get you started, some ideas could be Barbie and Friends, Thomas the Tank Engine, Children's Toys, Crayola Art Supplies, Hershey's Chocolate, John Deere collectibles, the color purple, Lighthouses, Longaberger Baskets, Pampered Chef, Pumpkins, Bath & Body Works, Yankee Candles, Sports, Gardening, Bird Lover, Expecting a Baby?, Teddy Bears and Friends, Tailgating, School supplies, Scrapbooking and Veggie Tales. The possibilities are endless.

In the SB each year is a registration form for anyone preparing a theme basket. From the

When ten-year-old Josh Murray heard the announcement about Grow Money at the 2000 BDRA, he decided he would like to try this idea using his talent to bring honor and glory to God. Within a couple days after he got an envelope with $10 in it, he decided to create a Theme Basket with Penn State memorabilia. As his family learned about his project, they wanted to help him. His grandma came across a Penn State tin container which he used as his "basket." Throughout the year, Josh and his mother would look for items to fill the basket. Using blue and white basket filler to line the container, they soon filled it with envelopes, tablet, sticky notes, pen, magnet, cup, plates and napkins, mug, glass filled with candy, flag, soda can holder and finally a bag of Penn State pretzels. By July, Josh was ready to register his basket, named "We are—Penn State," with the Theme Basket Committee, and it was to be number 54 to be sold.

Josh and his mother were at the 2001 BDRA on Friday evening, and as the time grew closer for his basket to be sold, he became more nervous and excited. When it sold for one hundred dollars, he was so proud that a boy, now eleven, was able to contribute that amount for disaster relief.

Before he left the Expo Center that day, he picked up another Grow Money envelope with $10 in it so he could begin planning his project for the next year.   *(2002 SB, p. 40)*

❖ ❖ ❖

X. Used Tools, Furniture, Appliances, etc.

Donations of good, "lightly used" items, have always been welcomed to be sold at the BDRA in a building commonly referred to as the Pole Barn. In 2006, on the 30th Anniversary of the BDRA, a large advertisement with the appearance of a "Wanted" poster like one would see hanging in a post office was printed in the SB. Instead of a wanted criminal, in this case what was wanted were "Good, useable items for the Pole Barn Sale." In the advertisement, Randy Hostetter, from the Florin COB, the Chairperson, stated that the motto of the Pole Barn Committee is: *If you have not used it in the last year, please consider donating it to the Auction.*

Sold at the Pole Barn Auction are such items as tools (power tools, hand tools–from hammers to wrenches), lawn and garden items (lawn mowers,

> *An old Pennsylvania Dutch axiom:*
> *"Use it up, wear it out, Make it do, or do without."*

weed-eaters, snow-blowers, long-handled tools, chain saws, hoes and rakes), furniture (tables, chairs, sofas, bookcases, chests), electrical appliances (toasters, coffee makers, microwaves, fans, irons, etc.), small items (bicycles, sports equipment, collectibles, household and garage items), and larger items (cars, trucks, tractors, motorcycles, trailers–all in good operating condition). They do request that NO large appliances, older TV's, or tires be donated.

The Pole Barn attracts all those interested in new or "lightly used" furniture, garden tools, household items, etc.

❖ ❖ ❖

As a resident of Cross Keys Village, one day I saw an announcement on the bulletin board that a bicycle was for sale. What motivates an aging person to consider buying a bicycle? It is not only the spirit of youth within them, but also the anticipation of using it as transportation in getting the mail, making visits, and relaxing in leisure time.

Since the Schwinn bicycle appeared to be well cared for and had a headlight, a horn, and a metal basket to place packages, I bought it at what I felt was a bargain price.

I used it once a month to go for a haircut, to visit my vegetable garden, and sometimes, on a summer evening with a friend, would use it to circle the Village on the newly paved streets and sidewalks. In winter, it was in a dormant state in my garage.

One spring day, having had too little exercise during the winter, I discovered discomfort in my knees as I pushed the bike up an incline. Since this arthritic condition didn't get better, I discontinued riding the bike. In time, I decided to sell it or give it away.

At the 1994 SOPA District Conference, in speaking with Robert and Ruth Henry, I mentioned that I had a bicycle that I was willing to give for the BDRA. Since I wasn't planning to attend, and it wouldn't fit in my car anyway, he agreed to come and deliver it. I then asked, "Could you let me know how much it brings?"

In the meantime, I asked several friends what they thought the bike would bring. One said $20 and another raised it to $25. I didn't tell anyone that I had paid $40 for it.

About a week after the Auction, I received a card from Bob Henry stating: "Your bike that you gave for the BDRA sold for $120. Thank you for helping us meet our goal. We made $353,000 as of Saturday night."

Praise the Lord!

(Excerpted from an article by Bernard N. King, 1995 SB, p. 9)

❖ ❖ ❖

THE "RUBBERMAID" STORY

For many years, a common sight at the BDRA was a large collection (often located in a tent) of all sizes, shapes and styles of plastic garbage cans, waste baskets, plastic storage boxes, etc., made by the Rubbermaid company. How did these products get to our BDRA?

Rubbermaid is a trade name for a quality product of injection-

At the BDRA, one can even buy a supply of wood for the winter!

molded plastic articles. Because the company, known world-wide, has very stringent inspection standards, about two percent of their manufactured products are found to be slightly inferior or sub-standard and are withdrawn from the retail market. Many of the flaws are barely noticeable to an untrained eye.

In time, the Rubbermaid Company had an accumulation of these rejects. If they would allow them to be sold to certain businesses, they might reappear on the market at lower prices than the "perfect" products, and in competition to them. The company didn't want to encourage that.

To solve the problem, Rubbermaid suggested that interested employees form a new business called "Specialmade" and find a way to distribute these surplus items. The owner of "Specialmade" was Mitch Orendorff, and he, as well as several others on his board, were members of the Church of the Brethren. After much discussion, they came up with a win/win solution for the Rubbermaid Company. The "seconds" or surplus items were donated by Rubbermaid to the "Specialmade" group and by doing this, Rubbermaid could have a tax write-off. In turn, the "Specialmade" group donated them to various charity auctions and the money raised by their sale was used to benefit needy people. The buyers, who attended the BDRA, were able to buy Rubbermaid products at a discount–and at the same time, to help those needing disaster relief. What a great idea!   *(2000 SB, p. 65)*

When Ken and Carroll Kreider, Elizabethtown COB, became involved with mak-

ing Aunt Ellen's Caramel Corn at the BDRA, their grandchildren were still quite small. During setup time at the caramel corn stand, their grandson, Rod Barlet, 3, would occupy his time riding his tricycle in the Big Hall and circle around to help where he could.

In subsequent years, Rod would be sent with a basket of popcorn and some change bills to sell caramel corn throughout the Auction Hall. At times, he would pest his grandpa, Ken, to go with him to the Pole Barn where the tools, bikes, utensils and whatever were sold because there he was permitted to bid. He loved that Auction and wanted to be there for that activity, so he would beg to not have to go to school on the Friday of the BDRA.

Eventually, his grandma, Carroll Kreider, gave him permission to attend the Pole Barn Auction of new and used items—and to use his discretion to purchase what he felt would be useful for the family. People were shocked that his grandma would permit this young boy (in 5th, 6th, and 7th grades) to participate in bidding without supervision. The auctioneers knew who he was and that he had been given permission to bid with his grandparent's number. People would ask Carroll, "Aren't you concerned that he will spend too much money?"

However, she had decided that whatever he would spend would be going to a good cause, and in addition, it was a learning experience for him.

He was very responsible and purchased some very nice, useful things like rakes, scrub buckets, work tools, brooms, garden tools, toolboxes—and a few useless items.

Oft times it would be very warm at the popcorn stand. On one occasion, he thought that a fan would be a good purchase for the work environment there. When the auction in the shed was completed, he would return to the caramel popcorn stand to share his purchased "treasures" and to help pop or sell the popcorn.

During the past two years, in 2007 and 2008, he has lamented that he can't be present at the BDRA since he is now enrolled as a student at McPherson College.

(Shared by Carroll L. Kreider)

Y. Winross Trucks

In 1990, at the height of the Winross Truck craze, the BDRA had its first Winross Truck Auction in East Hall. Many popular collectible trucks were donated and purchased during the years it was held, including the following: N.G. Hershey & Son, Paul Kurtz, Miller's Bar-B-Q, Manheim Auto Auction, Service Star, Martin's Hardware, Gehman's Feed Mill, Elm Tree Acres Dairy tanker with jug, KoKaLeKo Egg Range, and G & D Repair. Three examples from the year 1993 were trucks from these businesses: L. H. Brubaker, Elm Tree Acres, and Messick Farm Equipment, Inc.

Due to the volume of items donated to the Main Auction, the Center Hall Auction was created in 1995 and included the Winross Truck sale as well as ERTL and handcrafted toys, artwork, baseball cards, gift certificates and sports collectibles. Fine furniture pieces were also added in 2000 and this expanded sale was returned to the East Hall.

Z. Woodworkers

MARVIN AND JANE BENNER

Since 1991 Marvin and Jane Benner and their son, Jeff, have been sending both new wooden crafts and refinished old furniture to the BDRA. Doll highchairs, washboards, porch swings, towel racks and rocking horses are some of the hand-crafted items they have made. In 1997, the Benners created a wooden replica of a log cabin that could be used as a doll house or for decoration.

Besides the craft items, Marvin and Jane work together to restore antique chairs to contribute for disaster relief. Most of those old chairs require Jane's talent of caning to complete the seats. Some chairs have been salvaged from the streets, set out to be picked up for junk. Others have been donated by people who recognize the gifts the Benners have to transform the old battered pieces into beautiful, useful furniture.

What do the Benners do to change an ugly, broken chair into one that's ready for the BDRA? First, the chair is completely taken apart and broken pieces are replaced. After stripping off the old paint or varnish, the pieces are re-glued and stained. Then the seat is caned. Finally, the polyurethane is applied. A minimum of ten hours goes into re-doing each chair.

When asked why they donate so much time into items for the BDRA, both responded, "We like to help people in need." Jane added that they no longer are able to go to disaster sites as they once did. In the past, they helped flood victims clean up in Johnstown, Wilkes Barre, and Lewisburg. Not feeling called to serve the church in ways such as teaching, Marvin says, "We do things like this–anything we feel we are qualified to do." Jane also admits, "We enjoy what we do, or we wouldn't do it."

Members of the Buffalo Valley COB in Mifflinburg, Jane has been a part of that church since she was born, and Marvin joined shortly after marrying Jane 43 years ago.

Next to the Benner's home, which is off a quiet country road near White Springs, is their workshop, an old one-room school house built in 1908. They have owned it for forty years, and guess what? Jane went to that school for four years! Today the workshop contains various saws, a lathe, and other woodworking tools. As their son was growing up, they kept various animals there, and Marvin also operated a sharpening business from that shop for eighteen years.

Recently retired, Marvin had worked for forty years at Chef Boyardee as a truck driver. Jane had also worked for Hi Li Sewing factory for twenty-six years. Both agree that they need to keep busy and they enjoy working together. Marvin teases, "Jane's the boss, but I don't listen!"

Jane responds with a laugh, "He always says that!"

It's obvious they get along well, whoever is the boss--and victims who are helped from the BDRA benefit from those like the Benners who do "what they can" in response to the need.

(Fay Richards. 1997 SB, p. 6)

JOHN BOLLINGER

From 1980 to 1985, John Bollinger served as the Middle Creek COB coordinator for the BDRA. In that role, he and his wife, Mary Emma, were enthusiastic supporters and continued to be until he passed away.

Woodworking was his gift and he used that ability to create useful and decorative items that he would donate. Among his contributions over many years were a miniature thrashing machine, Conestoga wagons, hay wagons, a hand-crafted barn, and in 1988, at the age of 72, he made communion bread rolling pins.

Around that time, he also frequently was asked to drive members of the Team Mennonites to various locations. While he waited for them, he would use the time to do some whittling. One of his bigger projects, a 20-horse team and hay wagon, required lots of whittling!

John also helped the BDRA in other ways. One Thursday before the Auction, he arrived at the Lebanon Fairgrounds and discovered that the grass was in need of mowing. After making some inquiries, he mowed the entire grounds.

After a devastating flood in the Harrisburg area, John recalled working with other Middle Creek COB members helping to clean up. When they were getting ready to leave, the flood victim inquired as to whom he should pay. John responded, "There's no charge. We were glad to be able to help you in your time of need, and we feel good about it."

Upon hearing those words of kindness and caring, tears filled the man's eyes.

As he got older and his physical problems limited his volunteer work and other activities, John continued as long as he could in his shop, making items for the BDRA and serving God by sharing his talent for the benefit of others.

(Excerpted from an article in the 1988 SB, p. 31)

KIRBY K. KELLER

Few people understand and appreciate the grace of God as much as Kirby Keller does. In his early years, he was a rebellious, feared, Pagan Motorcycle gang leader, who rode down the wide road to destruction, coming to a stop only after he had committed murder and ended up at the Correctional Institution in Dallas, PA. In his incarceration, as long as he had access to woodworking tools and machinery, he made numerous wooden articles, from pen and pencil sets to a cherry schoolhouse clock to a roll-top desk, for the BDRA. Obviously, his life had changed!

In his own words, he says: "In summarizing my sin-filled past, I guess you could say my search to find Jesus led me down many paths.

A desk that was made by Kirby Keller and sold at the BDRA in 2006.

Most of the time, I tried doing things my way. When the right time came, God showed me the correct path and revealed the futility of going my own way. In October 1989, I chose to serve the Lord Jesus Christ, and on July 19, 1992, the Lord provided an opportunity for baptism and I then became a part of God's family at the White Oak COB. I'm so thankful God is still working miracles in lives today.

"I want you to know that all men and women in Pennsylvania's prisons are not hopeless villains. There are many who care, care about their victims, care about their families, and care about saving the souls of others who are lost in this world. Most of all, I want to make sure God gets all the credit.

"Tough times are inescapable in life, and we all experience them. These times can develop us or destroy us, depending on how we respond. I see many who respond with hostility to all around them, but all tough times are conquerable, no matter how bad they may appear. We must learn to walk in the continuing awareness that we're walking in the presence of God. Sometimes we listen and take advice from the wrong people (friends, people at work, etc.). We must turn and listen to God, focus on Him, and give Him our full and undivided attention.

"Even in prison, I can observe the fast-paced world and see how quickly new things become obsolete. These things are discarded and become things of the past. However, no matter how much change I see taking place, I see the Bible, God's Holy Word, remaining the one sure means for getting the right answers to the complicated problems of today's society. I urge you all to look to God's Word for all your answers today, tomorrow, and always. *The Bible may be old, but its truths are always new.*

"I may never receive forgiveness from society for my sin-filled past, and that's saddening, but thankfully, God has the last word. As my final word to you, I will quote 1 Timothy 6:18: *Command them to do good, to be rich in good deeds, and to be generous and willing to share.*"

(Excerpted from an article by Kirby Keller, 1994 SB, p. 25)

HIRAM MINNICH

One of the high points in the BDRA's history occurred in the 2006 Auction when a tall-case walnut grandfather's clock made by Hiram Minnich was sold five times earning $25,000 for Disaster Relief!

Hiram, a White Oak COB member, was not a newcomer in donating wooden creations to the Auction. The first item he gave to the BDRA was a two-seated child's rocker with adjustable seats. Next, he made and donated a balloon mantel clock, resting on a mahogany base, decorated with ebony wood, and run by an 8-day German clockwork, which was bought by his brother, John, at the 1997 Auction.

After that, Jay Witman approached him about making a tall-case grandfather's clock for 1998, the 22nd Anniversary of the BDRA, and Hiram promised he would. The result was an 8-foot walnut tall-case clock with immaculate inlay which was sold twice bringing in a total of $6,700. A music box in a case decorated with hand carvings brought $1,200 in 2001.

Hiram Minnich working on the Grandfather's Clock that brought $25,000 at the 2006 BDRA's 30th Anniversary Sale.

Because 2006 was going to be the 30th Anniversary of the BDRA, Jay Witman approached Hiram again in 2005 and asked him if he would consider making another grandfather's clock for the next year's Auction. Having spent much time in the Minnich home while growing up, Jay and the Minnich boys felt close as brothers. Since making a clock requires about six months of work, Jay made his request early, and Hiram agreed to do it.

Hiram observes, "The Lord knew what He was doing," because in working on that clock, he had a "never-before-experienced" drive to get it finished. He often worked on it until 2 a.m.; it was like a part-time job. This finished walnut tall-case clock was also eight feet tall with immaculate inlay decorations. But building a clock wasn't the only thing going on in Hiram's life.

When he was eight years old, he was diagnosed with Type 1 juvenile diabetes and was afflicted with this disease for the next thirty years. During those years, he was insulin dependent, and had an insulin pump for six years. However, in spite of that, he was growing progressively worse. He would have blackouts and experience periods when he didn't know where he was and realized this could be dangerous. Fortunately, he could usually tell when an episode was coming on and quickly drink something sweet.

During these years, he had married Lori Martin and they were the parents of four children. Because of his problems, he was involved in two serious automobile accidents. Sometimes his sugar would dip at night, and his wife would have to hurriedly get him a sweet drink or orange juice to keep him from passing out. Then he started going unconscious without a warning, and they felt something had to be done.

One day Hiram left his work in Lititz during his lunch break and went to a local deli, but didn't return for two hours. His fellow workers became alarmed, and his wife tried to call him. Although he heard his cell phone ringing, his brain didn't register that he needed to answer it. This was his "wake-up call."

Since his wife, Lori, worked in the renal dialysis unit of the Lancaster General Hospital, she asked hospital personnel what one needed to do to get a pancreas transplant, and was advised to contact Johns Hopkins Hospital in Baltimore. Knowing that there was a long list of persons waiting for transplants and simply having a consultation required a

long wait, Hiram and Lori began the process anyway.

To be eligible for a transplant, one has to meet a list of criteria, and Hiram met all the requirements. Consequently, he underwent numerous blood tests and one day when he had 26 vials of blood taken from one arm, he kidded the nurse, "You're dehydrating me so much I'll soon look like a prune!"

After that, he was officially put on the transplant list and had to wear a pager. However, he was still facing a possible wait of one to three years before an organ would be available. He says, "Fortunately, and I can only thank the Lord for this, my blood type was a little on the rare side. The doctor told me in May that he guessed I may have my transplant by the end of the summer."

On August 18, 2006, Hiram was repairing his back door and putting some screws back in it when the phone rang. It was from Johns Hopkins, and they had a pancreas. That news hit him like a brick wall. He was told everything but the name of the donor who was a male, age 26, who had died in an auto accident in St. Louis, MO. Everything matched, and they said if Hiram wanted to take it, they'll do some final tests and then fly it in. He responded, "Let's go for it." With high expectations, Hiram and Lori headed for Baltimore.

Hiram says, "I knew people were praying for us, and I could feel it, because I was calm like it was a 'walk in the park.' Although I had never had any kind of surgery before, when going through the final preparations, I wasn't really scared. I was just feeling God would get me through this."

On August 19th, on the way to the operating room, they had difficulty getting his gurney through the door, so Hiram offered to get off and walk in, and that is what he did. On his right was the surgeon scrubbing the pancreas in a stainless steel bowl. He said, "Mr. Minnich, would you like to see your new pancreas?"

So Hiram walked over and had the unique experience of observing his pancreas prior to getting on the operating table. After that, he remembered nothing.

The next two weeks were somewhat traumatic as the doctors tried to determine if his body would accept or reject the new pancreas. While he experienced ups and downs, Lori and the children had difficulties making the long trip to visit him.

Hiram had been home from the hospital about three weeks when the BDRA was held. Although he was still very weak, he didn't want to miss watching his clock being sold, so to protect himself from catching any illness, he wore a face mask. As he recalls that day, he says, "The generosity of the people just kinda overwhelmed me as they sold it and the bidders kept saying, 'Sell it again,' 'Sell it again.' It sold for $5,000 each time for five times, so the clock brought in $25,000! The final buyers were my wife's parents, Wilmer and Elaine Martin, and that's kinda neat! After the clock was sold, Jay Witman asked everybody to stand and sing *"How Great Thou Art"*, and that's when I broke down. Wow! I knew it wasn't the normal thing for people to give like that. I want to give God all the glory, but it was so neat how it all turned out."

Since then, Hiram has not required insulin shots. In fact, he thanks God that he hasn't had any low blood sugar reactions or blackouts since the surgery. However, diabetes is such an insidious disease that having had it for over 30 years has taken its toll.

Usually, diabetes isn't what kills you, but it's what it does to your organs. Hiram explains, "It messes up your heart, damages your kidneys and affects your eyes. In my case, my feet are pretty well shot, and I can't run. Within the last year or two, I developed an intestinal problem as a result of the surgery and I still take medication for that monthly. About a year and a half ago, I was very sick and almost didn't make it. Jay and I have always been close, but that's when we really connected with one another because we were both struggling with intestinal problems. If my health holds up, I would like to make something for Jay—in his memory—and donate it at a future auction."

Hiram is employed at the Lititz Planing Mill Company and enjoys working with wood. Each of his productions is a unique and original creation. He explains, "All my blueprints come from inside my head."

This gifted man, with a strong faith and a positive attitude, has certainly learned to make lemonade out of the lemons in his life.

RONNIE LEWIS REBER

Carrying on the tradition and skills of his great-great grandfather, Ronnie Reber continues to enjoy building Reber wagons, sleighs and Conestoga wagons, and has generously donated a number of them to the BDRA through the years.

J. G. Reber, the founder of the Reber Wagon Works in Centreport, PA, built the first Reber wagon in 1892. Known for their top quality farm implements, the Reber vehicle replicas made by Ronnie continue that reputation. A

A Reber Wagon made and donated to the BDRA by Ronnie Lewis Reber, a fifth-generation Reber wagonmaker.

Reber sleigh was sold at the 1993 BDRA for $950, another at the 1996 BDRA went for $1,100. In 1993 a Reber wagon was sold for $2,350 and in 1996 another wagon brought in $2,200.

EDDIE SWOPE

After the Gruber Wagon Works went to rubber wheels in the late 1940s, many farmers took their ancient hay and box wagons into the fields and burned them. A person like Eddie Swope of Bernville, who reveres the vener-

able wooden farm vehicles, could cry when he thinks of that.

Swope, who as a kid lived near Gruber Works in Mount Pleasant, has turned his nostalgia and woodworking ability to a practical level. As a hobby, this owner of Heidelberg Kitchens, has bought, repaired, restored and made miniatures of Gruber wagons. Without boasting, he says, "They are pretty near perfect as far as detail is concerned."

In 1994, at the 11th Heritage Celebration held in the Berks County Heritage Center, some of his pin-striped restorations and reproductions were on display, including: a restored 1913 Gruber hay flat, a $350 purchase which

Swope candidly admits was a "steal," a restored two-horse Weber box wagon built sometime before 1904 and purchased for $35, a miniature hay flat which took him 250 hours to craft, and a miniature Gruber wheelbarrow.

People who wonder what Swope starts out with have only to look in his shop wherein resides the skeleton of a Gruber box wagon, a "basket case" the cabinet-maker hopes to restore and exhibit at a future heritage exhibition.

As a youngster, Eddie, at the indulgence of Franklin Gruber, would wander through the Gruber Wagon Works, immersed in the buzzing of saws and fragrance of sawdust. The Grubers made their last wagon in 1956, and closed in 1971. Located in the Tulpehocken Creek Park near Reading, PA, the Gruber Wagon Works was declared a National Historic Landmark in 1977.

After working for Yatron Brothers, Eddie established his own cabinet shop in 1980. "It was a challenge, and I just like old things," he said, replying to why he chose wood reproductions and restorations of old farm vehicles as a hobby. "It was something I wanted to do for a long time—and, until lately, never had the time to do it," he explained.

In 1993, a Gruber wagon and sled were donated by members of the Indian Creek COB, and the wagon brought $1,550. That same year, a Swope wheelbarrow was donated by members of the Hatfield COB.

OTHER FINE WOODWORKERS

A sampling of other expert woodworkers and a partial listing of the things they have made and donated to the BDRA would include:

- **Mark Bollinger** – Miniature coops, 1989 Reproduction of antique rocking horse, 1990
- **Edgar Martin Brandt**, Brandt's COB – Cedar chest, 1991, Oak deacon bench/toy box, 1993
- **Herman Brandt**, Midway COB – Oak roll top desk, 1991
- **Isaac Bucher, Jr.**, Indian Creek COB – Child's walnut corner cupboard, 1991
- **Jay Buffenmyer**, Palmyra COB – 3000 piece model of the "Star Barn" which brought $1,500 in 1993; model of the "Star Barn" in 1994
- **L. B. Ebersol & Sons**, Amish – Child's walnut settee, one each year from 2004 through 2008
- **Ken Garver**, Poland, OH – Buggy, 1997; carousel, 1998; 1/8 scale horse-powered treadmill and threshing machine, 2000
- **Alan R. Hoover**, Shippensburg COB – Solid oak desk
- **Sam Martin**, Mennonite – Numerous handcrafted wooden trucks, tractors, trains. In 1996 two of his trucks sold for $1,900 and $1,000 respectively.
- **S. H. Martin**, Cocalico COB – Numerous bowls made of blended woods
- **Donald Maugle**, Quakertown COB – Sleds in 1990, 1991
- **J. Hershey Myer**, Little Swatara COB – Walnut table
- **Landis Myer**, Conestoga COB – Oak table with 6 boards, one each year from 1998 through 2003, cherry 4-leg drop-leaf table, 2001, cherry extension table with 6 boards, 2002, cherry table with 12 boards, one each year from 2002 through 2008, and a butcher block table nearly every year!

Landis Myer has made and donated many butcher tables and extension tables like this to the BDRA and the SDDA over the years.

- **Jeff Shirk, Lancaster COB** – Oak 2-drawer filing cabinet, old-fashioned jelly cupboard, 1995, cypress wood pie cupboard made from a pew out of the Conestoga COB, 1996, 1997, wooden bookshelf, 1999
- **John P. Stumpf** – Conestoga wagon, 1991
- **Charles Wagner,** Mechanic Grove COB – chest, 2004
- **Mark Wampler,** Mt. Zion Road COB – Black walnut corner cupboard
- **Leon Wenger,** Middle Creek COB – Rocking horse, 1990; walnut drop-leaf table, 1997
- **Lloyd Wenger,** Conestoga COB – Pine toy chest, 1995, 2005
- **Art Wert,** Middleburg – Handcrafted wooden house and barn, 2007, handcrafted wooden barn, 2008, One-room schoolhouse, 2008
- **Marty Witman,** Florin COB – Marble roller, 1990, corner cabinet, 2006

- **Marvin Zimmerman,** Reading COB – Colonial style wall clocks, 2000
- **Raymond Zimmerman,** Conestoga COB – Ash game table, 1999, lady's walnut desk, 1999, oak spice wall cabinet, 1999, corner cupboard, 1999

SOME OF THE MAKERS OF INTRIGUING "MECHANICAL CONSTRUCTIONS":
- **Ken Garver** – A ¼ scale replica of an old player piano from the Greenwood Piano Company with a double-hinged folding cover for the keys, sliding doors to cover the music roll, and pedals. The sound produced is that of authentic piano roll music. The male player moves his arms and legs as he plays the piano. Ken only made one, built over a period of several months and donated it for the 1995 BDRA.
- **Lester Hoffman** – Fully detailed, fully operating, scale model replica of a steam tractor engine, 1989
- **Scott Hufford,** Lancaster COB – Handcrafted backhoe, 2005
- **Charles Lake,** Hanover – 1/8 scale replica of a Conestoga wagon with every detail included, 2002
- **Olen Landes** – Steam engine and thrashing machine, 1995
- **Moses Stauffer** – 16" hot air fan operated by an alcohol wick flame, 1990; Miniature handcrafted hit and miss engine, 1996, 1997

CHAPTER NINE
_____

Leaders Who Made a Difference

"Anyone can steer the ship, but it takes a leader to chart the course."
Unknown

A. The Originators

JAY M. WITMAN

A 1995 Tribute to Jay M. Witman:

During the nineteen years of the Brethren Disaster Relief Auction, many persons have given of their time and talents, making it possible for the Auction to achieve its stated goals. Among those thousands of persons is an individual who deserves special recognition for having devoted his time, energies, spirit, and resources to the Auction far beyond what might be expected. That person is Jay M. Witman.

Although many of the auctioneers were excellent, Jay Witman had the gift of inspiring the highest prices giving the glory to God! Someone observed that Jay was the "Walter Cronkite" of auctioneers in this area.

Jay has been involved with the Auction in various capacities since its conception in 1976 and the first Auction of 1977. During those years he has served as auctioneer extraordinaire, as chairman of the Publications Committee which is responsible for publication of the annual sale booklet, as a member of the Executive Committee, as host for the Kick-Off dinners at his home which more than twelve hundred persons have attended since 1993, and as host for the wrap-up meetings for all committee members following each Auction. In addition, he has volunteered to speak publicly to various groups about the Auction, and he initiated the idea of the cookbook which will be available at this year's Auction.

Jay's determination and commitment in all he has undertaken on behalf of the Auction, his leadership, his enthusiasm, his Christian spirit and character, his seemingly unlimited energies, and his dedication to the goals of the Auction have been an inspiration to all who know him and have worked with him. Truly he is an example of the scripture: *"Show me your faith without deeds, and I will show you my faith by what I do." (James 2:18b, NIV)*

To recognize his special contributions and to express its deep appreciation for his years of service on behalf of the BDRA, the Publications Committee dedicates this 1995 booklet to him.   *(1995 SB, p. 2)*

A name which has been almost synonymous with the BDRA is that of Jay M. Witman who was a motivating force in moving church members in two districts to share his vision of helping those less fortunate, those who have been struck by natural and/or man-caused disasters. With this persistent goal and his contagious enthusiasm, Jay repeatedly emphasized that the ultimate purpose of his efforts was to help people see Jesus, feel His love, and come to know Him as their own Lord and Savior.

Since he was about thirteen years old, Jay was afflicted with Crohn's disease, a chronic debilitating condition which was hardly known when he had its first symptoms. Ulcerations of the small intestine, as well as almost constant inflammation, made frequent hospitalizations necessary. Although Jay appreciated the care, he did not like hospitals and always returned home as soon as possible, often with continuing weakness and pain. With added complications, such as back problems and kidney stones, he also experienced a stroke on April 1, 2008. Much prayer, therapy and effort brought him a long way, but he still had difficulty expressing himself and saying the words he wanted to say.

Nevertheless, he never allowed his physical problems to deter his service to Christ and the church. Although, as Jay said, "I do wonder sometimes, 'Why me?' *I have determined that, with Christ's help, I will be in charge, not the disease."* In retrospect, he grew able to see that God used his physical difficulties to bless others in that they opened doors for Jay to witness and to challenge others to give sacrificially. His brother, Luke, observed: "Every doctor that he ever had knew about his faith because he witnessed to them."

Although he was usually an up-beat, get-things-done type of person, Jay did have his moments of discouragement. One of his most thrilling experiences came during a longer than usual hospitalization when he received more than four thousand cards! "That," he understated, "was a real inspiration."

Licensed as an auctioneer in 1969, Jay began very early to do some of the selling at the ANE District COB Youth Auction held at Root's Auction near East Petersburg. When interest in the auctions dwindled in the early 1970's, the vision was transferred to Jay, Jacob Ruhl, a Manheim businessman, and Jim Gibbel, then youth secretary. These three, and especially Jay, saw a BDRA as a means for Christians to show unconditional love, to reach across miles and oceans, as well as cultural, racial and religious differences, to show and tell the good news of Jesus.

"People came to me with new ideas, and some were good and some were bad, and I tried to listen to them, hoping that Jesus was always lifted up—that all would be to the glory of God," he said. "People wanted to push themselves and their interests, and they wanted to put up signs or hand out flyers, and we wouldn't allow that—no matter who they were or what cause they represented."

"For instance, one time I brought in a U.S. flag, and I gave the green light to do it. We had just gone through 9-11, and this was about two weeks later—in September 2001.

We had it up, you know, displaying it, and I must have had a hundred people calling me saying that was bad. I had made the decision to display it simply to thank people—not that we were different but to show that we care for people and to tell the whole world that Jesus loves them. So I sold the flag—for about $2,500, and that made people mad also.

"Whether what I did was right or wrong, time will be the judge on that, but I didn't do it to make anybody mad but to help people

understand. At that time the whole world was involved, the president had visited the 9-11 site, everybody was disturbed, and it was sad. I think sometimes you have to make a decision, and I hope God will never hold that against me because my main thing has always been to honor and glorify God."

One of the traditions of the BDRA (and one that upset Jay's mother) was that Jay, as head auctioneer, always dressed in a white suit. When asked how that got started, Jay explained that in the 1980's he was president of the Manheim Rotary Club. That led to an invitation to speak to a national Rotary Club gathering in Philadelphia. Along with the invitation was a request that he wear a white suit. Although he had owned one for several years, he very seldom wore it. Using as his subject, "You Are the Key," he complied and dressed in white. He gave a key to all attendees stating that they have in their hands the key that can make a difference in the world when they unlock their hearts and allow Jesus to come in. He concluded, "If each of us does this, we'll find that *Jesus is the Key to a better world, a world of peace and joy for everyone.*"

His audience applauded, and those who knew Jesus told him, "You are right, Jay. Believing in Jesus *does* make a difference!"

They also liked the image of the white suit, and Jay began wearing it for the BDRA. He explained, "When I am dressed all in white, I seem to speak with more authority. Without words, it says to others that I am doing my *best* for Jesus—not second best. We are to give Jesus our first-fruits, not our leftovers. We are to give our tithe, not what is left after we have bought everything WE wanted. It is a reminder of the respect and love for God that we should all feel. It also gives a look of professionalism. You can go to a doctor who comes to you with his shirt open and dressed in jeans, but when he is dressed in white, it makes a difference. It looks more professional. That's what my thinking is on this thing. We should appear as professionals, not that everybody should dress in a certain color, such as red or white, but I think *it's important to give Jesus your best.* You've gotta put Jesus first, and the minute you've got that, you have your priorities straight and you are a winner."

He continued: "When the SDDA began, they requested that I wear the white suit when I come to their sale in Harrisonburg, and so I wear it there, also. For most auctions and occasions, I don't wear it, but when it's a special thing, for God's glory, I will wear it as a witness of my faith and hopefully inspire others."

(Personal interviews)

Despite his constant pain, his failing kidneys, and a recent hospitalization, Jay attended the May 15 and 16, 2009, SDDA—accompanied by a nurse and concerned friends—but wearing his white suit. Wanting to say goodbye to his Virginia friends and determined to sell a wagon made by his long-time friend, Olen Landes, Jay was assisted to the platform. In a brief statement of encouragement, he said that he wanted to go and be with Jesus soon. Then he began auctioning the wagon, but after several bids, he got mixed up in his numbers. Realizing it, he sat down, saying, "I'm so sorry. I just can't finish it." The crowd stood and applauded in appreciation of his courage and his life of service to others. He had been an inspiration to so many.

On Sunday evening, June 7, 2009, he died quietly at his home near Manheim.

Long-time friends, Jay Witman and Olen Landes, sat together at the SDDA on May 16, 2009. Three weeks later, Jay died and Olen was one of the four ministers who spoke at his memorial service.

JACOB H. RUHL

No one is indispensable. After a great man dies, the world continues to revolve with thoughtless regularity; no storms, no volcanic eruptions announce his passing.

But in the living room where he talked and laughed with his family and friends, in the church where he worshipped, in the workplace where he exchanged ideas with colleagues, the jolt is felt, and it resonates throughout the lives of those he touched.

Jacob H. "Jake" Ruhl, who died on September 12, 1987, following a brief illness,

Jacob H. Ruhl

was present with us for 75 well-spent years. A multi-talented man, he put not merely a few but all his talents to use in the service of his family, friends, acquaintances, and most graciously, in the service of people he would never even meet.

Jake was one-very-important-third of a trio who, in 1977, revived the BDRA, which had been organized during the late 1960's by the Youth Cabinet of the Eastern District. With James C. Gibbel and Jay M. Witman, Jake took on the responsibility of acquiring the sponsorship of the ANE district of the COB. Following district approval, the three rekindled the original spirit of the Auction by soliciting donations that would raise $11,000 that year.

For the next 10 years, Jake served as an auctioneer for the Auction, volunteering valuable time and energy to make each suc-cessive year's event more successful than the one before.

In his church, the East Fairview COB, he was director of the choir for 30 years, served as a Sunday school superintendent and teacher, and was church moderator and deacon emeritus. He served for three years as a representative to the Eastern PA COB District Board.

For many people, those activities would have been enough. After all, Jake was also an industrious businessman. At the time of his death, he was chairman of the board of Jacob H. Ruhl, Inc., Manheim, insurance brokers, president and director of the Lititz Mutual Insurance Co., Lititz, and co-founder and director of Datcon Instrument Corp., Lancaster.

Known locally as one of the founders of the Manheim Auto Auction, he later served as corporate secretary for the board of the company, now Manheim Services Corp., a subsidiary of Cox Broadcasting. In 1962-63, he was president of the National Auto Auction Association.

A former director of Fulton Bank, Jake put his business acumen to work for his home community of Manheim, serving as the first president of the Manheim Chamber of Commerce and on the Manheim Zoning Hearing Board. He also served as past district governor for Rotary International.

For 30 years, Jake's most committed interest was the Brethren Village retirement community, Neffsville. At the August 1972, trustees' meeting, he made the motion that the name be changed from "Brethren Home" to "Brethren Village."[9] When the chapel was

---

[9] Johnstone, Mary Ann. *A Pattern of Love: Brethren Village, 1897-1997* (Masthof Press, 1997), p. 160.

added in 1978, the costs "were covered by the generous contributions of the Jacob H. Ruhl family"[10] and others. From 8/7/1980 to 12/31/1983, he served as Executive Director of Brethren Village.[11] In 1985, the PA Association of Non-Profit Homes for the Aging recognized Jake with the "Distinguished Service Award" for his years of active support for the home. This support took many forms: director, executive director, director emeritus, pastoral associate and general benefactor.

In May of 1987, Jake was the recipient of a doctor of humane letters degree from Elizabethtown College and, in 1964, was elected to the college board of trustees.

But the true greatness of a man is measured by his day-to-day response to life. In this, Jake had few peers. In the October, 1987, issue of the "Villager," a publication of Brethren Village, a writer who surely must have known him well offered this simple tribute: "Jake made the least of us feel as if we had … his full attention for the moment, and his interest that gave one a sense of approval and belonging.… Jake could quickly recall one's name, lend an encouraging word, and give a smile."

He has been missed.

(Excerpted from an article by Henry H. Gibbel, 1988 SB, p. 2)

"I would love to have the knowledge and wisdom of Jake H. Ruhl," Luke Witman commented recently. "Many years ago he taught me an invaluable lesson: He came up to me and

stood right in front of me. Taking a dollar bill out of his pocket, he held it with both hands, holding it between himself and me. Then he said, 'Luke, as long as you never allow dollars to come between you and Jay, you'll be successful.' I never forgot that. What a wise man he was!"

(Luke Witman, personal interview)

JIM GIBBEL

When the BDRA was begun in 1977, James C. Gibbel from the Lititz COB served together with Jake Ruhl and Jay Witman as one of the originators, serving on the planning committee as treasurer for about three years. Upon his resignation in 1980, he was succeeded by Jim Nelson who served as treasurer the next twenty years.

An insurance agent by vocation, Jim has been married to Elaine for 34 years and they are the parents of Janice Sommerhoff, Joel and Ethan Gibbel and have one grandson. While he enjoys collecting Brethren books and traveling, he continues to be active in his church as a deacon and Sunday school teacher, and in addition, serves as assistant treasurer of the Brethren Encyclopedia, Inc. In the past, he has also been on the Boards of Brethren Benefit Trust and On Earth Peace and served as moderator of the Lititz COB.

Through the years his passion to help the cause of the BDRA in giving honor and glory to God and helping those stricken by disaster never waned, and he still heartily supports the Auction by donating items to be sold and as an active bidder. He states: "I am thankful that I

---

[10] *Ibid*, p. 162.
[11] *Ibid*, p. 131.

can share my life with my family and the church community."   *(Personal Interview)*

B. The Coordinators

J. GERALD (JERRY) GREINER
1977-1980

"With every end, there is a new beginning!"
Ideas are born every day, but like seeds falling from trees, they only grow if there is fertile soil, gentle rain, and abundant sun. The auction idea, as started by the youth of the ANE District of the COB, was about to die when some courageous leaders gave it new life.

Through their efforts, at an auction held at Roots near East Petersburg, the youth had raised about $5,000. However, with the enthusiasm waning, the three "J's," (Jay Witman, Jake Ruhl, and Jim Gibbel) were not willing to let it die. Seeing the potential for a larger and more widely supported fundraising activity, they invited Jerry Greiner, (who had worked with the youth earlier and was now serving as chaplain at Elizabethtown College), Marilyn Sanko (Ebel), Mark and Marty Hershey and Henry Riest to join them to form a committee to see how they could build on the foundation already established by the youth.

One of their first decisions was to ask the ANE District Board for their blessing. Not only did the Board approve, but they selected the fourth weekend in September as a permanent date so calendars would be free of conflicts with other activities. Looking back, this was a very important first step, giving broad support and credibility to this new venture.

Jerry Greiner

In God's kingdom, the ladder to success is always climbed by faith. The assignment of finding a location was given to Jerry Greiner who grew up near Lebanon and had taught in their schools. This led him to pursue the use of a newly developed county fairground near Lebanon. Although it had only one building and very little parking space except on the grass, the committee gave their approval. Marilyn Sanko saw the need for a logo and designed a fitting symbol.

When it came to setting a financial goal, Jay Witman challenged the committee by suggesting a goal of $10,000. At first, he was met with silence, as the members remembered the struggle the youth had in raising half that amount. On the other hand, they all were aware that the Mennonites had raised $250,000 at their most recent Farm Show Auction. Jay added, "If the Mennonites can do it, so can we."

So, with fear and trembling but with a strong faith in a God who knows no limits, the committee accepted $10,000 as their goal for their first BDRA in 1977. That first year, mainly donated used home furnishings, antiques and household goods were sold. After not only making but exceeding that goal and raising almost $12,000 for disaster relief, the financial goal each succeeding year continued to grow and grow as we continued to praise and honor God, and even now, He continues to bless our efforts.

Today Jerry Greiner serves as pastor of the Shippensburg COB in the SOPA District.

(Excerpted from articles in the 1993 SB, p.3; 2006 SB, p. 6, and an email article from Jerry Greiner)

Mark and Marty Hershey

MARK AND MARTY HERSHEY
1981-1983

Mark and Marty started their journey with auctions in the late 1960s when they served as youth directors for the Lititz COB and helped organize an auction to raise money for church related activities. Consisting mostly of people's well-used household items, this auction was abandoned in 1969. Even though that project had ended, the seed of an idea for a more ambitious annual event to help others had been sown in the minds of some youth leaders.

Later, the Hersheys received a call from Jay Witman, one of their co-workers for the youth auction, asking them to serve on a committee to help start a BDRA. The money raised would support volunteers, building supplies, medicine, and whatever else was needed for the

victims of calamities in the United States and throughout the world.

That first year, everything was located in one large building at the Lebanon Fairgrounds, and $10,000 was raised! Marty still remembers how excited she felt. She was "on top of the world!"

In 1981, Mark and Marty accepted the responsibility of a 3-year commitment as coordinators of the BDRA. Their goal was to realize a profit of $100,000 by the end of those three years. Several people felt that goal was beyond reach.

During their first year, over $37,000 was raised, almost half from the sale of quilts. In 1982, after branching out and adding livestock, the sales reached $95,927. In their third and last year, 1983, the sale topped all expectations with a grand total of $103,243.

From the beginning of their planning for the BDRA, the Hersheys experienced changes including increased participation, spirit, interest, and enthusiasm among the denomination members as well as significant increases in the number of items for sale and in the funds raised for disaster relief.

In the first BDRAs Marty tended the baked goods stand which, along with all the other BDRA activities, was located in the old (first) fairground building. Tents were provided prior to their term, and the baked goods and crafts were the first moved to those facilities. Craft sales were first held in the pig barn. They remember the first foods served included turkey barbecue, soups and French fries while hot dogs and other foods came later.

Most parts of the BDRA then were the same as today, but the number of the items was much smaller. For example, fruits and vegetables were on one table. Mark and Marty recall their concern on Fridays of the BDRA about having sufficient items to offer. Yet, their faith in the aims of the BDRA and their belief that the goods would come always held, for without fail, items began to arrive in the afternoon and ample amounts were there when the sales began.

During the 1982 BDRA, it rained hard on Friday night, and they were concerned about its effect upon the attendance. Yet, in the morning the sun came out, and it was a beautiful and successful day.

Even after they "retired" as coordinators, they remained involved. Marty scheduled the auctioneers for six years, and for two years helped organize the packing of health kits and school kits. Although her vocation today is marketing health industry products and

managing real estate, she remains very active in her church at Lititz COB where she and Mark serve as deacons, ushers, fund-raising organizers, and on various committees. Mark has served as a volunteer at the Lititz Community Park Information Center, and for over ten years, Marty has helped to organize their church's annual New Year's Day Pork and Sauerkraut Dinner.

The Hersheys consider the BDRA to be one of the largest meetings of Brethren (with the exception of Annual Conference) in the brotherhood. It was and still remains a time for reflection, worship, and fellowship for all who participate. The basic goal: "Brethren gathering for a Purpose–To Honor and Glorify God" has been proven valid by the BDRA's continuing growth and success.

(Excerpted from articles in 1993 SB, pp. 3,4, 2006 SB, p. 6, and Personal Interview)

THOM AND SUE KELLER
1984-1987

I Cor. 10:31: *" … Whatever you do, do all things to the glory of God."*

When we became coordinators of the BDRA, we felt that our primary objective should not be raising money. After all, if God owned the cattle on a thousand hills (as well as the thousand hills), for Him, to come up with the money was not a problem. Although God certainly delights when we, His children, work for our neighbor's good, we believe He delights even more in our praises. Our committee felt that if we focused on glorifying God, that He was "big" enough to take care of achieving

Thom and Sue Keller

whatever dollar amount He felt would best accomplish His purposes.

Well, some interesting things happened as a result. First, we found an incredible spirit of unity and oneness of purpose among our committee. We believe that the spirit of a Christian so closely identifies with the desire to glorify God, that it brings people together in one heart in a way no other objective could.

Secondly, although we did set a monetary goal each year, it became an almost avoided subject. We remember many times being asked, "So what is the BDRA's goal this year?" We would always respond, "Our primary goal is to glorify God. Our monetary goal is $75,000." And through all this, God did something amazing. Every year our committee kept moving the monetary goal up, and every year God kept hitting it! Imagine that!

We remember one year, when our monetary goal was $125,000, Jim Nelson, our treasurer, gave me (Thom) a slip of paper at the District Conference in October, right before we gave our Auction report. On it he had written the final Auction total: $125,000.25. That same type of thing happened year after year. As George Mueller has said: *"God's work, done God's way, will not lack God's support."*

We also remember seeing people unconnected to church asking us, "Why do all these people do this?" When we'd explain that the entire event was run by volunteers and that no one received a salary or remuneration, they were usually left in awe. *(Thom and Sue Keller. 1993 SB, p. 3 and 2006 SB, p. 6)*

Although Thom is the President and part-owner of the Keller Brothers Company in Buffalo Springs, near Schaefferstown, he also serves as the Senior Pastor at the Calvary Chapel in Lebanon. After being a volunteer counselor at the Susquehanna Valley Pregnancy Center for ten years (1989-1999), Sue now heads up the Women's Ministry in their church and does other church volunteer work. For their recreation, Thom and Sue both enjoy bike-riding and skiing. In addition, Thom likes playing soccer and reading, while Sue enjoys swimming and playing piano.   *(Personal interview)*

The Kellers have said, "We oft-times forget how *true service with pure motives is such an intriguing mystery that draws people toward Jesus—If we will only get out of the way and let people see Him!"*

Dave and Belinda Graybill

DAVE AND BELINDA GRAYBILL
1988-1990

As we assumed the responsibility of assistant coordinators of the BDRA for two years under Thom and Sue Keller, then as coordinators for three years, 1988–1990, followed by one year giving assistance to Ken and Deb Weaver, perhaps the one thing that was evident to us was the working together of many individuals to bring honor and glory to God.

Our committee's theme was the words from the chorus:

> *"We are one in the bond of love; …*
> *Let us feel His love begun.*
> *Let us join our hands that the world will*
> *   know*
> *We are one in the bond of love."*
>   - Otis Skillings

We believe the BDRA reaches out in love and touches people's lives. It's a time of serving, a time of fellowship, a time when many individuals, young and old, share out of hearts of love and caring. It's showing God's love to those in need. It's a time when those who have been so blessed can share and say as the song writer penned, "To God Be the Glory, Great Things He Has Done."

The auction sale booklet was started in 1987 and as assistant coordinators we worked very closely with the booklet committee in writing articles, compiling information and helping to organize this new adventure. Those responsibilities continued throughout our term as coordinators. Being involved with the BDRA was certainly a team effort. Both of us appreciated the many wonderful people we met.

Even today, when Belinda recalls the auction, she says, "One word that comes to my mind is people–individuals reaching out and touching lives."

In 1988, the Farmer's Market expanded with fresh produce and canned items attractively displayed, appealing to both the eye and the appetite. To illustrate: 60 bushels of green beans and 7 bushels of turnips were sold!

The 1989 BDRA was held in the shadow of Hurricane Hugo. High winds Friday evening provided some tense moments as men throughout the night worked to keep tents from blowing down. It was a welcome sight to arrive at the Fairgrounds early Saturday morning and see the tents still standing! But through all the adverse weather that year, people generously supported the BDRA, giving out of hearts of love and compassion for those devastated by the storm. That year also saw the inception of two new ideas: GROW money and buttons indicating, "I Gave 1 Hour to DRA."

1990 was the start of a two-day Auction to alleviate having a long Saturday. Along with this change, the committee felt that beginning the weekend events with a worship service would be appropriate. During the Graybill's term, the ANE and SOPA Districts became co-sponsors of the BDRA.

Galatians 5:13 states that we are to "… *serve one another with love.*"

Dave and Belinda felt this is the spirit of those involved with the BDRA. It truly is "Brethren Gathering for a Purpose." So many individuals give so much to make the BDRA possible, but our prayer would be that those in attendance wouldn't see individuals, but would see Christ.

(Dave and Belinda Graybill. 1993 SB, p. 4, 2006 SB, p. 7, 1988 and 1989 ANE District Conference Reports, and Personal Interview)

Dave and Belinda were married for 35 years when he passed away suddenly on September 12, 2002, at the age of 58. Since then Belinda has continued serving in the Middle Creek COB as a Sunday school teacher, Women's Bible Study leader, and facilitating "Wisdom for Widows" classes throughout the district.

With two children and five grandchildren, Belinda, an Elizabethtown College graduate and former elementary school teacher, now delights in being a grandma, supporter and encourager to each member of her family. Skiing, walking, reading, and cross stitch are also activities she continues to enjoy. Most of all, she thanks God for her biological family, her church family, her many friends and for His great faithfulness.

(Belinda Graybill. Personal Interview)

Ken and Deb Weaver

KEN AND DEB WEAVER
1991-1993

We served two years as assistants under the leadership of Dave and Belinda Graybill, and they provided us with an excellent example of the job as coordinators of the BDRA. With their guidance and accurate notes, we were able to move into this three-year position following their term.

As people became interested and wanted to help, the BDRA continued to grow. After experiencing a few years of rather crowded conditions at the fairgrounds, 1992 brought the welcome addition of a new building there. In 1993 the Lebanon Fairgrounds completed another phase of new construction, adding inside space and a new kitchen.

It was exciting to see the creative ideas and talents people used to raise funds for the BDRA. The GROW money project was an example of this. The participation of the SOPA District kept growing considerably, for which we were very thankful. The Farmer's Market continued to grow with generous offerings of home canned items and homegrown produce. Food preparations had to be expanded to accommodate the growing crowds. It really took thousands of people to make the BDRA possible, and we merely tried to coordinate all their efforts.

The job of coordinators would be impossible without those who serve on the BDRA committee and the church contact persons. Many serve behind the scenes without any acknowledgement of their contributions or services. Please continue to pray for the Auction, that we may continue to serve the Lord and give Him the Honor and Glory for it all!

(Ken and Deb Weaver.
1993 SB, p. 3, 2006 SB, p. 7)

In 1993, three sets of Coordinatoers were given plaques in honor of their years of service (left to right): Ken and Deb Weaver, Dave and Belinda Graybill, and Sue Keller. Earl Ziegler (right) and Jay Witman (front) also participated in the ceremony.

Today Ken and Deb have been married 32 years and are the parents of two children and members of the Middle Creek COB where they are active in the choir, church committees, trustees, etc. They are grateful for having had the opportunity to serve and to learn to know so many wonderful, caring persons.

MEL AND GLORIA BURKHOLDER
1994-1996, 2000-2002

We would like to express our sincere appreciation to the many people whose contributions have helped to provide a bright spot in the lives of victims of disaster. We heard that *"Love wasn't put in your heart to stay. Love isn't love 'til you give it away." (Oscar Hammerstein, Jr.)* Over the past 18 years—1977 to1994—the BDRA was made possible because YOU were willing to show your love by giving.

(1995) One of the highlights this year was the new house which was sold with the proceeds going to benefit disaster victims. Also new this year was the Brethren Disaster Relief Cookbook with approximately 1,000 recipes to add to your collection.

(1996) This year the BDRA celebrated its 20th Anniversary. In reminiscing about our involvement for the past 15 years, I remembered, *"When you feel grateful for something others have done for you, why not tell them about it?"* The BDRA's success is because of God working through people. *"A man plans his course, but*

Mel and Gloria Burkholder served as Coordinators for six years.

the Lord determines his steps." (Proverbs 16:9, NIV) The God-directed person came in many ways: a grandmother quilting, a grandpa building something, an uncle sharing his farm produce, an aunt baking, a sister and brother giving their time and money, a son and daughter helping where they're needed most—and on and on. Thank you for getting involved to help those in need.

(2000) As I leafed through the SB, I discovered anew its powerful message and purpose. The motivation was not, "How can I help myself?" but, "How can I help someone else?" Sure, the goal was to raise money, but the main purpose was to Honor and Glorify God.

(2001) This year the BDRA celebrated 25 years. Were we successful? Did we lend a hand, lift a burden, give a cup of cold wa-

ter? Is somebody's life and circumstance better today because of us? I'm convinced God brought us together to reach out to those in need.

(2002) The BDRA is all about people—people working together to change people's lives. Think of a quilt, made of many different pieces, colors and sizes of material. Sewn together, how beautiful they are. The BDRA is like that quilt–different people from different walks of life, brought together in unity by God, the Master Creator. What a beautiful quilt they become! Thank you so much for your very important part in the "people quilt"

(1994 SB, p. 2; 1996 SB, p. 2; 2000 SB, p. 2;2006 SB, p. 7)

Today, Mel Burkholder, owner of Dutch Valley Foods, attends the Reamstown Church of God. While he and Gloria are the parents of three children and have seven grandchildren, in addition to her family, Gloria enjoys growing flowers, serving elegant Victorian Teas, spending time at the beach and several winter months in Florida. Mel enjoys fishing and 3 G's—Giving, Golf, and his Grandchildren and thanks God daily for His mercy and grace.

MARLIN AND JANE SNAVELY 1997-1999

The BDRA is a special event in the life of the church as we come together to give of our first fruits to God. In Exodus 35:4, 5 (NIV) Moses said to the people, *"This is what the Lord has commanded: From what you have, take an offering for the Lord." Exodus 35: 21 (NIV)* re-

Marlin and Jane Snavely

cords their response: *"Everyone who was willing, and whose heart moved him came and brought an offering to the Lord."* This is the picture that we see as the body of Christ gives of their varied talents to help those in need. It is exciting to see God's children, people of all ages, coming together to bring projects they have made, using the gifts God has given them.

Most people in our society today think only of themselves. God has instructed us to remember our neighbor. The Good Samaritan story in Luke 10:27-37 exemplifies showing compassion to our neighbor. Through the BDRA during the last 22 years (in 1998), you have shown this Christ-like love to many.

My heart was blessed a few years ago by a young boy who had taken railroad spikes, cleaned and painted them and brought them

to the BDRA. They were sold as paper weights, giving all the proceeds to disaster relief. The memory of this young boy's enthusiasm has encouraged me many times.

As members of the COB, we have so many things to share with the world. Let us continue to be the Good Samaritans in today's world, helping those who need food, clothing and shelter. As we share with those in need, may these people see Christ working in us.

(Marlin and Jane Snavely. Excerpted from the 1998 SB, p.2; 2006 SB, p. 7)

Marlin and Jane remain active in the White Oak COB.

DUANE AND TINA NESS
2003-Present

During my tenure, the Board of Directors of the BDRA has authorized and implemented a variety of new facets and ideas. One of my goals was to have an up-to-date and user-friendly web site whereby the news and work of the BDRA would be available for review throughout the calendar year to disseminate information. It is now a reality at *http://www.brethrenauction.org*

In 2002, the first BDRA Hymn Sing was held on the Sunday night after the auction, and it is a tradition that we've continued. For 2004, the goal was to have a three-bedroom modular home built during the auction. When that goal was realized, the home was then donated to a mother with young children who had lost their home as a result of a flood.

As an aftermath of Hurricane Katrina, 2005 was the year of substantial destruction

Tina and Duane Ness and Chloe (left) and Maxwell (right).

in the South. As the name "Brethren Disaster Relief" implies, it seemed appropriate to reflect our willingness to get involved. (The story of how we managed, with God's help, to get 30,000 Gift of the Heart health kits assembled is told in Chapter Six of this book.)

In 2005, the pace at the auction quickened a bit with the addition of two new auctions: the Alabaster Auction especially for the sale of very unique items, and also a Children's Auction exclusively for bidders under 12 years of age. The goal of involving younger generations increasingly demands our attention as the ones who have worked and supported the BDRA over the last 30 years begin to grow weary. Have you ever wondered why some of us look tired at the end of the day? At the peak, there will be five auctions operating at the same time with nearly 1,600 bidders!

From the perspective of natural disasters, we were rather fortunate in 2006. However, that was the year of the Nickle Mines school tragedy within our own neighborhood, and it had a direct impact on our auction family as we shared our love and resources with them.

(See our response in Chapter 11 in the section on TURF activities). Because you provide substantial funds for the BDRA, we are able to partner with local congregations and ministries as needs arise, and to do so on an emergency basis, if necessary. We are always in need of volunteers who are willing to get involved and make a difference when disasters strike. Many folks overlook the fact that although the auction itself operates just two days of the year, many volunteers spend substantial time and effort year round in support of the BDRA effort. The TURF Committee, which is part of the BDRA, works tirelessly year 'round responding to disaster needs in your neighborhoods. Your help with this massive effort is always appreciated.

As our world continues with many examples of craziness, I would encourage you to consider how blessed most of us are to have health and wealth far beyond most. Part of what the BDRA does is present the opportunity to share our blessings. Your good health allows participating in the physical work of the BDRA. Your accumulation of wealth, however large or small, provides an opportunity for you to bless others who are in need.

(Duane Ness. Excerpted from the 2004 SB, p.2; 2005 SB, p. 2; 2006 SB, p. 7; 2007 SB, p. 2; 2008 SB, p. 2)

Duane is the founder and owner of Advantage Security Inc., an electronic security and fire alarm company near York. He and his wife, Tina, live in York, where they enjoy family times together with their two children, Chloe Noelle and Maxwell Grey.

❖   ❖   ❖

C. A Few (of the Many) Major Workers

BOB AND SALLY BINGAMAN

As an Amish host for a Share-a-Meal was holding the door open to his house and greeting his guests warmly, he suddenly said, "Oh, I see someone coming. Watch out, as I must quickly shut the door." And he did it!

When the latest arrivals knocked on the door, the Amish man opened it and was immediately "reprimanded" in fun by his guests, Sally and Bob Bingaman. Everyone had a good laugh.

Known to be fun-loving by all of their friends, including the Amish, Sally and Bob Bingaman are an energetic, enthusiastic pair who have left a strong imprint on the BDRA since the beginning of their involvement in the 1990's, when they were recruited by Sally's brother, Dave Jenkins, and his wife, June.

Reared in the family of Jesse O. and Thelma Jenkins, a well-known SOPA COB minister and his wife, Sally grew up with an interest and involvement in the church, a love for Christ, and a spirit of caring and sharing with those less fortunate.

Today, she and Bob are active members of York First COB, where Sally serves as president of the Chancel Choir, a member of the Spiritual Gifts Discernment Committee, a Refugee Resettlement Committee member, and Chairperson of the Music Committee. Both are members of the Lamplighter's Class and Bob is Church Treasurer.

Despite being a busy homemaker and churchwoman, with a part-time job in Kimman's Gift Shop in downtown York, Sally has found time to be a part of The Moss Roses (an organization for admirers of the art of P. Buckley Moss), and to be a volunteer at Memorial Hospital's gift shop.

Growing up also in York County, Bob has a life-long passion for sports, helping to establish the York Youth Soccer League for which he refereed for about 20 years. Wrestling was another interest, and he officiated for about 15 years at matches involving youths up to and including high school age. In recent years, he has enjoyed being captain of First Church's golf team in the York County Sunday School League.

Bob's employer for 42 years has been Precision Custom Components (formerly Allis-Chalmers) and he presently is Business Manager there.

Their family includes three children, ten grandchildren and two great-grandchildren.

Sally's involvement with the BDRA includes being Co-Coordinator of the Annual Faith Dinners, Publication/Publicity Committee, Board member and secretary of TURF, and Co-Chair of Information at the Auction. In addition to being a BDRA Board member, Bob is Chairperson of TURF.

In an article Sally wrote for the 2006 Sale Booklet, she related how her faith was tested in undertaking the project of planning, preparing and selling tickets for a Faith dinner in April, 2006, sponsored solely by her church. It turned out to be a huge success with 350 persons attending and raised $10,000 for the BDRA. When it was over, Sally prayed this prayer, "Thank you, dear God, for allowing us to do Your work and provide comfort for those less fortunate. We give You all the glory for all You give to us. Please keep us ever mindful of the needs of others. Amen."

And all of us can add our "Amen's" to that!

(Excerpted from "The Power of Prayer and the Faith Dinner, 2006 SB, pp. 42,43, and an article by Pat Gibble in the 2007 SB, p. 4)

EARL AND CHARLENE FAHNESTOCK

Like most of the others featured in this chapter, Earl and Charlene are among those who have worked faithfully behind the scenes at the BDRA for years and still play an important part, yet are not well known by those who attend. From 1990 to 1997, they served on the Baked Goods Committee, and beginning in 1998, Charlene served the BDRA Board of Directors as secretary and in inter-church communication for seven years. Today both serve on the BDRA Board of Directors and the Main Hall Auction Committee.

As a Longaberger Basket Branch Advisor, Charlene has been responsible for providing these collectible baskets to be sold at the BDRA each year. She has also been the contact person with various pottery-makers for the numbered collectible pieces that have been featured annually at the BDRA.

Members of the White Oak COB, the Fahnestocks have been married 41 years and have four children and six grandchildren. Although Earl is self-employed in renovations, they have taken the time to go on disaster response projects and help to get items ready for the Main Hall Auction. They also enjoy travel and have organized and led many tours in the United States and abroad.

One reason they've enjoyed working with the BDRA is all the different people they have met there and learned to know. They have observed, "It takes so many different people with so many various talents to pull the whole thing together and make it a success." As a result, they thank God for the good health they enjoy, enabling them to be active in helping and serving others when they are facing disasters.

DAVID AND CAROL FARMER

If you ever have an opportunity to purchase Share-A-Meal tickets for a meal at the David and Carol Farmer home, buy them! They are gourmet cooks, and you can expect an unusual, memorable, bountiful and very delicious meal. But that is only one facet of this creative couple's many interests and skills.

Dave, a professor at Harrisburg Area Community College (HACC), is also an author, having written two books, "The Learning Book" and "The Cancer Diaries," and is currently working on his third. Other interests include: oil painting, photography, cabinetry, and antique auto restoration.

Meanwhile, Carol, his wife of 46 years, mother of their two daughters, and the grandmother of six, is chairperson of the Children's Auction. Both are members of the Board of Directors and the Publication Committee where Dave does writing and proof reading of the annual SB's and is the unofficial media liaison.

Carol recalls, "Our first Children's Auction was interesting. I was a complete novice on auctions, but Jay Witman and his brother, Luke, assured me I would have help. Although I was relieved to hear that, I still knew nothing of how an auction should be run. However, everyone was so helpful: my committee, the runners, and Luke, who was the auctioneer. The parents and kids were so excited. Because of this, I did not feel intimidated and the task became easy. Seeing the kids' faces and their enjoyment during the special Auction just for them was a wonderful reward."

Carol, who was a business owner and self-employed in the area of retail management, still works part-time in retail sales. In addition to all of these activities, she serves as the team leader for a Good News Club at the Bainbridge Elementary School often hosting youth activities in her home, and enjoys creating with stained glass, reading, playing badminton, and traveling.

When the Farmers list the things for which they are most grateful to God, the first thing mentioned was "Our Savior, Jesus Christ." In addition, they include their family, friends, health, and living in a country where they are free to worship God. Dave adds that he is willing to serve "wherever the Lord leads."

CHRIS AND AMY KELLER

Did you ever wonder who sets up all the chairs for the bidders, the tables for the registrars, baked goods and produce? Who puts all the trash cans around the fairgrounds and arranges for them to be emptied regularly? Chris Keller can tell you.

After serving two terms on the BDRA Board, beginning shortly after the Auction began, he became a member of the Arrangements Committee in 1989 and has been its chairperson since 1995. This means he not only takes care of all the setting up but also cleans and

puts everything back in place when the Auction is over. Although it is one of the most essential tasks of the entire BDRA, it is a behind-the-scenes and often thankless job, requiring long hours. When people call for "help," Chris responds calmly and does his job, making sure everything is in place for all who need space, tables, chairs, supplies, and more.

Meanwhile, Amy, his wife of 15 years, is busy organizing the Theme Basket Auction. She still recalls the first year that theme baskets were featured. In June 1999, Marlin Snavely, the BDRA coordinator at that time, called the Kellers and asked them if they had any new ideas for the Auction. She says, "We had seen theme baskets auctioned at several different events so we suggested that idea to him. The first year, we had about 20 theme baskets."

The following year more theme baskets were expected, so the BDRA Board planned to have a Theme Basket Auction separate from the main auction hall and in a different location. Consequently, in 2000, over 100 theme baskets were donated and sold.

After 9/11/2001, the response in donations of theme baskets and the amount of money raised by them was almost overwhelming. One theme basket, filled with holiday paper products, brought over $3,000.

Amy's memories of the BDRA go back to when it was held in what is now West Hall, getting her face painted, running around and having fun with the other young people during the Auction. Today, as members of the Midway COB, the Kellers are the parents of two: Cody and Mikaila. Chris works as a truck salesman for the Keller Brothers Car Village at Buffalo Springs, and Amy is Director of Advancement and Admissions at the New Covenant Christian School in Lebanon.

Top priority for both of them is spending time with the family, but it is no surprise that Chris also enjoys riding bike, fixing things and helping people, and Amy adds playing the piano and working at crafts. While both are active in their local church as deacons, Chris also teaches Sunday school and Amy plays the keyboard for the praise team.

One year that Chris will never forget was the first BDRA after North Hall was built. After a series of bountiful rains, all the cars parked in an area of new ground fill and recently seeded grass. As a result, they were stuck in the mud and had to be pulled out one by one!

Another lasting impression on Chris has been the witness and commitment of Allen Scott who has come from Vermont to the BDRA for years to empty the trash cans during the Auction and then drive home again.

Amy adds: "Ever since I knew Chris (my husband), he has taken some of his annual vacation days to help with the Auction. Each year when we plan for our vacation, the Auction days are always made a priority."

Both Chris and Amy praise and thank God because He has blessed them so bountifully, and in turn, they have been a blessing to the BDRA and grateful disaster victims.

ALVENA AND LEE KNEASEL

Alvena's role in the history of the BDRA can be summed up in three words: advertisements and cinnamon buns! For over twelve years, Alvena worked with the BDRA Publica-

tion Committee, selling about twenty ads each year to businesses in the Lebanon area, and for at least seven years, she made sticky buns to be sold at the sale.

With both working in the food industry, Lee distributing foods and Alvena working twenty-seven years in the Cedar Crest High School cafeteria as the official baker, it surprised no one when she volunteered to get up at 3:30 a.m. on auction days to head the annual production of 120 dozen of sticky buns.

In wanting to better her community, Alvena served as a 4-H leader for 27 years and her concern for the diminishing availability of arable lands led her to promote agriculture at Penn State and land preservation at political events in Lebanon, Harrisburg and Washington D.C.

A member of the Lebanon COB, she served several terms as their clerk as well as president of the Women's Fellowship. In addition, Alvena taught kindergarten children in Sunday school and cared for nursery children on countless occasions. She was especially pleased to be able to represent her church as an Annual Conference delegate for two years and has also served on the ANE District Women's Cabinet.

Alvena always enjoyed working on puzzles, doing left-handed crocheting, and walking their beloved cocker spaniel. Together, the Kneasels have enjoyed traveling to see the Oberammergau Passion Play in Europe in 1990, the Bahamas, and exploring the East Coast of the U.S.

During the time when Poland entered the free market and Alvena was serving as a Penn State leader helping a group of Polish visitors learn about U.S. farming, a memorable coincidence occurred. In conversation with some of the men, she wished the visitors could attend the BDRA. To her surprise, one of the men had first-hand knowledge of the COB with Brethren student exchanges in Poland and with his own experience in helping to sort and pack clothing at the New Windsor Service Center.

Serving Christ and the church is a wonderful way of growing a larger family of friends, brothers and sisters. It is a joy to have Alvena and Lee Kneasel in God's family and to see the joy they receive while bringing aid to others. As a result, the 2000 SB was dedicated to them.

(From an article by Charles Bieber, 2000 SB, p. 5)

CARLOS R. LEFFLER
October 10, 1922–August 14, 1994

From being raised on a farm to becoming one of the most successful men of Lebanon County in this century, Carlos R. Leffler's life epitomized the fulfillment of the "American Dream." Since he was not a good student, he left school in 1937 when he was in ninth grade. Instead of becoming a hired man on his father's farm near Reistville, he borrowed money and bought a truck to haul coal from Schuylkill County to homeowners of Lebanon County, often working sixteen hours a day.

Although he was deferred from military service during World War II for physical reasons, he served his community in other ways, such as watchman, guard, family helper and encouraging parents whose sons were serving their country.

After his marriage to Georgiana Balsbaugh in 1947, they became the parents of two daughters. When his wife developed walking difficulties, he helped and encouraged her.

During the latter part of the war years, the Texas Oil Company asked him to deliver gasoline to dealers in the Lebanon area. Before long, he purchased additional trucks and established an oil and gas delivery business of his own in Richland. Continuing its phenomenal growth, his business expanded into a multi-million dollar operation, which at the time of his death in 1994 consisted of 800 employees, 60 or more delivery trucks, and about 65 CR's Friendly Stores.

Carlos is not only remembered as a capable businessman but also as a generous philanthropist. As a member of the Richland COB, he helped build a new sanctuary and remodel the old church for Sunday School rooms and a social hall, serving as chairman of the building committee. As chairman of the finance committee, he helped to keep the Richland COB among the top twenty-five of the national COB churches in financial efficiency and in the sharing of resources with others.

"From the day the Lebanon Valley Brethren Home (Palmyra, PA) was dedicated on May 29, 1979, Carlos Leffler was a solid anchor on our board. Wherever Carlos was, things happened. Carlos was the originator and chairman of the board of the Good Samaritan Fund. He presented excellent programs for the fund each year. On June 14, 1994, Carlos and Georgiana presented gifts of $100,000 to the fund." *(From "Echoes from Lebanon Valley," Column 15, Number 4)*. He also purchased the organ for their new chapel.

Elizabethtown College, where both of his daughters graduated, was also a recipient of Carlos' generosity. With his wife as an active auxiliary member, he served as secretary of the Board of Directors and chaired an endowment campaign, providing funds for the Student Union Building and for the $4.5 million, 900 seat multipurpose facility named Leffler Chapel, in honor of Carlos and Georgiana. In return, the college granted him an honorary doctorate degree.

At the BDRA he not only shared his time, equipment and personnel, but he also purchased many items. Not only did he buy them, but he often immediately donated them back for resale, and then would buy them again.

If you had seen Carlos or talked with him, you would never have suspected that he was wealthy. This quote from George Bernard Shaw exemplifies his philosophy: *"I am of the opinion that my life belongs to the whole community, and as long as I live, it is my privilege to do for it whatever I can. I want to be thoroughly useful as long as I live."*

(Excerpted from an article by Ray Kurtz, Richland COB. 1995 SB, p. 19)

❖   ❖   ❖

JOHN AND LOIS MINNICH

If you ever attended the BDRA and noticed a guy going around carrying a large camera and capturing everything he can get on film, that was John Minnich! His love of photography began as a hobby, then evolved into a part-time job taking family portraits, weddings, and still shots of antiques. When you look through back copies of BDRA sale books, his work is evident in the collages on the covers, the photos of quilts, specialty and Alabaster Sale items. In addition, most of the photographs in this book are from his extensive collection.

Despite his compulsive trigger finger in the area of photography, John is diversified

with many other interests including gardening and biking. His vocation is that of an electrophysiologist at Lancaster General Hospital, and in that capacity, he often is a medical conference speaker. Both he and Lois are members of the White Oak COB where he frequently uses his medical knowledge in combination with down-to-earth explanations to convey heart object lessons in his Sunday school class.

Married for 33 years, and parents of two children, the Minnichs enjoy traveling through the United States, riding rail trails, doing backyard gardening and sampling the delicacies of a variety of restaurants, often with other couples. Lois enjoys employing her gifts of decorating, hospitality and gourmet cooking by serving multi-course teas. In addition, she works as a medical transcriptionist for Lancaster General

John and Lois Minnich

John Minnich (right) the BDRA photographer for many years, has been like a brother to Jay Witman (left).

All three are totally committed to giving God first place in their lives and it is difficult to get any of them to admit all they do for the BDRA. They have truly learned and daily practice *the secret of JOY: Jesus first, Others second, and Yourself last.*

In 2008, Landis and Audrey, the parents of three and grandparents of three, celebrated their sixtieth wedding anniversary. In their local church, the Conestoga COB, they serve as deacons, and Landis is disaster coordinator. Besides that, they are always on the lookout for someone needing help or assistance. One of their friends has said: "When someone is in need of a helping hand, Landis and Audrey are there." Sometimes that means traveling to a disaster area to help clean up, rebuild or help in any way that they can. Other times, it may mean preparing and delivering a food platter

Hospital and creates beautiful handiwork using a blanket stitch.

For many years the BDRA has benefited from the contributions that John has made using his studio and camera and Lois has given with her kitchen and baked goods – so that God could receive the glory, and needy people could receive aid.

(From an article by Nathan Minnich in the 2008 SB, p. 4)

LANDIS AND AUDREY MYER

Almost from the beginning, the names of Jay M. Witman and Landis and Audrey Myer have been linked with the BDRA. When a job has to be done, a decision has to be made, or an experienced person has to show the way, these are the three people who lead the pack.

Landis and Audrey Myer

or meal to someone who has had an operation, or perhaps just being there for someone to offer support. When God calls, like Isaiah, this couple replies, *"Lord, here am I. Send me." (Isaiah 6:8 NIV)*

In helping with the BDRA, they have served in many capacities, from the Publication Committee where they helped to gather advertisements and put the booklet together, to planning, making and serving the annual Kick-Off Dinners from the very beginning. They are both involved with the Share-A-Meal program, hosting and being guests at many meals. In fact, Audrey chaired the Share-A-Meal Committee for many years until 2001 and continues to remain active on it. As co-chair with her daughter, Candy, she was instrumental in gathering and organizing recipes and having them printed into the BDRA cookbook in 1995. Living in the heart of "Amish Country," the Myer's have been instrumental in encouraging and persuading many of their Amish friends and neighbors to participate in the Share-A-Meal program and even agree to come to the Auction to make their unique and delicious donuts and soft pretzels which have proven to be very popular items. Landis always helps his Amish friends set up their equipment so they'll be in great working order for the Auction.

In his workshop, Landis has produced top quality wooden furniture from footstools to butcher block tables to drop leaf and extension tables and donated many of them to the BDRA. He even uses his woodworking gifts to make and donate his handcrafted wooden furniture pieces to the SDDA in Virginia. For example, an extension table with 12 boards that he donated for the May, 2009, SDDA, brought $3,100.

Through the years, Landis has served on numerous Disaster Response Teams in many states with a two-fold desire: to physically assist in the cleanup, repair and rebuilding and to share the love and compassion of Jesus to those who were struggling, feeling discouraged and hurting. After Hurricane Andrew struck Florida, Audrey went with him—with neither of them knowing what they were in for, but going in faith, ready and willing to help and encourage.

As a team, they have faithfully served the Lord and touched many lives over the years, and are still always ready to listen, to offer their friendship and a helping hand.

(Personal Interview)

JIM AND CAROL NELSON

What happens to the funds raised at the BDRA each year? Jim Nelson could answer that question. For over twenty years, he served as BDRA treasurer, receiving all monies raised, paying all expenses, preparing financial reports, and sending out funds to TURF and the Elgin COB Headquarters for local, national and worldwide disaster relief.

Jim, a graduate of Cheney State University, and Carol, a graduate of Shippensburg University, met one summer when both were volunteers at Camp Swatara. Married in 1971, they have continued serving God in their church, the Ridgeway COB. Participating in dramas at their church and in the Community Theater of Harrisburg is an interest they share.

But their Christian service doesn't stop there. For several years Jim served as treasurer of the ANE District, and later, in addition to being BDRA treasurer, he also served on the TURF Committee. Meanwhile, Carol's commitment was recognized when she was elected to the Annual Conference Standing Committee representing the ANE District. Wherever God calls them, they like to serve Him.

In addition, they enjoy travel, having visited Europe several times, and love Windjammer cruises in the Caribbean. As their daily jobs, Carol works with Capital Area Blue Cross and Jim with the Mechanics Savings and Loan of Steelton.

A final interesting bit of information about the Nelsons is that both Jim and Carol are twins! Jim has a twin brother and Carol has a twin sister!

In 1998, the SB was dedicated to the Nelsons in appreciation for their twenty years (at that time) of service to the BDRA.

(1998 SB, p. 4)

LEONARD AND HELEN STONER

Leonard and Helen Stoner, residents in the Brethren Home Community at Cross Keys and members of the York First COB, originally came from Mechanicsburg and Lewistown, respectively. Their journey together began in 1980 after the death of Leonard's first wife, Lucy. They have two children: Dan, (married to Raquel), and Rebecca.

After Hurricane Agnes hit the Wilkes-Barre area in 1972, Leonard became involved with disaster response teams. He continued helping to clean up and rebuild after the John-

stown flood in 1977, to Pensacola and OH following Hurricane Ivan's rampage, and to Wichita, KS, after tornado destruction there. More recently, he has served as SOPA District Disaster Coordinator.

In 2006, Leonard and Helen completed two weeks of training to become Disaster Response Project Directors and in March, 2007, they began a month's work in MS. Helen served as overseer for the kitchen, preparing meals for the volunteers using food donated by the food bank and the COB, while Leonard's responsibilities included seeing that the volunteers had work to do, that materials were on site, and renting space for the volunteers to call "home."

From his years of experience, Leonard has observed that wherever it goes to help, the COB has a good relationship with people in crisis. For example, when he came into a hardware store in Mississippi to get supplies, the female clerk always remarked, "Here come the Brothers!" *(From an article by Peggy Metzger in the 2008 SB, p. 4)*

MARTY AND LOIS WITMAN

The adjectives of "fun-loving, hard-working, go-getting, and faithfully serving" could all be used to describe both Marty and Lois Witman. Both personify Christianity in action, showing their love by their deeds.

Members of the Florin COB, the Witmans have been married for 58 years and have three sons and five grandchildren. In their church, they serve as deacons, Sunday school teachers, and Marty is on the Missions Team.

With his many woodworking and mechanical gifts, Marty started out farming, then became a carpenter and ended up working for Kevin Zurin, a contractor. Lois has cleaned for others for years in addition to being an excellent housekeeper, cook and seamstress. In their "spare time," they enjoy antiquing and traveling.

However, the activity that gives them the most joy and satisfaction is helping people. Consequently, they are familiar faces and workers who can be counted on at the annual BDRA's. Marty has helped with the pole barn, washed dishes, donated his handcrafted furniture and was one of the builders for all five of the BDRA Charity Houses, while Lois served on the food committee for 27+ years. She remembers starting out in the little pavilion and transitioning to the beautiful kitchen facilities the Lebanon Expo now has.

Every year Marty and Lois can be counted on to be at the Auction site by 5 a.m. to make coffee for the breakfast, and they stay until about 6:30 p.m. when everything is cleaned up and put away.

Some of their memories include the year that there was a hurricane on Friday evening, and many people stayed overnight to hold down tents and watch that the food was protected. Marty also fondly remembers the wonderful volunteers who helped build the BDRA house project for which he was in charge. He still marvels at how people would call and offer their help with such willing hearts.

They also remember those times when things did not go well, like when roasters wouldn't work or there would be electrical problems. Sometimes schedules got mixed up, but always, by the grace of God and His providing willing hands and helpers, the BDRA happened anyway!

Marty and Lois Witman

In addition to serving in the kitchen at the Auction, Marty and Lois have been active supporters of Share-A-Meals as hosts and as guests. Those lucky enough to get one of their tickets can be sure they will be served a bountiful and delicious meal.

But their outreach activities include even more. Their love for God has given them a contagious joy and a deep desire to be involved in helping people. Consequently, Marty serves on the TURF Board, the COBYS Board, and has been on more than thirty disaster response projects which have taken him to the Dominican Republic three times to build churches and to Puerto Rico to help put on a roof. Brethren Village has also been a recipient of their many gifts, with Marty serving on the Woodworking Shop Building Committee and Lois as president of the Brethren Village Auxiliary for almost twenty years. In that role, among other things, Lois was in charge of all the beautiful indoor Christmas trees and decorations that bring so much holiday cheer to the Village residents. In their community, Marty has served on the East Donegal Township Planning Commission and the Rainbow's End Youth Services Board, and Lois served for twenty-five years as part of the Ladies' Auxiliary of Elizabethtown College.

Although so many could testify that their lives have been blessed by Marty and Lois, they feel that they are the ones who have been most blessed—by meeting so many wonderful people and having had the privilege of living and working together for so many years for the honor and glory of God.

If you are ever traveling with adults on a bus or in a group where there are some children, and you happen to hear a little dog barking, look around and you just might see Marty trying to look innocent but with a very naughty twinkle in his eye!

(2004 SB, p. 4 and Personal Interview)

CHAPTER TEN

The Role of the Sale Booklets

"Reliable communication permits progress."
- Proverbs 13:17 (TLB)

I N THE BEGINNING, the main ways of publicizing an upcoming BDRA was to print one-page cards or hand-outs, insert notices in church bulletins, publish an article in the newspaper and by word of mouth. Each year more means of communication were discovered, including bookmarks, radio announcements and placemats. Nancy Diffenderfer (White Oak COB) remembers well the times that she and her husband, Harold, would travel all over Lancaster and Lebanon Counties delivering stacks of BDRA placemats to area restaurants.

Seeing the need for sharing more information about what would be offered at the next BDRA and about the COB, a magazine-sized Sale Booklet was published for the first time in 1987. Although it changed in format in 1991 to a 56-page newspaper style, a Sale Booklet has been published annually ever since. Each issue typically contains photos of select quilts and specialty items that have been donated to be sold, a dedication of that issue to a faithful worker, messages from leaders of the COB denomination and ANE and SOPA District Executives, plus articles about Disaster Response Teams, COB denominational and local church history, commentaries on Biblical characters and doctrines, current and future BDRA projects, thumbnail sketches of local and regional ministries, favorite hymns of COB musicians, etc. Anyone who has saved all their issues has

quite a storehouse of information. For persons doing research about any of these topics, the executors of Jay Witman's estate have promised to follow his wishes to donate a set of all the Sale Booklets to Elizabethtown College so that they will be accessible.

The cost of publishing the Sale Booklets is covered by selling advertisement space, and persons on the Publications Committee are kept busy most of the year contacting businesses, hoping to make sales. Ads about different aspects of the BDRA, such as the Baked Goods, Produce Stands, Theme Baskets, Share-A-Meal, Heifer Auction, Alabaster Auction, Crafts Tent, Gift-of-the-Heart Projects, Building Events, Children's Auction, etc. are also included.

Although many people have given countless hours to make the Sale Booklets a success, only a few can be featured here, but the work of everyone has been and still is much appreciated.

❖ ❖ ❖

A. Those Who Made It Happen

CHARLES AND MARY BETH BIEBER

Mom was a people person. When I was a child, I was sure she influenced the entire world.

Our house in Nigeria always had people coming and going. She liked to talk, and I think was well chosen to be the radio correspondent in our Lassa station. I loved to tag along and listen to her share the news. And she

Charles and Mary Beth Bieber at their 60th Wedding Anniversary celebration on June 26, 2004. Mary Beth died 24 days later on July 20, 2004.

had friends, all sorts of "aunts" and "uncles" for us to know. If there was ever a conflict between missionaries, we never knew about it. In our family's eyes, everyone was beloved.

Loving service was a major part of her personality. It was so common that it took adulthood for me to realize how uncommon it was. She always took food to people who were in some sort of crisis. She maintained correspondence with hundreds of people. I remember her telling me once that she wrote about 25 letters a day. Her letters were full of ordinary life—the weather, the laundry being hung out, news of other people. And they were usually ended with a personal note of encouragement.

She rarely arrived at our home without some gift. The grandchildren could expect regular letters (often with money inside) and care packages when they were at college. Now, Mom was no ordinary shopper, but she liked a lot of items for her money. We still laugh over the rice krispie bars she sent my son, which were "for sharing with your pet." Dog food or human food? He ate them.

Giving stuff away was her big mantra. I tried to hold this in check if the gift was a family heirloom. Nevertheless, I would return to their house and say, "Where is _____?"

"Oh, I donated that to the Auction," was the frequent reply.

I would also find out the most recent donation when I picked up the latest sale booklet. Too late then. We children knew that about as soon as we sent her a gift, it would be sent on to someone else. The weather radio I gave her ended up at my sister's house. I received gifts that others had given her. She just didn't need the new gadget—or clutter—and it soon got handed on.

We all had to keep the Auction in mind as well. She would look over our stuff on visits and wonder if we wouldn't mind donating this or that. There were two acceptable replies: "I'm using it," or "I'm giving it to the church, someone else, etc." She carted boxes of my canning jars from Ohio to the Auction where a few dollars could be gained for relief.

My mom did not easily take "no" for an answer. If she thought one should do something, it was simply assumed that it would be done. I could talk to her for five hours about an issue, and then Mom would act like she had never heard a dissenting word, and do what she had originally planned. I always felt a little sorry for the people she solicited for ads for the booklet, as I am sure she used the same technique on them.

Mom believed we are here to love others, to give ourselves away. She had a positive attitude to life and no conditions or barriers to

her love. New additions to the family were always warned, she will hug you the first time she meets you. Giving hugs was normal.

My mother's faith ran true and deep. She prayed for everyone. I knew that all of us were lifted up by name every day. No theological arguments, no questions, she just went to God with her concerns and joys. The Auction and Relief were frequent words in her vocabulary. I am sure she will never miss an auction—if God allows sightseeing from heaven. I know she rejoices still when people contribute in any way, from baking shoofly pies, as she did, to giving embroidered gifts, or family heirlooms, or purchasing items that come for sale.

For several years, Mom sold about 50 ads per year to the sale booklet, writing letters to each former advertiser with a copy of their former ad, and being sure to invite the advertiser to come to the auction, experience the fellowship, food, and opportunities to give and add to disaster relief.

What we can do for others is never lost. I know now, for certain, that my mom *did* influence the world! *(Marla Bieber Abe. 2005 SB, p. 4)*

Mary Beth (High) and Charles Bieber were married June 24, 1944 and celebrated their 60th Anniversary on June 26, 2004. Twenty-four days later, on July 20, Mary Beth died after knowing only since July 16th she had acute leukemia. Together they had served for 13 years as missionaries in Nigeria.

Charles has been a nurse, pastor, District Executive, and served as Moderator of the COB in 1977 in Richmond, VA, and as pastor of the Ephrata COB, 1992-1996. Besides reading and playing games, Charles enjoyed caning chairs and making wearable badges for BDRA attendees. Both he and Mary Beth were members of the BDRA Publications Committee with Mary Beth securing ads and Charles editing the SBs and writing articles for eleven years (1997–2007). The Biebers are the parents of five children (3 doctors, one clinical psychologist and one pastor) and have 14 grandchildren and seven great-grandchildren.

Although he turned 90 on September 11, 2009, Charles still has a quick wit and remains active in the Ephrata COB as a Sunday school teacher, writes monthly "Thoughts for Senior Citizens" for their church letter, and lives at Brethren Village where he presents devotions once a week on the inter-village TV system, teaches Sunday school occasionally and leads weekly Bible studies.

(Personal Interview)

CHARLES M. FORRY

Charles M. Forry, Lancaster, didn't have what many people would call an ideal childhood. Some might even say it was a disaster.

After his father died when Charlie was nine years old, he was sent to the Milton Hershey School at age twelve to take advantage of the free room and board and the school's reputation for preparing boys to enter the work force. Graduating with a solid education and experience in printing, he surely must have expected easier times ahead.

But World War II was on the horizon, and Charlie enlisted in the U.S. Air Force. Following several months of training in California, the twenty-two-year-old B-17 aerial engineer was shipped to Clark Field, near Manila. Here he experienced the horror of a surprise bomb-

ing raid by the Japanese, only hours after the attack on Pearl Harbor.

Could things get any worse? They could. Sent to Mindanao, Charlie was taken prisoner by the Japanese in May 1942. At first confined to a prison camp in Manila, he spent the remainder of the war at hard labor in Formosa stone quarries and coal mines.

The prisoners' only food was rice, and not much of that. Mine cave-ins were a reality that followed them through their days of work and terrorized their dreams at night. Charlie still has nightmares about his more than three years at the mercy of sadistic guards and the pervasive feeling of hopelessness brought on by the suppression of new reports about America's war effort.

In February 1945, the prisoners were moved to the Japanese Island of Hokkaido. They had already seen U.S. Navy planes in the sky and knew their own forces were attempting to reclaim the Pacific. Hopes rose.

After the Japanese surrender, Charlie and the surviving prisoners spent another month in captivity before being released. The ordeal has left indelible memories, the kind that can scar a soul.

But Charlie is a man who doesn't let bitterness rule his life. He has chosen to heal himself by helping others. He credits his training and experiences at Milton Hershey for the self-control he was able to display during his wartime incarceration. "I knew how to discipline myself," he says, a trait that probably saved his life.

Following the war, Charlie finally was able to use the printing trade he had learned as a youth. He joined the old Conestoga Publishing Co. in Lancaster. A few years later, with partner Lavinia Hacker, he founded Forry & Hacker,

Inc. in a three-car garage. Through the years, the business moved twice to accommodate its growth. Charlie sold the business in 1982, retiring from 16-hour work days, but not retiring from work.

Today, Charlie's business is helping people. His extensive volunteer calendar includes one day a week working at the Milton Hershey School. He lives on Roseville Road in Manheim Township, Lancaster County, with his wife, Virginia.

"Charlie is committed to Christ and the church out of an appreciation to the Lord for His getting him through and out of World War II prison camps," says Ralph Moyer, Pastor for Special Ministries at the Lititz COB. Charlie has been a member of the Lititz Church since 1947, when he transferred from the West Greentree COB.

A decade ago, in space provided by the Lititz COB, Charlie donated the equipment and established a complete print shop for the primary purpose of teaching youth the art of printing, and to do printing for the church. "He is at the church often by 5:30 in the morning, two or more days per week," continues Moyer, "to do volunteer printing, not only for the church, but for others as well."

When an honorarium is given for printing, Charlie gives it to the church's Youth Club. "We don't know what we'd do without him," says Moyer. "We are very fortunate to have him."

A 10-year member of the BDRA publicity committee, Charlie is responsible for the printing of 80,000 sale bills, 10,000 bookmarkers, 2,000 posters, 20,000 bulletin inserts and 3,000 quilt papers, in addition to a variety of other printing jobs for the project. Thank you, Charlie.

At 71 years, with a warm smile and a willing heart, Charlie happily continues to fulfill Christ's wise reminder to His disciples: *'Inasmuch as ye have done it unto one of the least of these my brethren, ye have done it unto me.'"*
(Henry H. Gibbel in the 1990 SB, pp.18,19)

(Charles Forry died December 20, 2005, at the age of 86. His widow, Virginia (Ginny) Forry is an active member of the Lititz COB).

CARL AND DOROTHY SHULL

When we think of Carl and Dorothy Shull, we often think of music, but they have touched lives in other areas as well. Their work with the BDRA began about 1990, bringing organization to the publications. With the cooperation of the Publication Committee, Carl tackled the task of coordinating data for the SB for almost twelve years, working closely with the Engle Printing Company of Mount Joy.

Among their tasks were the selling of advertisements, planning the lay-out, editing, and proof-reading. All this was done with the ever-present dual-purpose goal of helping the needy and "so that one soul might be saved through its publication."

A Bridgewater graduate, Carl earned his Master's from Northwestern and a doctorate from Florida State. After moving to Elizabethtown in the early 1960s, Carl became chairman of the music department at Elizabethtown College until 1988. Interestingly enough, during some of those years, Dorothy's uncle, Nelson R. Huffman was chairman of the music department of Bridgewater College. One of Carl's major contributions at Elizabethtown College was instituting and developing its music education major. At the same time, he served as minister of music at the Lancaster COB for many years and even today, although he is retired, he is not only a lay visitor but also a substitute organist and Dorothy is a pianist at the Elizabethtown COB where they are members.

In addition to their music and BDRA interests, Carl enjoys golfing and woodworking, while his wife of fifty-six years, Dorothy, likes to make flower cards.

They have three children, five grandchildren and three great-grandchildren. Otis Kitchen, a thirty-year colleague in the Elizabethtown College music department, has described Carl as "a very dynamic leader with keen insight and a strong work ethic."

The 2000 SB was dedicated to this devoted couple who have shared so generously of their time and God-given gifts and continue to praise God for "each day and its blessings."

(From an article by Wayne Zunkel. 2000 SB, p. 5)

ROBERT AND ELLEN YOUNG

On July 27th, 1996, the BDRA lost one of its very dedicated volunteers, Robert S. Young. Bob was originally from the Salunga/Landisville area, one of five boys who grew up in the Mountville COB. Ellen, his wife, also an active and dedicated BDRA volunteer, was born on the William Longenecker farm near Mount Joy, one of eleven children.

Bob and Ellen were married on July 14, 1934, by Samuel Shearer at the Florin COB. Bob worked on a Milton Hershey farm between Campbelltown and Palmyra as a house parent and was a college student at the same time, attending Lebanon Valley College and later the University of Pennsylvania. Subsequently, Bob and Ellen raised three children.

Bob was ordained at the Spring Creek COB about 1949, and he and Ellen became members of the Bachmanville COB in 1960. Taking an active role in the life of his church, Bob filled the pulpit, conducted revival meetings and love feasts. Sixteen people committed their lives to Christ at his first revival.

In 1952, Bob was hired as a development officer at Elizabethtown College, and he served that institution until his retirement in 1983. He was awarded the Elizabethtown College Educate for Service Award in October, 1983, in recognition of his years of service and dedication. A statement from a college program of 1984 honoring Bob stated: "He epitomizes a refreshing creed in his insistence that *we must think and not talk of negatives but of the positives which make a college, a church, and a community strong.*"

After his retirement from the college, Bob served as a fund-raiser for Brethren Village in Neffsville (1985-1988), the Lebanon Valley Brethren Home (1988-1996), and he also supported financially and physically the Brethren Housing Association in Harrisburg. Ellen Longenecker Young supported Bob's fund-raising efforts with her many famous delicious meals in their home for persons donating to the above organizations.

Bob and Ellen became volunteers at the first BDRA in 1977 when Ellen was asked by Gerald Greiner to assume responsibility for the food stand. She was overwhelmed with the response of many churches to provide food, which included one church donating chicken soup, another chicken potpie, a third baking 100 pies, a fourth preparing 400 apple dumplings and a fifth sending a roaster filled with turkey barbecue. Ellen served as chairperson of the food committee through 1979, and then she and Bob introduced the BDRA to caramel popcorn, an item which became very popular. Ellen and Bob supplied the equipment for popping the corn, and the copper kettle for mixing the popped corn and caramel, using a recipe for the caramel which Ellen had received from her mother. With the assistance of forty helpers, Bob and Ellen operated the popcorn stand until 1991 when Ellen was 82 and they passed those responsibilities to Ellen's niece and her husband, Janice (Longenecker) Holsinger and John, and to Carroll (Hall) Kreider and Ken. Ellen believed the amount earned at the popcorn stand in 1977 was $180, and the amount entered from the 1996 stand was $2,900.

Bob also was an active member of the BDRA Publications Committee, writing and soliciting articles and advertisements. His enthusiasm, ideas, insights, and contributions to the SB were deeply appreciated. In 1995, he secured the first gift of $5,000 to establish the BDRA Endowment Fund, which by 1997 totaled about $198,000.

In the summer of 1996, Bob and Ellen sold their home in Bachmanville and on June 1 moved into an apartment in the home of one of their sons in Lititz. On July 26, Bob worked in his garden and then drove to Harrisburg to help paint and clean a house owned by the Brethren Housing Association. While working there, he suffered a severe stroke and was taken to Hershey Medical Center where he died the next day.

For their years of work on behalf of the BDRA, for the many ways the Youngs demonstated their Christian spirit, and for the inspiration their lives were to countless persons, the 1997 sale booklet was dedicated to them.

(1997 SB, p.4 and information
shared by Janice Longenecker Holsinger)

B. Index to Church Histories and Reports Listed in the BDRA SBs from 1987 through 2008:

C. Ministries Mentioned in the BDRA SBs from 1987 through 2008:

D. Favorite Hymns

*"Next to theology, I give to music
the highest place and honor.
Music is the art of the prophets, the only art that
can calm the agitations of the soul;
It is one of the most magnificent and
delightful presents God has given us."*
(Martin Luther)

❖ ❖ ❖

Starting with the 1996 SB, an interesting feature in each succeeding issue was that musicians within the two BDRA sponsoring districts wrote articles about their most-loved hymns. **Joan Fyock** wrote the first one listing three perennial favorites of those who attend the BDRA as: *Great Is Thy Faithfulness, To God Be the Glory,* and *Move in Our Midst.* She gave the stories of how and when and by whom they were written and pointed out that all three can be considered "newer" hymns since two were written in the 20th Century and the third did not become popular until 1954.

(1996 SB, p. 20)

Other musicians featured in succeeding years and the hymns they chose were:

1997 – **Arlene S. Keller** – (Midway COB) whose "favorite" has changed through the years, from *Jesus Loves Me* in childhood, *We're Marching to Zion* in Bible School, *I Ain't Gonna Study War No More* as a youth, *The Family of God* after a love feast service, second verse of *This Is the Day* when she was alone in a foreign country with her husband hospitalized, and finally *Great Is Thy Faithfulness,* after cardiac surgery and her all-time expression of praise for each day of life. *(p. 51)*

1998 – **Carolyn Fitzkee** – (Chiques COB) gave the story of how *Great Is Thy Faithfulness* was written. *(p. 17)*

1999 – **Floy M. Hess** – (Chiques COB) chose *Abide With Me,* not only because of its message but because it has such beautiful harmony and all four parts "move" in its tune. *(p. 42)*

Arlene Keller, a former music teacher, was choir director at the Midway COB for 50 years. She continues to lead the Brethren Village Male Chorus, the "Village Voices." The wife of Norman Keller, she is the mother of Thom, Cindy, Dan, and Jane.

2000 – **Verna Sollenberger** – (Annville COB) looked for hymns that inspire the persons who sing them. Although she named *Great Is Thy Faithfulness* as the hymn she finds herself humming most, she also named *My God and I* and *Move In Our Midst* (the latter, especially mentioned because she was present at Camp Harmony when Ken Morse and Perry Huffaker finished its words and music.) She concluded with this comment: "The real privilege as a choir director is to direct a large group singing *The Hallelujah Chorus.*" *(p. 41)*

2001 – **Mildred Grimley** – (Akron COB) liked lots of hymns as various ones ministered to her "just when I needed it most." A few that she mentioned were: *Deeper, Deeper, in the Love of Jesus, I Am Weak and I Need Thy Strength, Joyful, Joyful, We Adore Thee,* and *For the Beauty of the Earth.* The thrilling songs of Christian celebrations such as *Come, Ye Thankful People, Come, Joy to the World,* and *Christ, the Lord, Is Risen Today* are also her favorites. *(p. 49)*

2001 – **Lois E. McWilliams** – (Pleasant View COB) picked *What a Friend We Have in Jesus* because the words are so personal and speak to many situations in which she has found herself. *(p. 49)*

2002 – **Paul W. Brubaker** – (Middle Creek COB) – In his article, *You Are What You Sing,* Paul selected *Marvelous Grace* because its words helped him to gain the assurance of salvation. *(p. 56)*

2002 – **Tom Ford** – (Midway COB) – chose *O the Deep, Deep Love of Jesus* because he grew up on the southeastern coast of Taiwan and enjoyed floating around and swimming in the vastness of the Pacific Ocean. He wonders if the writer of the words used to describe God's love as "underneath" and "all around" him had a similar experience. Just as the ocean never stops rolling, God's love is constantly flowing to all who are willing to receive it. *(p. 59)*

2003 – **Deanna Crawford** – (Codorus COB) – In her work as a Music Therapist, Deanna has seen the way music touches the soul, sometimes causing persons who are virtually unrespon-

sive to actually sing along with an old familiar hymn. As a result of observing this happen and her own enjoyment of music, Deanna picked *How Can I Keep from Singing?* as her favorite. *(p. 31)*

2004 – **Joanne Swords** – (Lancaster COB) – Unable to choose just one, Joanne picked four hymns that "give her hope when she despairs, inspiration when the well is dry, and quiet focus when the noisy world invades." They are: *Great Is Thy Faithfulness, Blessed Assurance, O For a Thousand Tongues to Sing,* and *A Mighty Fortress Is Our God. (p. 13)*

2005 – **Donna Lerew** – (Codorus COB) – Although her all-time favorite is *When Peace Like a River,* Donna wrote more about *Joy to the World,* pointing out that it is appropriate for any season and is not simply a Christmas hymn. She likes it because the music is joyful, easy to sing and familiar, and "the message is one of joy and hope. The Lord is come, the Savior reigns, no more let sins and sorrows grow for He rules the world! Amen." *(p. 19)*

2006 – **Laverne Yeager** – (Ridge COB) – Her vote is another for *Great Is Thy Faithfulness* because the Christian walk is not always smooth and easy. During some rough times, the words of this hymn gave her reassurance and hope. She was especially blessed to hear the 2004 BDRA Choir sing a beautiful arrangement of it. "What a praise hymn!" *(p. 11)*

2006 – **Evelyn M. Brubaker** – (Middle Creek COB) – Evelyn says that to name her favorite hymn depends on the time of the year, the theme of the worship service, or the season of life she's experiencing. Favorites in the past have been *Open the Gates of the Temple, To Us a Child of Hope Is Born*, and *He Lives*, while her all-time favorite anthem is *The Hallelujah Chorus*. However, her all-time favorite hymn is *O God, Our Help in Ages Past* because "when the events of the day bring discouragement, worry or anxiety, the God of the Ages remains our Eternal Home." *(p. 26)*

2006 – **Penny Sanders** – (Buffalo Valley COB) – As a mother recalling with fondness the closeness of having pre-school children cuddle up to her, Penny enjoys the hymn, *Near to the Heart of God*. It reminds her of the joy in "staying close to God, within that perimeter where watching, talking and listening are a regular occurrence." *(p. 54)*

2007 – **Beth Hollenberg** – (York First COB) – Since Beethoven is Beth's favorite composer, she chose *Joyful, Joyful, We Adore Thee*, marveling at the fact that it was composed in silence as the composer was totally deaf by that time. Appreciating Henry van Dyke's poetry in the lyrics and the praise and adoration they express toward God, Beth and her husband, Keith, included this hymn as part of their wedding celebration in 1986! *(p. 22)*

2007 – **Bob Kettering** – (Lititz COB) – Bob selected #47 in the Old (1901) *Black Brethren Hymnal, I'll Count My Blessings*, with words by poet Carrie E. Breck and music by Brethren musician, George Holsinger (1857-1908). The music is a real "toe-tapper," and the lyrics, based on Psalm 73:1, end with the statement, *"I'll count my blessings, bountiful and free, yet I can never count them all—so good is God to me."* *(p. 62)*

Glen Ziegler, a retired nursing home administrator of 32 years and one of the choristers at the White Oak COB.

2008 – **Glen Ziegler** – (White Oak COB) – After spending 45 years of his life working in retirement/nursing homes and being present when the end of life came for some, Glen thought about the time all of us will make that transition. Consequently, he picked the Fanny Crosby hymn, *My Savior First of All*, based on I Corinthians 13:12. It reminds him that we choose our destiny, and can know and have the assurance of His presence and welcome Home. We will know Him by the nail prints in His hands–put there to redeem you and me. *(p.24)*

2008 – **Michael Baldwin** – (York First COB) – As a church organist and pianist, Michael has played hundreds of songs during worship services. Especially meaningful to him has been

intertwining two songs–playing them in the
same key–and noting the meaningful words in
their combined message. This duo can be sung
antiphonally and is one of his favorites:

> *Take my life, and let it be consecrated,*
> *   Lord, to Thee.*
> **Here I am, Lord, Is it I, Lord?**
> *Take my hands, and let them move at the*
> *   impulse of Thy love,*
> **I will go, Lord, if You lead me**
> *Take my silver and my gold, not a mite*
> *   would I withhold*
> **I will hold your people in my heart.**
> *(p. 61)*

CHAPTER ELEVEN

How We Helped in Disasters

Graybill Hollinger sums it up, "We went there to rebuild houses, but the most important building we did was bridges of understanding."
- Deb Walton, 1990 SB, p. 64

It does feel good to be a small part of a big effort when one feels Jesus climbing alongside.
- Earl and Susan Mull, 2004 SB, p. 45

A. Testimonies

Disaster is such a strange word. What really is a disaster? We come to the BDRA and we relate that word to those afflicted by the natural progression of the earth–floods, hurricanes and tsunamis. We know of earthquakes, fires, tornadoes and avalanches. Is that what we mean by a disaster? These are the natural ones that the BDRA money so lovingly supports, but what about the other ones? What about the disasters that come in the natural progression of life?

Each of us faces disasters which come in the guise of disease, sickness, handicaps, death, accidents, violence and/or acts of terrorism. They come costumed as bankruptcy, unemployment, homelessness, addictions, and/or marital and family difficulties. We face disasters in spiritual and emotional ways everyday. Do we *get* relief? Do we *offer* relief? The money we collect at the BDRA doesn't always cover disasters like these.

Let us reach out, better yet, let us SEEK those who are suffering in their own disasters daily. Let us continue to serve, love and support all those who need more than shelter, food and water and share with them the gospel, the joy and the love of Christ.

*(From an article by Larry O'Neill.
2005 SB, p. 13)*

Disasters are devastating. They are rarely anticipated. At least not to the extent of the many ways they affect people. Think of Baxter Mow (Anna's husband) who was caught in the Roanoke flood. He was home alone. The waters came up rapidly. In desperation, he climbed up on the table, stretched himself upward and was scribbling messages on the ceiling, assuming that someone later might see them, but he was rescued. The church spells relief by rescuing from the depths of despair.

(James F. Myer, 1987 SB, p 9)

WHEN DISASTER STRIKES

Destructive forces in air and on land.
Why does this happen? I don't understand.
Only God knows the ways of creation,
The cause of these dreadful aberrations.

Striking landscapes, homes and people alike,
Lord, how can I stand this horrible sight?
By showing compassion and offering aid
Hope arises, and lives are remade.

So, Creator of all, spur me to care,
To reach out my hand and somehow "be there"
For those who are hurting, scared and adrift.
Here I am—damage to fix and burdens to lift.
(By Lois Duble 2007 SB, p. 61)

This was my first trip to help someone less fortunate than myself. It was very rewarding. I am looking forward to doing it again. The people were very grateful for everything we did for them.

(Mel Von Stetton – 1993 SB, p. 31)

HERMAN BRANDT

Herman Brandt, from the Midway COB, began volunteering on Disaster Response teams in 1972 when Hurricane Agnes caused much flooding and destruction.

After a flood in WV in 1986, he spent seven weeks in one year helping there and "making lasting friends."

Shortly after that, hurricanes became very active in the Caribbean and he and his wife, Erma, went to help for one month in Puerto Rico, two months in St. Croix, and one month on the island of St. John's. After Herman and Erma were appointed as directors in 1993, they spent three months helping out in FL in St. Petersburg and Miami. That same year, they spent one month working in MO and one month in Western PA.

When the Brandts were scheduled to do a project in ID in 1997, their plans were changed by cancer, which also changed their lives forever. In 1998, Herman did volunteer for a week in WV, and in 2000, worked for another week in MS.

Now widowed, this father of four and grandfather of two has volunteered at the Hershey Medical Center for the last ten years and given them 6,000 hours of service.

❖ ❖ ❖

"What we do for ourselves dies with us. What we do for others and the world remains and is immortal." (Albert Price)

❖ ❖ ❖

The Lord changed my life this summer! He taught me many lessons. He spoke to me in countless ways. He poured His love on me. He showed me what it meant to truly share Christ's love with others. He did all this by leading me down to Matamoros, Mexico.

I found out about a 10-week mission trip to Mexico with an organization called Ad-ventures in Missions, and I was certain it was where God wanted me. I completed all the paper work and upon acceptance started writing support letters to my church and praying that God would provide.

Here is where I learned my first lesson. Our God is so amazingly faithful. I had less than a month to raise $2,000. In about three weeks I had reached that amount plus a great abundance to give to Mexican churches. On June 6, 1999, I got off a plane in Brownsville, TX, knowing no one and was nervous, excited, scared, and willing—all at the same time.

The first week we did a lot of training, and I met the fourteen other girls with whom I would spend the summer serving the Lord. Each had a unique gift and taught me something about the Lord.

I had expected to see poverty, but I never dreamed it would look like it did. The neighborhoods that we worked in were built on an old trash dump. On seeing their living conditions, I remember starting to weep as I prayed. How could I have not known that I was so lucky? Why did these people have to live like this while we lived like royalty in comparison? The Lord humbled me that day and stirred up a desire in me to bring the only hope that will ever truly bring light into their lives—the gospel of Jesus Christ.

I watched an 80-year-old man finally accept the Lord. I prayed with an 18-year-old girl to receive Christ in the streets. I saw over forty fishermen and children give themselves to the Lord after an evangelistic outreach. There are countless stories I could tell in which a heart was changed and the Lord's might was revealed.

The Lord answered every one of my prayers this summer in small ways and in huge ways. Prayers for little provisions like having the van start, or having enough sandwiches or water on a hot day (105 to 110 degrees) were always answered. Our God never ceased to amaze me.

This summer the Spirit of the Lord changed me. He chipped off pieces of me that were not pleasing to Him and filled the holes with His love and mercy. My life will never be the same. Now my challenge is to you. Seek out the Lord with all your heart. Let Him do a great work in you. You may need to step out of your comfort zone to do this. For me this was going to Mexico. For you, it may simply be stepping out in faith at work or in school or with unsaved family members. Whatever the call may be, the promise is clear. In Jeremiah 29:13 (NIV), the Lord says: *"You will seek me and find me when you seek me with all your heart."* May your journey be as rewarding as mine.

(Bridgett Heckman, Ephrata COB and star hockey player at Bloomsburg University. 2000 SB, p. 18)

Building one house won't shelter everyone,
But for that family, it will be a home.
Adopting one child won't change the world,
But for that child, the world will change.
Feeding some who are hungry won't feed
    everyone,
But for those who receive food, it means life.
Building a school won't educate everyone;
But for that country, it may produce future
    leaders.

Going to Florida this past January has made an impression on my life that I will never forget. I not only was able to see the damage and the deprived conditions which people endured, but I was able in a small way to experience the same conditions myself. I thank God for allowing me the privilege of going to Florida to serve others in need, and especially for giving me the opportunity to appreciate more than ever the blessings that I possess.

(Karen A. Nell, Pleasant Hill COB – 1993 SB, p. 31)

I was really shocked at the tremendous destruction. It made me really thankful for what I had at home.

(Leon Bierbower, Chambersburg COB, 1993 SB, p.31)

HARRY AND GERRY GRAYBILL

If you are a regular visitor to the BDRA produce stands, you will quickly recognize the faces of Harry and Gerry Graybill. Their many years of experience in raising fruits and vegetables in their own garden, have given them the knowledge to answer many questions asked at the BDRA.

Although they are members of the Black Rock COB, they now live at the Brethren Home in Oxford, PA, where they are both active volunteers. Gerry works in the gift shop and helps with the finances of the Auxiliary, while Harry assists wheelchair bound residents to activities and therapy.

Since 1980, they have volunteered regularly at the Brethren Service Center in New Windsor, MD. While Gerry has been their Volunteer Coordinator, Bookstore Manager, and Human Resources Office Assistant, Harry has worked in the Cut Garment area, SER-RV International and other Service Ministries. Once a week, the Graybills roll up their sleeves and help prepare meals at Provide-A-Lunch (PAL), sponsored by the Hanover Area Council of Churches.

Every other year, they organize a special service project (such as packing school and/or health kits) for those who attend NOAC (National Older Adult Conference) of the COB in NC.

During the 1980s, Harry made several trips to Central America with organizations such as Witness for Peace, and when he came back, he shared his slides and stories with church groups. He also has participated in the "Clean Your Desk" program which collects unwanted supplies at the end of the school year and ships them to Nicaragua, where paper and pencils are sorely needed.

By their own example and doing all they can to encourage youth to participate in work camps, BVS, service projects, disaster response teams, Christian Citizenship seminars, and short term mission experiences, the Graybills hope to ensure that the next generation will discover the joys of volunteering, sharing the gospel and caring for the needs of others.

(From an article by Marua Leiter, their daughter. 2006 SB, p. 4)

It makes me feel good to help the people down in the South.

(Jay Nonnenmaker – 1993 SB, p. 31)

Members of the White Oak COB have been volunteering one day a month for the last seven years at the Brethren Service Center in New Windsor, MD. Eight to ten dedicated people regularly get up early and make the 85 mile trip from near Manheim, PA, to work in the SERRV pricing department. SERRV Self-Help Handcrafts is a COB program that promotes the social and economic progress of people in over forty developing countries by purchasing and marketing their handcrafts in a fair and direct manner. The products are inspected, priced and repackaged by volunteers.

When the White Oak members were asked why they spend time volunteering, their comments tell the story: "I know I am helping others."

"It gives me a sense of belonging." "It is a change from the normal pace of life."

"I enjoy the fellowship with the other workers." And one member commented on the way home, "I like it because the 'pay' is so good." (Their "pay" is lunch in Zigler Hall and the warm feeling of helping make a difference in someone's life.)

(Kathleen Campanella. 1994 SB, p. 24)

Why do I go on a disaster work project? The fact that *"It is more blessed to give than to*

receive" was something I was taught from my parents at a very young age. I only realized what they were talking about when I was laid up with a fractured back in 1971.

God's healing power was wonderful, and so many people came to my aid to help me through that healing process. I never forgot what a blessing it was to have so many friends, and from then on, I was determined to try to help others as I had been helped. By retiring early to be more able to help others, I discovered that when you go out on disaster work, no two experiences are alike.

When we were in Florida after Hurricane Andrew, as far as the eye could see, there was little remaining of houses and other buildings. At one place, we put a tarp over the one remaining room of a dear lady's house. I told her I was sorry for her and she said, "I am so thankful for my one room. My neighbors have nothing." What a witness!

So often the question was asked: "Why would you do this for us?"

Our answer: "Because we love Jesus, and Jesus loves you, too."

(Landis Myer, Conestoga COB, 1995 SB, p. 11)

In the May 21, 1989, issue of *Parade* magazine, Edward Klein has an article on Barbara Bush and her personal crusade to help the illiterate. He quotes her as saying, *"Everyone has something to give."* To encourage people to get involved, Mrs. Bush said, *"Walk out your door and help someone. Whatever you do, you're helping me."*

How much more should we be motivated to help others by our Lord and Savior Who said,

"Whatever you did, [fed, clothed, helped, cared, loved], *for one of the least of these brothers of mine, you did for me?"* (Matthew 25:40, NIV)

(1989 SB, p.18)

I can distinctly remember our first refugee family from Uganda, Africa, in 1972. Their lives had been threatened, but they had no place to go. Finally, the doors opened and they discovered that someone cared. I can remember Samsudin Pabani's questions: "Why did you sponsor us? Why didn't you leave us there to die in Uganda?"

Our response was, "Because God has loved us so much we want to share that love with you and your family."

We need to continue to share that love wherever we go. Disasters are all around us, and we need to give of ourselves and pray for the broken-hearted, depressed, homeless, widows, our children and leaders in government.

(T. Grace Ziegler. 1993 SB, p.12)

"While faith makes all things possible, it is love that makes all things easy."

(Evan H. Hopkins)

"My week spent with Disaster Relief in the greater Miami area was indeed an eye-opening experience. I've never seen such extensive damage done to such a wide-spread area. There's no

doubt God is in control of our lives and that He is very awesome and powerful. This experience has taught me to be more thankful daily for the many blessings that we have."

(Mary Rose Good, Pleasant View COB,
1993 SB, p.31)

As a young child growing up in the Florin COB, I remembered hearing stories from missionaries as they came home from Nigeria. Later, as a youth in BVS in the early 70s, I was on a project in Dundalk, MD, and came in contact with former missionaries, Monroe and Ada Good and their family. Through these contacts, I became interested in visiting Nigeria. Although the World Ministries Commission sponsored annual work camps to Nigeria and I wanted to go, I could never find the time. However, in 1993, everything worked out right, and I headed toward a Nigerian work camp.

When you think of a work camp, you often get caught up in the "I want to go and do something for someone" attitude. Well, the Nigerian work camp was anything but that! During my time there, I visited many churches, and in one case, I was the first white person to ever worship with them in their church. I stayed in Nigerian western-style homes and mud huts, visited their markets, met a few local chiefs, and experienced the food.

In addition, I was able to work with many Nigerian church members. As a person whose vocation is construction, I can remember thinking, "Why in the world are we doing things this way? These are really dumb ways of doing things."

After analyzing what we were doing plus the materials and tools that were available, I realized that we were making the best use of all the resources, and amazingly, we accomplished much work. *Only by walking in another's shoes do you learn not to criticize.*

Just as I had experienced earlier in BVS, I came away from the work camp feeling that I had received more than I gave. Having been taught that it is more blessed to give than to receive, I returned to Nigeria for the 1994 work camp. The second experience was just as rich as the first, and if you can assure my wife that the winter of 1995 will not have as much snow, ice, wind and cold as 1994, I plan to attend the 1995 work camp. This could get to be a vicious cycle!

(Jeff Mummau. 1994 SB, p. 11)

For the past ten years, the SOPA District of the COB has cooperated with the Mid-Atlantic District in an annual meat canning project where volunteers have butchered and canned tons of meat and broth for distribution at home and abroad. In 1988, one hundred and one cows were slaughtered with 16,000 cans of beef and 4,000 cans of broth shipped.

(Warren M. Eshbach, SOPA District Executive.
1988 SB, p.6)

This is the sixth time that I have done disaster work as a cook for workers. I have met so many nice people, those working and those we have helped. It is real rewarding.

(Marilyn Miller – 1993 SB, p. 31)

❖ ❖ ❖

In July 12-16, 1993, The Indian Creek COB partnered with the First Haitian Fellowship in Brooklyn, NY, in their Vacation Bible School. The pastor, Verel Montauban, his wife, their four children and thirteen other Haitian children spent the week in the homes of nine of the Indian Creek families. As an offering project, $600 was collected and given to the Haitian Fellowship to purchase folding chairs to use in their worship.

Each day, after Bible School and a quick lunch, the children were taken on day trips and varied activities such as visiting a milking parlor, an outdoor picnic, a swim party, and touring in Lancaster County Amish country. When it was over, the church planned to do it again in July, 1994.

(1994 SB, p. 58)

❖ ❖ ❖

The love of God is often easier presented to someone who is warm, well fed, and clean. Offering a warm blanket often opens the opportunity to witness. During this past difficult winter, one of our members took blankets and went through the housing project where she lives, seeking elderly people who had been forgotten with the offer of a warm blanket and word about Jesus' love.

(Betty Foster, Brooklyn COB.
1996 SB, p. 58)

❖ ❖ ❖

In 2005, customers found it hard to get serious answers from Ivan Lutz (left) pictured among the apples with his partner in comedy, Harold Eckert (right).

IVAN LUTZ

For a small child in a homeless shelter, or an abused woman hiding from the terror she married, or a grandmother sitting in her room at a retirement home, simple pleasures are treasured. To them, a small thing–a smile, a gentle touch on a shoulder, a piece of fresh fruit–may seem heaven-sent.

Hundreds of people in situations like this in ten Pennsylvania cities must be thinking that God has finally reached out and brought them one of these little pleasures. But in this case, His hands are at the ends of Ivan Lutz' arms.

With his 65-year-old arms, Ivan brings 40-pound boxes full of fellowship to the people who need it most. Ironically, these boxes contain apples, traditionally thought to be, although mistakenly, the forbidden fruit of the Garden of Eden.

"They are something almost anyone can eat," said Ivan, who lives in Millway, near Lititz.

"Kids love apples; old folks love apples." With this fresh fruit, which he buys 15 to 20 cases at a time, Ivan is fulfilling a dream which he formulated years before his retirement at age 63.

"I just knew that when I retired I wanted to do something worthwhile."

Working in the warehouse at the Miller & Hartman Co., Lancaster, a wholesale grocer, Ivan envisioned delivering apples to the neediest of people. After he retired, he searched for an outlet for his "apple ministry." A talk with a friend at the Water Street Rescue Mission gave him the lead he sought. From one facility, Ivan has expanded his travels to include 100 different stops in ten cities. Centers for abused women and children, the Salvation Army, homes for children affected by AIDS, homeless shelters and other groups in Lancaster, York, Harrisburg, Lebanon, Reading, Pottstown, Norristown, Allentown, Bethlehem and Philadelphia are the targets of his giving.

For Ivan, the reason why is obvious. "I am 65 years old and my generation of 60 to 80-year-old people are the first generation of Americans to receive the good Social Security and pension checks. I really feel that we owe something back to this great land of America. If my generation fails to help with these problems, who will?"

One day a week he does his part to reach out to people who he sees as not very different from members of his own family. "They could

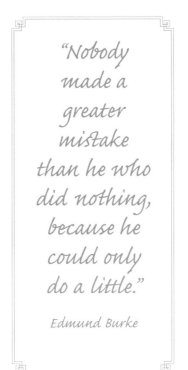

"Nobody made a greater mistake than he who did nothing, because he could only do a little."

Edmund Burke

be my children in there," he said. "There are a lot of good young boys and girls in these places."

Meeting the people who run the varied facilities has been an unexpected pleasure for Ivan. "They have hearts of gold," he observed.

To deliver his cargo, Ivan bought a 1986 Ford van, which, if seen once, is hard to forget. On both sides of the tan truck, he had a friend paint, *Jesus Loves You,* in 17 languages.

"I got the Chinese translation from a restaurant," he said proudly, as cars cruised by slowly to look at the van in the parking lot of a local shopping center. English, several African languages, Dutch, Hebrew, Arabic, Russian, French, Italian, Hindu, Korean, Portuguese, Spanish, German and Greek are represented in an informal style.

"It's an eye-catcher," he admits with a wide smile, but added that his wife won't ride with him in it. "You are a marked person when you drive in this thing." But for Ivan, the van helps to get the attention he hopes might inspire others his age to get up and out, to lend a hand when there might be no one else to do it.

"Oh me, we've got a problem," he said as he sat behind the wheel of his van. "There's a lot more we could be doing. We have to do something to mend the broken parts of society. Sometimes I have gripes with my generation. We've been so blessed."

But he does what he can, this native Lancaster Countian with a Dutchy accent.

He said he is at his limit at what he can handle financially, although with some outside help, he could probably do more. But the benefits for the people he visits, and also for himself, make it worth all the effort.

"You know, half of the good is the fruit, and the other half is just showing these people that someone out there cares."

(Reprinted with permission from the Intelligencer Journal, *Lancaster, PA March 13, 1995. 1997 SB, p. 17)*

We have been on nine projects…In March, 1990, Hurricane Hugo hit Copohee, SC, and every house but one was destroyed. Twenty-six of us went to work there, framing, putting on roofs, sheet-rock and dry wall, laying carpet and installing windows. It's hard to explain how people feel about us coming to help them. They thanked us over and over. One person said, "I wish you people could come and start a church here."

(Mark & Naomi Wampler, Mt. Zion Road COB, 1995 SB, p. 11)

Can carrying mud out of a 90 degree basement be fun? Can dragging a car out of a gully be fulfilling? Well, hardly, if you are stuck with such tasks all by yourself.

The church spells relief by developing fellowship from working together so that the drudgery actually becomes enjoyment. Relief workers have often said, "Those were some of the best days of my life."

(James F. Myer, 1987 SB, p. 9.)

LES SHOBER

Les Shober, from the Ephrata COB, began volunteering for disaster relief missions twelve years ago when Hurricane Hugo hit SC. That mission made a profound change in his life. Upon returning home, all he could do was pray for God's help for all the people who had been affected by that natural disaster. He felt as if he "had been blind, but now he could see."

Les has been on twenty-two missions of various types, including devastation caused by floods, hurricanes, ice flows, wind and rain damage. On these missions, he has enjoyed meeting and working with people from a variety of backgrounds and professions and has seen and felt the very presence of God in their midst. He has worked through the American Red Cross, the Mennonite Central Committee, The Presbyterian Church of Parksburg, Habitat for Humanity, and New Windsor (COB).

Many times, Les found it difficult to leave a project because of all the work remaining to be done. However, usually a fresh group of volunteers arrived to continue the clean up and rebuilding. Les plans to continue volunteering, giving thanks and praise to God for his own good health and for the opportunities to serve God and his fellow man in this manner. While doing this work, he feels he is witnessing for his Lord and Savior, Jesus Christ, and he has also gained a greater appreciation for the safety of his own home.

I had the privilege of volunteering with flood relief in Vanceboro and Rocky Mount, NC. When you see the widespread devastation, you realize one cannot fathom what these people have gone through, but by being there, you are showing that you genuinely care. What you accomplish in a week is but a drop in the bucket; however, in God's eyes, you are one of many giving a cup of cold water. Volunteering blesses those we help, makes us more aware of our many blessings, and brings Honor and Glory to God.

(Rachel Z. Good, Pleasant View COB.
2001 SB, p. 46)

I felt really glad I could help people that weren't as blessed as I am. We have everything we need and plenty of things we want. To think that I could give some of my time to help the less fortunate gave me a warm, happy feeling inside.

(Joanne Hilty, 16,
Pleasant Hill COB 1997 SB, p. 58)

On Saturday, November 24, 2001, Vicki and I had the opportunity to travel to Brooklyn, NY, for a Thanksgiving Memorial Service sponsored by the Brooklyn First COB. We had asked Pastors Earl Foster and Phill Carlos Archbold if it would be possible to travel into Manhattan and view Ground Zero. Little did we realize that God would take us into the heart of Ground Zero.

Brother Eddie Quijano, Church Moderator and a retired NYC police detective, met us at the church and graciously guided us through the subway into south Manhattan. As we emerged from the subway and turned the corner on a short block, Brother Eddie said, "There it is." Several blocks away appeared the ruins of the terrorists' attack on September 11. He continued, "Do you want to go closer?" Vicki jumped in with a quick but somber, "Yes."

As we proceeded, the ominous destruction of this horrible act loomed even more real. Brother Eddie stopped to talk with a couple of his former colleagues from the NYPD. After sharing with them the reason for our trip into the city–preaching at the Thanksgiving Memorial Service, a captain asked if we wanted to "go in." We quickly agreed.

We were ushered behind the police barricades to wait for the Police Community Service van to escort us into the perimeter of Ground Zero. After a brief tour, the Community Service officer stopped the van and asked Brother Eddie if he and his guests would like to "go further." We nodded.

Connections were then made with the National Guard Sergeant on duty to secure clearance for us to enter. We stood patiently for nearly forty-five minutes as family members were escorted into the grave sites of their loved ones. With hard hats on their heads, tears streaming down their cheeks, arms clinging to teddy bears and flowers clasped in their hands, family members slumped in. And then, like a casketless funeral recessional on a trip to nowhere, these husbands and wives, moms and dads, brothers and sisters, grandmothers and grandfathers, aunts and uncles simply filed out on their way back to grief-impacted homes and a long string of empty tomorrows.

Then it was our turn. We walked directly to the platform that had been originally erected for President Bush and Mayor Guiliani. We stood and gazed into the stinking, smoking pit of rubble that was once the World Trade Center–New York City's symbol of global grandeur. We silently surveyed the annihilated architectural magnificence, the worldwide prestige, and the international financial eminence now represented by piles of hellish, smoldering debris, chunks of strewn concrete, twisted configurations of steel, tons of shattered glass, secondary buildings shrouded with orange safety mesh, and the ashes of cremated human flesh. We cried. We prayed. We left.

On Sunday morning as I stood to preach, I looked into the eyes of some thirty New York City firefighters seated to my right; and I knew that my journey to Ground Zero had taken me to a place deep inside–the place where God alone works to impact the human soul.

As you come to the BDRA, take time to remember the events of September 11th, 2001. Remember the destruction. Remember the national pain. Remember the giving spirit. Remember the heroes. Remember the victims. Remember the grieving families.

Remember that *neither disasters nor Christ's love take a holiday.* Remember that your giving does make a difference in someone's life. I know—because I have looked into the eyes of

some of the survivors and seen the reflection of Christ's love and care.

(By Craig H. Smith, ANE District Executive, COB. (The primary text for this article first appeared in the Pastor's Memo of the ANE District. With slight modification, it was reprinted in the Brethren News. By popular request, it was adapted and reprinted again in the 2002 SB, p. 21.)

> *"You can't help the person in the gutter by looking out a second-floor window!"*
>
> *Shared by Bob Bender, Lititz COB*

❖ ❖ ❖

Within a few months after returning from a Brethren Disaster Relief effort to help an area in Louisiana recover from a hurricane, I received a Disaster Response Certificate that quoted Jesus saying in Matthew 25:40, *"I tell you this: anything you did for one of My sisters and brothers here, however humble, you did for Me."* I then came to the realization that my disaster relief efforts really amounted to working for the Lord!

I subsequently went on Brethren Disaster Relief trips to a flood damaged town north of Panama City, FL, to flood damaged Hampton, TN, to tornado damaged Birmingham, AL, to flood damaged Albany, GA, and to a church building project near Statesboro, GA. On those trips, I met many people. With many of them, I shared my conviction that I was there to help with the Lord's work.

I believe the Lord touched me through these experiences. As I look back, I have an ever growing closer relationship with Him and an increasing desire to help others in need. I have the desire to develop and learn more skills and have a much clearer focus as to what I want to do with the rest of my life.

(Terrill Myers, Harrisburg COB.1999 SB, p. 52)

Millard Fuller, founder of Habitat for Humanity, was visiting a community some time after a blitz build had taken place. When he came to the house former President Jimmy Carter had helped to build, he stopped. He asked the boy playing in his yard, "Do you know who built your house?" Millard thought, of course, that the little boy would say President Carter. But the little boy replied, "Jesus built my house." Who could have said it any better?

(Shared by Deanna Crawford in 2003 SB, p. 39)

WHO'S YOUR JOSÉ?

The biggest highlight of my 10-day mission trip to the Dominican Republic in July 2007, was seeing people come to a saving relationship with Jesus Christ. While we were there, over 30 people decided to follow Christ.

One guy, in particular, was José. He was hired to help with construction and was a hard worker and a good mason. We worked with him all week at the church site, and on the last night there, we participated in the first service in the new church building. The fact that it had no roof, doors, windows, or restrooms did not seem to deter anyone from praising and worshipping our awesome God and Creator! By the end of that service, José had given his life to Jesus Christ.

That night and many times since I thought about what it was that helped José make that decision. What did he see or hear that helped convince him that he should become a Christian?

Was it because we talked and preached to him all week about it? No—we spoke English; he spoke Spanish.

Was it because we shared the same vocation? No—he was a mason and by looking at our block work, it was pretty obvious that we were not masons.

Was it because he liked the Christian songs we played at the job site? Nope. They were in English.

Was it because we liked the same football team, hobbies, or TV shows? No—most of those things aren't even options for José.

So, what was it that helped move José to become a Christian?

John 13:35 (NIV): *"By this all men will know that you are my disciples, if you love one another."* I really feel that summed it up. We were a diverse group that came in love, in the name of Christ, and I think José could really see and feel that love. We didn't focus on our differences, our preferences, our personal likes and dislikes. No, we focused on what united us and that was our love for Jesus Christ. That is how he knew we were followers of Christ. We were united, and there was a love and caring among our group that could be felt by all who came in contact with us.

Who has God put in your life that needs to feel His love?

(From an article by Shane Keeny, Pleasant View COB. 2008 SB, p. 39)

Upon returning from the missions trip, I felt completely renewed. Despite the fact I had spent a week working for others as compared to spending a week doing things for myself, I found myself very fulfilled from the love of those I had befriended and those I had helped serve. Also, I gained such a respect for those who dedicate their lives to service, and most importantly, I realized how much glory is brought to the Lord through serving others. There is an extraordinary joy in wholeheartedly serving, and since the trip, it has become a personal commitment of my own to continue serving those in need. After all, we live in a world that is desperately crying out for service, and I realize God has given me personal gifts which are not to be wasted but are to be used toward bettering the lives of others."

(Brandi Benzel, an Elizabethtown College student who went on a missions and service trip to NC on her spring break in 2004. 2004 SB, p. 9)

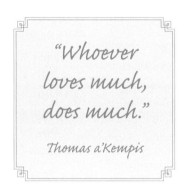

"Whoever loves much, does much."

Thomas a'Kempis

"What is a math teacher from Florida doing at a construction site in Nebraska?"

I was asking myself that question my first day on the job as a BVSer in Hallam as I was hammering over my head getting a sore wrist putting up trusses. I soon bought myself a nifty little tool belt and began learning the tricks of the trade from the other volunteers. God showed me that it isn't how much construction experience you have but what really mattered was having a willing and obedient heart.

I've really enjoyed getting to know the families that belong to these houses. Their stories are amazing. For example, the only picture that was found salvageable after the tornado for one family was a painting of Jesus holding their baby boy who had died at a young age. While the house was leveled, this one irreplaceable item was found to be in almost perfect shape.

Another man lost his mother in the tornado and has questioned God since that traumatic event. At first, he was very reluctant to let a church group rebuild his house, but since then, he has developed a trust and whole new attitude toward God and His people.

Another lady had her wedding ring taken right off her finger by the low pressure during the tornado and was very saddened by that loss. However, when they were cleaning away the debris on the other side of the house, her tiny ring was found! While it was very unfortunate that the tornado happened, it's neat to see God's hand in the little miracles that happened there.

I won't be missing the cold, windy Nebraska weather, but I sure will miss those warmhearted people. To see people working together like that to restore a community in the name of Christ is what life is all about for me.

(From an article by Kevin Dibert, a member of Chambersburg COB. 2005 SB, p. 48)

A small boy in church with his parents listened to the minister describe his visit to a poor home. He pictured the bare rooms, the ragged clothing, the empty dishes on the table, the pale, hungry children. When he finished his story, he announced the closing hymn. But the little boy, with tears in his eyes, cried out to his father, "But, Daddy, aren't we going to *do* anything about it?"   *(1989 SB, p. 19)*

When my son, Jim, felt the desire to help flood victims in Rocky Mount, NC, my wife suggested that we make it a *father-son effort.* I think the Lord was leading us in that direction, not only to help others, but at the same time, giving the opportunity to spend a week working together. We enjoyed the fellowship of the group with whom we worked and received much satisfaction and joy in helping those in need. The blessing we received was far greater than what we anticipated by answering the call of the Lord.

(Harry J. Cleaver, New Fairview COB.
2001 SB, p. 46)

In the early 1990s, I volunteered to help in a Harrisburg Habitat for Humanity project. In the midst of removing some rock lath with a pry bar and a hoe, the dust made visibility almost zero. In spite of using goggles and a dust mask, I knew I was still consuming

"We can do great things for the Lord if we are willing to do little things for others."

(2000 SB, p.28)

a lot of dust. Since my vocation was being a hospital manager, while taking a break, I casually remarked to the man with whom I was working about the apparent health hazard of what we were doing. He quickly responded, "Terrill, this is *the Lord's* dirt. You'll never get sick from the Lord's dirt."

That comment had a lasting effect on me.
(Terrill Myers, Harrisburg COB. 1999 SB, p. 52)

It has always amazed me what happens on these disaster response trips. You take a group of people, most of whom you have never met. Send them to a location with a Project Director who usually doesn't know who is coming or what skills they have. In the course of a week, those diverse people come together and accomplish amazing things. This reminded me of vegetable soup. A lot of different ingredients, stirred together in the situation, and how good it turns out! Of course, to make good soup, you have to have a good stock to start with, and that stock is GOD! 'Nough said.'

(John Ryman, Shenandoah COB District, VA.
2002 SB, p. 38)

As a young child, I was awakened one night by the fire sirens and a bright light reflecting in my bedroom window. In fear, looking out the window, I saw our neighbor's barn being destroyed. They had just harvested their new crop of hay and now it went up in smoke. My parents immediately responded by helping to clean up and rebuild–mother with food and dad with his carpenter skills. Their example and response made a lasting impression on my life. Their acts of love to us children and others have been a motivating factor in my life. I have vivid memories of my dad taking a load of choice alfalfa hay to our neighbor after the barn was rebuilt, and unloading it in their empty hay mow. At that moment, I learned the joy of helping people.

*(Floyd Myer, Jennersville COB,
1995 SB, p. 10)*

One evening, my wife, Shirley, and I were with our pastor and his wife. He said to me, "Glenn, if you were to say what is the greatest thing you've learned this past year since the fire destroyed the Sight and Sound Theater, what would it be?"

And I said, "The one thing that stands out in front of everything else–I have learned to trust in God, no matter what! I have put my faith and trust in Him as never before. I *know* He does not fail. I *know* He is an ever present help in times of trouble. I *know* He is the great I AM. He is here today. He was there yesterday. He'll be here tomorrow. He'll always be there for His children.

"I leave you with this message: whatever you do, do it in faith. We live in fantastic times, with fantastic opportunities. There's a hungry world out there. Feed them. Not only bread from the bakery, but Bread from heaven. Give them Water to drink, for which they'll never thirst again. Follow the desires of your heart, remembering the words of the Lord: *'Delight yourself in the Lord, and He will give you the desires of your heart.'"* Psalms 37:4, NIV.
(Glenn Eshelman, owner of the Sight and Sound Millennium Theatres in Strasburg, PA, and in Branson, MO. SB, 1998, p. 38)

In an article reporting about the work of a 17-member flood relief team that helped the Vanceboro, NC, area for five days in March 2000, Rachel Good concludes by saying: "We arrived back in York, PA, tired but feeling blessed for having lightened the load just a little for many people. We all realized none of us can imagine what they lived through, *but we cared."*
(2000 SB, p. 51)

The closing worship at the Tidewater, VA, work camp was especially meaningful. It was going to be tough to say good-by to the people we worked for and to this new group of friends. Sitting on the floor in a circle in candlelight, we reflected on the events of the past week. There was no denying that God was at work in us and through us during our week at work camp. God was made very real to us and to those for whom we worked. We went to serve and we were served. Indeed, the experience would change each of our lives.

When you support or sponsor youth to go to work camps, you are giving them a wonderful gift–an encounter with God.

(Twyla D. Rowe. 1996 SB, p. 9)

If you are considering helping with a Disaster Response team, Habitat for Humanity, or some other volunteer experience, long-term or short-term, I have two words of advice–DO IT! But I must warn you, you'll never be the same again. You will see scriptures come to life, and you will look at what it means to be a Christian in a whole new way.

(Deanna Crawford. 2003 SB, p. 39)

B. The Brethren Disaster Response Services

The history of the COB Disaster Response Service goes back to the founder of the denomination, Alexander Mack himself. Although he was a rich miller, according to tradition, he died a poor man because of his generosity in helping religious refugees.

Christopher Sauer, another early COB leader, spent much of his time and money working with new immigrants as they arrived in Philadelphia from Germany.

After the Civil War, churches in the North raised monies to be sent to needy persons in the South. A principle was established (and still continues) whereby charity funds were to be used to help *all* persons and not limited to members of the German Baptist Brethren (an early name for the COB).

In the nineteenth century, Brethren could often be found helping neighboring farmers to rebuild a burned-down barn or a storm-damaged house, but these deeds of kindness were seldom recorded.

At the 1917 Annual Conference, collections at local levels were approved "for relief of those unfortunate sufferers," referring to the needs of the Armenians.

In 1932, the Brethren Young Peoples' Department petitioned Annual Conference "to build up a church program of international goodwill, to investigate and provide a program of service—of neutral relief work in time of war and periods of national crises." Their request was granted.

A plan was presented in 1939 to establish a Brethren Service Commission and to have a Committee on Peace and Relief. It was passed, and M. R. Zigler served as secretary for the new committee. In 1942, the myrtlewood service cup was adopted as a symbol for Brethren Service at the Asheville, NC, Annual Conference.

Ministry in the early church had a service motif. The Greek word for ministry was "diakonia" and literally meant "to wait on tables." The Community of Faith was comprised of persons who had allowed God's grace to transform their lives into servants.

Though seen today in more professional or sophisticated terms, ministry still needs to be servant oriented. The Holy Spirit activates our gifts at baptism to be used in service for God and others. God's grace is translated into deeds of kindness.

(Warren M. Eshbach, SOPA District Executive. 1992 SB, p. 8)

Ralph and Mary Smeltzer began a program of public education to Japanese-Americans who were taken from their homes and placed in relocation camps in the desert. That same year, 1942, the COB spent nearly $2 million in Civilian Public Service (CPS) Camps, where young men worked as firefighters, dairy testers, human guinea pigs in starvation experiments, and many other hospital and community development programs.

In 1946, the "sea-going cowboys" began with Heifer Project International, accompanying live animals to Europe and China, and material relief was sent to the European survivors of World War II. International work camps began in 1948, the same year that Brethren Volunteer Service (BVS) was approved at the Denver, CO, Annual Conference.

An international youth exchange occurred in 1949 at the request of the U.S. military in a program whereby the COB provided homes and administrative personnel for almost 100 German youth who were brought to the U.S. to live in American homes for one year while U.S. students lived in German homes.

As a part of its statement on civil defense on March 22, 1957, the General Board made

this recommendation: "We urge our members to study carefully all Brethren plans to help the needy, such as Brethren Disaster Service. We urge the establishment of classes and other efforts to train our people for readiness to help effectively."

The Brethren came to the aid of the victims of flooding in Stroudsburg, PA, in 1955, Yuba City, CA, in 1956, Shelbiana, KY, in 1957, Miami Shores, OH, and Peru, IN, in 1959. Then in 1960, the Emergency Disaster Fund was established so funds would be available immediately when urgently needed.

Almost yearly, from that time until today, they responded to disasters occurring around the world. In 1978, a Director of Disaster Response Services was appointed, and in 1980, the Disaster Child Care Program was established.

Each time I hear of tornadoes and hurricanes, the memories of May 6, 1965, surface. We were a young family, my husband, myself, and our two-year-old son, Dan. The excitement and apprehension of making a major move from PA to MN was still fresh on our minds when less than two weeks later, we were hit by two tornadoes. A beautiful spring day ended with a night of terror and fear. Dan was separated from us, and we did not find him until 6:30 the next morning.

The following days were difficult at best for adults. There was no way Dan could understand the sudden changes in his life. He had to eat Salvation Army sandwiches while we cleaned up debris from our home and the Red Cross food at a local church when we finished work for the day. Later there was a new apartment to live in, but his express wagon and toy radio were gone.

(Jean Myers, 1990 SB, p. 35)

Along with other volunteers, Jean Myers responded to the Lord's call after Hurricane Hugo struck SC, where one child responded, "Why you be so nice to me?"

(1990 SB, p. 35)

In the aftermath of Hurricane Floyd, which caused the worst flooding in NC history in the fall of 1999, disaster childcare was provided in several locations. Caregiver Fran Holcomb relayed a story about a little boy who was worried because he saw his daddy cry. He wanted to know what he could do to make him feel better. I said, "Help me, Lord."

I began by asking the little boy what his daddy did when he cried. He answered, "He took me on his lap and hugged me and told me he loved me."

I suggested that when they got home that night, he should crawl up on his daddy's lap, give him a big hug and tell him how much he loved his daddy."

(From an article by Jane Yount, 2000 SB, p. 20)

When Sheryl Faus of the Chiques COB heard the tragic news of the attack on the World Trade Center on September 11, 2001, she immediately contacted the Brethren Service Center in New Windsor, MD, to indicate her availability to help. Sheryl, a volunteer with the COB Children's Disaster Services since 1985, had trained three years earlier for Childcare Aviation Incident Response (CAIR), a division of the Red Cross which works closely with the COB childcare program.

Usually the volunteers go to the site with hands-on activities for the children. In Manhattan, however, only four miles from the attack area, the childcare center was very large, fully equipped, and looked like a page from a toy catalog. Play items had been contributed by several companies. "Besides," Sheryl reported, "we were often asked what else we needed, and any request was filled in short order, including baby beds and many blankets."

Later, in reflecting on her experience, Sheryl noted: "Our role was to provide a safe, fun place for the kids. There's no way to know the ramifications this horrific disaster has and will have in the future for the thousand plus children who lost parents."

She added: "Even my own life was touched by the many who were suffering and by those who were caring for the suffering. Those faces will remain in my mind's eye for a long time."

(2002 SB, p. 38)

Sheryl, who succeeded Jean Myers from the Little Swatara COB as ANE District Coordinator of Children's Disaster Services, is a retired elementary school teacher. Living near Manheim and married for 48 years to Glen Faus, this mother of three with one grandchild, is active in her church as a Sunday school teacher, choir member, serving as a member of the Vision Builder Committee, and on the Music Commission. She has also served on the ANE District Women's cabinet and the Senior Adult Committee.

During her years with Children's Disaster Services, she has responded to emergencies from California to Maine to Florida and is thankful for the many volunteers who so willingly give of their time "to serve those in need as Jesus taught us to do."

Each year, the funds raised at the BDRA are divided between: (1) The COB Emergency Disaster Fund distributed through the national COB offices at Elgin to give worldwide relief and to support disaster ministries within the U.S., and (2) The United Relief Fund (TURF) which gives aid to crises situations within the two sponsoring districts and is distributed through an appointed TURF Committee.

The significance of the BDRA cannot be overstated as it raises more than one-third of the total amount of money contributed to disasters throughout the COB in any one year. Therefore, the BDRA is the major source of contribution to the Brethren Disaster Program.

Contributions from the BDRA go to disasters around the world, overseas as well as domestic. The largest domestic amounts recently have gone to the victims of Hurricane Andrew. The largest overseas amounts have gone to the Horn of Africa, particularly the Sudan.

(Donald E. Miller, General Secretary of the COB, 1993 SB, p. 4)

Each SB contains a listing of what has been spent for the various aid projects during the past year by both disaster ministries. For example, in the 2003 SB, p. 16, the Emergency Disaster Fund Allocations for January 1–December 31, 2002, are listed by disaster world-wide and the dollar amount sent to each, with a total of $338,874.33 sent that year. The amounts spent for aid through the Emergency Disaster Fund has grown from $9,500 in 1962 to over $718,000 in 1985 to $799,800 in 2007.

(2008 SB, p. 36)

In the 2008 SB, p. 16, are also listed interesting statistics about the activities of Brethren Disaster Ministries during the year 2007. Included are the projects (and in parentheses the total numbers for 2007) (to which a response was given: disasters - 4 hurricane and 1 flood (5), number of volunteers who helped (1,554), number of workdays given (11,168), number of hours of work (89,344), and the number of families served (154).

After a week on a Disaster Response team, Tim Ritchey Martin wrote: "The Spirit of God was evident in the work that was accomplished and in the eyes of those who said 'thank you' through their tears. What a wonderful week!"

(From an article by Jane Yount, 2000 SB, p. 20)

C. The United Relief Fund (TURF)

The United Relief Fund (TURF) is a joint disaster response effort of the ANE and SOPA Districts of the COB and is responsible to the BDRA Board. Since the early 1990's, funds allocated from the BDRA each year are used to work in partnership by COB congregations and related agencies in the two districts to meet urgent needs. Over $1,873,433 has been disbursed for TURF grants and programs since its founding.

The TURF Committee, in reviewing grants already awarded to congregations in the two districts, noted that only sixteen of the 118 congregations have applied for and received TURF grants. In an effort to get broader congregational involvement, early in 1998 the committee awarded a one-time $500 grant to each congregation "to offer immediate aid to those in need within the congregation and/or church community."

Conditions of the grant require congregational participation "in a way which gives appropriate witness and glory to Christ," provision of volunteer service and/or congregational funds to the project(s), and reporting on the use of the funds expended by the end of the year. A total of $59,000 was distributed to congregations, inviting them to participate in this effort. *(1998 SB, p. 63)* Four congregations elected not to participate and returned the funds.

According to the congregational reports, the monies were used for needs, expenses related to home fires and one church fire, counseling for a mother of five, help for a visually-impaired student who was sexually abused, 16 youth and five adults working at a disaster project in TN, providing seed money to establish a community credit union for disadvantaged families, clothing for work released prisoners and contributions to food banks.

Many congregations reported that these grants increased their awareness of needs in their communities, that helping meet needs was a means of showing their faith and God's love to others, and in one instance, gave the inspiration to start a food bank and a "Pastor's Caring Fund" using 1% of their Sunday morning offerings. One recipient family later returned the funds with an added $100, and these monies were then used to help three additional needy families. Some recipients began attending that church, and most congregations were challenged to add funds or services to expand the use of the grant.   *(1999 SB, p. 67)*

Grant applications may be submitted by a COB congregation or related agency in the two partner districts. Guidelines have been established for TURF to follow in awarding grants to respond to individual, family and community needs.

The TURF Committee, made up of representatives from the two participating districts, urges all congregations to become more involved in ministry to those in need in our communities. Those currently serving on the TURF Board are:

ATLANTIC NORTHEAST DISTRICT
Marty Witman, Disaster Auction Appointee
Kay Weaver, District Disaster Coordinator

Dean Lengel, District Witness Commission Member

Aaron Martin, Jr., District Witness Commission Member

Craig Smith, ANE District Executive

SOUTHERN PENNSYLVANIA DISTRICT

Bob and Sally Bingaman, Disaster Auction Appointees

Lutricia Zerfing, District Disaster Coordinator

Ray Lehman, District Witness Commission Member

Jake Myer, District Witness Commission Appointee

Georgia Markey, Associate District Executive

(2008 SB, p. 6)

TURF AND THE TRAGEDY AT NICKLE MINES

On October 2, 2006, when the news of the Nickle Mines Amish School tragedy came through the news channels, Jay Witman, Duane Ness, Landis and Audrey Myer and other TURF Committee members got together and agreed unanimously that they wanted to support and help their Amish Christian brothers and sisters in their time of grief. A committee visited the parents and grandparents of several of the little girls who had been injured or killed and joined the Amish relatives, church leaders and the Amish Bishop who had gathered to minister to them in their grief and loss.

After the BDRA group stated their purpose in coming–that they were offering to share the love of Jesus by giving funds to help in rebuilding their school, the Amish seemed

stunned and didn't immediately accept the gift. Realizing they were surprised and humbled by the offer, Jay explained, "We don't want to push you. Whatever you want to do is okay. We're just here to help."

After more discussion, they agreed to accept this love gift of funds. Then the Amish bishop, deacons, family and the TURF committee members stood in a circle there in the family's kitchen. Each shared as they felt led and closed by sharing in prayer together.

Jay says, "It was the most touching day of my life, and I've seen a lot of things. It was a day of crying and yet of celebrating. It was a day I can't even comprehend. I knew God walked in for I saw Him there, and I felt Him. And He is still there."

At the beginning of TURF in 1991, Martha M.D. Hackman served as Coordinator, assisted by Henry and Helen Patches. Each year, from 1991 through 1996, Martha wrote an article in the SB describing the goods and grants that TURF had given during that year. In 1997 the format for the summary report changed, first to a full-page chart, and later to the present time, a half-page chart. Whatever the form, a full report is published in the BDRA SB annually as to how the TURF funds were distributed.

For example, in the 2007 SB, the money shared through TURF in late 2006 and early 2007 totaled $80,223. However, another

$76,100 was planned to be used to cover the travel expenses of volunteers serving on denominational disaster projects, bringing the total to $156,323 given by TURF during that year for those needs and expenses.

(2007 SB, p. 6)

In the 2008 SB, the money dispensed since last year's report to relieve individual and community disasters amounted to $46,551 with another $76,600 to be used to cover the travel expenses of volunteers serving on denominational disaster projects.

(2008 SB, p. 6)

TURF grants given to relieve individual and community disasters since June 2008, totaled $15,054. Another $70,000 will be used to cover the travel expenses of volunteers serving on denominational disaster projects. Since its beginning, TURF has contributed a total of $352,923 for these expenses.

(2009 SB, p. 28)

CHAPTER TWELVE

Saying "Thanks" in Many Ways

"You men are working here like busy little bees; we are so glad
you people came here to help us."
(Women in Louisiana – 1993 SB, p. 31)

"HELLO! WE ARE the family that resides at _____ Street in Wilson, NC. We are back in our home now, and words cannot express our deepest thanks for all you have done to our home. We are so pleased and happy with everything! Your kindness was appreciated very, very much. We will never forget this outreach of kindness from all of you. May the love of God always be with you all."

(Willie, Anna, Joseph and Jessica Knight. 2002 SB, p. 38)

Dear Friends,

On Oct. 16 and 17 seven wonderful men from Lancaster County, PA, appeared at my home to clear my yard which had been devastated by Hugo, a force 4 strength hurricane with 110 mph winds. These men spent countless and exhausting hours of time and energy sawing, hauling and clearing thirty-five or more uprooted or broken pine trees which were more than a hundred years

- 227 -

old. It was a wonderful feeling to know that there are people ready and eager to help out their fellowman in this way. They really exhibited the true Christian and American spirit. Four of these men are members of your parish (Conestoga Church of the Brethren). They are as follows:

Leo Snader					Landis C. Myer
Ben Landis					Allan C. Bewley

I am enclosing a small token of my appreciation in each man's honor to the church which he represents.

May God bless these wonderful caring men.
In Christ's love,
Betty Gibson
Sumter, SC
(Written October 25, 1989. 1990 SB, p. 27)

THE FRIENDS

They came from places far away
And labored tireless day after day
To make my home a better place
To live and share with humble grace.

I never shall forget the ones
Who painted, swept and fixed the floors
And climbed the roof to patch up some
Annoying holes that wet the floors.

The love that shone from every face
To show to all God's amazing grace
Will ever burn and live within
Because it shows the love of Him.

"Church of the Brethren" so aptly named,
For everyone that I have met
Are truly worthy to be so named
For no truer friend will I ever get.
(By Bernice Holmes, Bonifay, FL. Tropical storm Alberto survivor. 1995 SB, p. 38)

"God knew the best way to express His love to me, and He did it through you. It is a very special home built by so many loving hearts and hands. I thank God daily for bringing you all into my life and pray for your group, so that you each might feel the joy of peace and contentment in your lives and for continued prosperity in your mission. You bring glory to God through your servant heart. Thank you for giving of yourselves for the good of others. God bless you for all that you do."
(Ann Lang and her daughter, Eva, Poquoson, Va., recipients of the modular home built at the 2004 BDRA. 2005 SB, p. 44)

"I read recently about how a man had a change of heart after a flood had devastated his home area. He had been strongly opposed to a church being built near his house, but he relented when he saw truckloads of food and other supplies sent by Christians. He commented that seeing what believers do 'outside the walls' of the church building changed his mind."
(Sandra Lentz, 2000 SB, p. 28)

In 2004, a delegation of Nigerian government and church leaders visited the BDRA to express their appreciation to the Church of the Brethren for bringing the Gospel, digging wells, starting schools and giving medical aid to their country. They reported on the growing churches in Nigeria and brought a donation of their native handiwork to be sold to aid disaster victims wherever most needed in the world.

Some samples of the skilled and beautiful leather craftwork brought to the BDRA by our Nigerian brothers and sisters as a token of gratitude and their way of saying "thank you" to helping those in distress.

GOD HEARS THE PRAYERS OF THE NEEDY

In February 1999, the staff and I began to pray that God would enable us to give needed articles to our clients when they left the York Rescue Mission and Children's Shelter. Although Bob Henry had been bringing blankets to the Main Mission for the men for six years, by the time the blankets had trickled down to us, we never had enough to meet our needs. The first clear answer to our prayers came in the form of 150 blankets that Mr. Henry brought from the BDRA. Since that time, God has provided for our needs continuously through His people.

Mr. Henry, his wife, and another couple were able to see the shelter and pray with our staff. We were so excited to watch how God would supply our needs. Since that time, all our blanket needs have been supplied, and we rejoice together how God hears the cries of His people and uses each of us to fulfill His plan.

(Melinda Gorog. 2001 SB, p. 44)

In a July 7, 1994, letter of appreciation:

"Words are hard to find to give you the praise you deserve, but I will try to let you know how very much we appreciate what you did in building our new home. Had you not come forward and done the job, we would still have nothing. It is really nice to know there are people like you still around, willing to help someone who is less fortunate. People used to help each other when I was a young boy, but a lot of folks have kinda gotten away from that–too busy, not enough time, or something to that effect. May God bless you and smile down upon you as you go along your way. God has surely blessed us."

(William & Leona Covey, Orrick, MO. 1995 SB, p.6)

About five years ago a wedding was held in the home of some Amish neighbors of Landis and Audrey Myer from the Conestoga COB. The groom's grandmother, two uncles and their wives, all from Indiana, attended the wedding. During the time they were here in PA, they received word that their houses and barns had

What remained from an Amish home in Indiana after a tornado passed through.

been leveled by a tornado that struck the part of Indiana in which they lived.

Hoping it wasn't true, they hurried home as soon as they could, only to discover that the grandmother's house and both barns of the uncles were totally destroyed. The only things that were still intact were a motto with the words, "God Bless Our Home," painted on it and a glass jar containing an arrangement of artificial flowers. The motto had hung in the grandmother's kitchen but now it was dangling in a tree and the decorative floral-filled jar was wedged between some branches.

This event raised some questions. How did they get there? And unbroken? Were the words an ironic message from God?

Since this was a true disaster, their plight was brought to the attention of the TURF committee who decided that a significant contribution would be made to the family to help pay for the expense of rebuilding their house.

The Indiana grandmother, Sarah, (not her real name), was deeply appreciative and asked Landis and Audrey, "What can I do to show my gratitude for what these people did for us?"

It was suggested that perhaps she could make and donate a quilt to the BDRA. That next year she sent a quilt and said, "I don't know if it's good enough for you's, but if you don't want it, just send it back to me."

It turned out that it was more than "good enough." The Indiana Amish grandmother's quilt was sold twice, bringing a combined total of $6,000. Upon hearing that, she was so pleased that she made another quilt the following year, and that one sold for $975.

And the young married couple, Sarah's grandson and his wife, still live in Lancaster County and the groom's parents have hosted several BDRA Share-A-Meals.

David and Belinda Graybill received the following letter from the White House, written on December 19, 1989:

> *Dear Mr. and Mrs. Graybill:*
> *Thank you for sharing with me the results of the Atlantic Northeast District of the Church of the Brethren's 13th Disaster Relief Auction. I am heartened by your efforts to ease the suffering of disaster victims.*
> *Through your generosity and hard work, you have shown that the tradition of neighbor helping neighbor is alive and well in our country. Although we cannot prevent events like Hurricane Hugo and the San Francisco earthquake, there is much we can do to support the unfortunate victims of these tragedies.*
> *Your efforts serve as a shining example of the kind of humanitarian aid that people can rely on in their time of need. Barbara joins me in sending best wishes to you as you dedicate yourselves to helping others. God bless you.*
> *Sincerely,*
> *(Signed) George Bush*
> (1990 SB, p. 29)

"People who are kind, people who make time, people who share, people who care: There really is a God!"

(Bill Dochat. 1993 SB, p. 31)

"In communities devastated by mud slides, ice storms, flash floods, or tornadoes, volunteers have opened their hearts and homes to offer shelter, hot meals, building materials, and–most important–the hope and support that people desperately need to begin putting their lives back together. This spirit of citizen service has deep and strong roots in America's past, and by nurturing this spirit we can help to ensure a better future for our Nation."

(President Bill Clinton,
National Volunteer Week, 1998)

One elderly black man, whose home was markedly improved, smiled and said, "I feel like real people again."

(After a group from Lititz COB went to SC to rebuild following the destruction by Hurricane Hugo on Sept. 21, 1989. Quote is from the 1990 SB, p. 64)

An elderly couple, after flood waters rose to within six inches of their kitchen ceiling, stood in awe and disbelief as Brethren workers carried bucket after bucket of mud from their "life savings" house. Their only searching question was, "We don't even know you. Why would you do this for us?"

The seven-year-old boy who lives with his mother and sisters in a shanty at the edge of an Ethiopian village walks daily to the center of the village to stand in the once-a-day food line for rice and soup. Their hunger, helplessness and poverty is etched in their faces. "Who cares enough to provide this food for us?" is the grateful question asked in the recesses of their spirits. On the rice bags are three words:

"Church World Service." The COB in 1987 and early 1988 provided $87,500 worth of food and supplies to our needy African brothers and sisters in Ethiopia, Mozambique and Sudan."

(Earl K. Ziegler, ANE COB
District Executive. 1988 SB, p. 5)

"As the flood waters were coming up and as I struggled to move my furniture to higher places, plenty of our local people were driving back and forth with four-wheel drive equipment and with cameras, and they were gawking and looking around. But not one of these local people offered to give me any help. If you are ever in the area again, don't think of getting a motel–our home will be your hotel!"

(Resident of Lewiston, Maine, after the spring of 1987 flood there, commenting to the people who came from PA and MD to help. Quoted by James F. Myer, 1987 SB, p. 9)

"They say money can't buy love, and I guess that's true enough, but let me tell you, the supplies we received when we were hit the hardest had to come from love more than anything else. And there had to be contributions behind it all, money to get it done, from an awful lot of people we have never met. That's love. They brought us a truckload of supplies, and they brought us a whole lifetime of love."

(Geri Dean, after her mobile home in Albion, near Erie, PA, was devastated by a tornado and Arthur and Marion Boltz drove to Albion with a truckload

of supplies from the BDRA Fund and the Lebanon Food and Clothing Banks. 1987 SB, p. 6)

"I was recently informed by Federal Emergency Management Agency officials of the incredible work that your group accomplished during the recent Jones County, Miss., disaster. I understand that your child care program is exemplary and that your practical thoughtfulness and spiritual support have again alleviated much suffering.

Thank you for all of the people of Miss., and if I may ever be of assistance to you, please don't hesitate to let me know."

(Letter written by U.S. Senator Thad Cochran following the February 28, 1987, tornado in Jones County, MS, and quoted by Verna Forney in 1987 SB, p. 37)

"As a recipient of Disaster Relief from the COB volunteers, we want to extend our heartfelt thanks to each one who gave a part of themselves to help our family recover from Hurricane Andrew.

Without the reconstructing assistance from the COB volunteers from PA and surrounding states, we would probably still be renting, but it has a happy ending. We are HOME!"

(Bruce Saucier Family, Franklin, LA – 1993 SB, p. 31)

Someone recently asked, "With all the natural disasters, human tragedy, war and violence, what difference does the BDRA make?"

My reply was simple, "It makes a difference to each person who is a recipient of the aid given in the name of Jesus Christ!"

(Warren M. Eshbach, COB District Executive of the SOPA. 1996 SB, p. 16)

CHAPTER THIRTEEN

The Amounts Raised Each Year

"You may give gifts without caring – but you can't care without giving."
(Frank Clark in *Quotable Quotes*,
Reader's Digest Association, Inc., c1997, p. 41)

FROM ITS BEGINNINGS in the early 1970's when the youth raised $5,000 at an auction for disaster relief, the proceeds raised by the BDRA each year have grown steadily. The unanimous response from those who made it all happen is simply: "To God Be the Glory!" The total amount raised each year is listed here:

Year	Amount (US Dollars)	Year	Amount (US Dollars)
1977	$ 11,714	1987	$ 259,853
1978	$ 15,085	1988	$ 252,458
1979	$ 19,594	1989	$ 330,000
1980	$ 25,018	1990	$ 338,301
1981	$ 37,725	1991	$ 327,372
1982	$ 95,927	1992	$ 335,068
1983	$ 103,243	1993	$ 343,329
1984	$ 125,000	1994	$ 370,802
1985	$ 162,000	1995	$ 635,934 H
1986	$ 209,149	1996	$ 670,208 E

1997	$ 585,893 E
1998	$ 611,720
1999	$ 462,000
2000	$ 693,320
2001	$ 738,000
2002	$ 695,153
2003	$ 502,000
2004	$ 557,750
2005	$ 634,500
2006	$ 580,515
2007	$ 497,274
2008	$ 458,203

H = Includes House
E = Includes Part of Endowment Fund

In its first 31 years, the BDRA has raised over $11,500,000, which has been divided between the COB Emergency Fund (nationally and internationally) and TURF (needs within the two sponsoring districts).

CHAPTER FOURTEEN

Chronology & Summaries of Brethren Disaster Relief Auction Events

"I command you to be openhanded toward your brothers and toward the poor and needy in your land." Deuteronomy 15:11 (NIV)

A. The Brethren Disaster Relief Auction (BDRA)

1948, Feb. 7 – A public sale for World Relief sponsored by the COB Eastern District Men's Work Council was held at Root's Country Market near East Petersburg, PA
(Sale bill is printed in the 1987 sale booklet, p. 56)

1960s – Eastern District youth conducted an auction for charitable purposes. They raised $5,000 the first year, but abandoned the project after several years.

1977, Sept. 17 – First BDRA, sponsored by ANE District of the COB and held at the Lebanon County Fairgrounds. Attended by almost 2,000 persons, it netted over $11,700.

1979 – First apple dumplings made by Chiques COB women for BDRA – Total: 200

1982 – First Heifer Sale with 42 head selling for $42,565 (1997 SB,p. 28 says $46,565)

1984 – Motto: "To Bring Honor & Glory to God" was adopted

1984 – First Auction to be a two-day event

1985 – First Share-A-Meals (In 1987, they sold for $7.50 each).

1986 – Farmer's Market was added, selling fruit, vegetables, flowers and processed foods

1986 – Emergency Disaster Funds were shared with 17 areas outside the U.S. and 9 areas within the U.S. 1800 volunteers contributed 4500 work days to help to clean up in flood and disaster areas.

1987 – First Sale Booklet was printed.

1987 – "Silent auction" was begun for sales of cars, time shares, service and gift certificates.

1987 – NBC's Willard Scott and Bryant Gumbel sampled some delicious shoo-fly pie sent to them by organizers of the BDRA on their morning Today Show.

1988 – Winross Truck Auction was added.

1988 – "Hot Potato Bar" was available.

1988 – Alternative Gift-Giving Certificates could be purchased with a contribution.

1989, Sept. 22 – Hurricane Hugo strikes in South Carolina.

1989, Sept. 23 – Remnants of Hurricane Hugo hit Lebanon Fairgrounds and the 13th Annual BDRA.

1989 – Grow Money Fund was started by two businessmen who contributed $2,200 to fill 220 envelopes with $10 each.

1989 – (SOPA) Southern District of PA (45 churches) and Atlantic Northeast District (ANE) (67 churches) became sponsoring partners for the BDRA. 125 congregations were now participating.

1989 – First "I Gave One Hour to DRA in 1989" buttons, received by dropping one's earnings for one hour in a specified container.

1989 – "Hoops Day" was sponsored by the District Youth. All entrants got 20 shots at the basket. For each basket made, sponsors pledged an amount. All monies collected went to the BDRA.

1990 – First auction of baseball cards

1991 – First large format booklet (56 pages)

1992 – First house was started – on Fruitville Pike with Harold Diffenderfer as contractor

1992 – Golf-a-Thon began

1992 – First in series of "Collector's Pottery" – 200 one-quart "Fruits of the Spirit" pitchers made by Rockdale Union Stoneware in Edgerton, WI

1992 – Korean & Hispanic foods were offered.

1993, May – First Shenandoah District Disaster Auction (SDDA) was held at Harrisonburg, VA with 1500 attending.

1993, June 12 – First Fundraiser/Kick-Off Dinner (300 people) sponsored by Jay Witman and held annually for the next 5 years on the lawn of Jay's home near Manheim, PA.

1993 – First Winross Truck/Handcrafted Toy/ Art Combination Auction in East Hall

1994 – Endowment Fund is established by Mary Grace Martin with an initial donation of $13,000.

1994 – First special table for eight at the 1995 Fundraiser/Kick-Off Dinner was auctioned. It was to be served solely by Jay Witman.

1995, August 17 – The first BDRA Golf Tournament with 124 golfers on Par-Line golf course in Elizabethtown raised $4,771.

1995 – Disaster Relief Cookbook is published. Fifty copies were numbered, autographed and auctioned.

1995 – First house was completed along Fruitville Pike in Milton Estates at 1153 Suffolk Drive, Lititz, PA 17543. Selling Price: $240,000

1995 – Center Hall Auction was created due to volume of items donated to Main Auction.

1995 – Decision was made to hold the livestock sale Friday evening and move the Heifer sale to Friday noon.

1995 – An "Incredible Edible" was a 200 lb. cherry pie baked by Oehme Bakery of Lititz and sold by the slice along with a dip of vanilla ice cream. (They donated one again in 1996 and 1997.)

1996, May 2 – First Memorial Dinner was sponsored by the Wenger Foundation as a tribute to Renee A. Layser, deceased.

1996 – First Chicken Barbecue dinner was served by the Conestoga COB members at the Auction. They continued doing this annually for the next ten years.

1996 – Unknown man brought back empty pie plate with $20 attached.

1996 – "Noah's Ark" visited the BDRA: a petting zoo and pony rides by Paul Zimmerman's exotic animals

1997 – Sale of 2nd house – built by the SOPA District of COB at 104 Pleasant View Court, East Berlin, PA was sold for $146,500.

1997 – Built 3rd BDRA House in Pleasant View Estates, Manheim, PA, on land donated by Wilbur and Marion Brubaker. It sold for $179,000.

1997 – Basket-weaving demonstration. Baskets were signed and dated by an on-site weaver.

1997, Sept. 26 – Center Hall special session was held to auction contents of Mohler's Meeting House located between Harrisburg and Gettysburg along route 15.

Last service held there was Palm Sunday, 1996.

1998 – First pottery piece (basket-shaped) in new series by Eldreth Pottery, Oxford, PA

1999, April – Ground-breaking for the 4th BDRA house to be built at 1015 Huntington Lane, Elizabethtown

1999 – First theme baskets

1999 – First Longaberger basket (with a hand-painted lid) in the 6-year Generations Series was sold – a different sized basket each year.

2000, June 11 – First Kick-Off dinner to be held at Yoder's Restaurant in New Holland

2000, September 11 – Sale of BDRA House #4 on Huntington Lane, Elizabethtown

2002, Sunday, Sept 29 – First BDRA Hymn Sing, "An Evening with a Treasury of Great Hymns," Lebanon Area Fairground

2004, March 27 – First FAITH dinner was held at York First COB and sponsored by SOPA District.

2004 – First time a modular home was built on the Expo grounds during the Auction. Planning Committee: Elvin Wagner, Marty Witman, Bob Wolgemuth

2004 – First time for Obie the Clown, Larry the Clown, Train Rides, Children's store, Face Painting and Free Child Care

2004 – ANE and SOPA Celebration Tent highlighting ministries within the Districts

2004, Sept. 26 – "Sing To the Lord": The Second Evening with "A Treasury of Great Hymns" with a 400-voice choir – at Lebanon Area Fairgrounds

2005 – First Children's Auction for ages 5 to 12

2005 – Alabaster Gift Sale for specialty (beyond the ordinary) items

2005 – 30,000 Health Kits were assembled at the Auction.

2005 – Second modular home (1,300 sq. ft.) was built at the Lebanon Fairgrounds.

2005, Nov. 13 – Concert for the BDRA was held by the Craig Smith family at the Hempfield COB.

2006 – In honor of the BDRA's 30th Anniversary, attendees could buy one piece of the 30th Anniversary cake and one dip of ice cream for $2.50.

2006 – A 3-bedroom modular home (1,312 sq. ft.) was built on auction grounds in four days.

2006, Sept. 24 – "An evening with a Treasury of Great Hymns" celebrating the 30th Anniversary of the BDRA – at Lebanon Fairgrounds

2007, July 28 – BDRA Golf Tournament at Cool Creek Golf Club, Wrightsville, PA- Cost: $75

2007 – First pieces in Rowe Pottery Series offered for sale

2007 – New this year: Amish-made pretzels and donuts

2007 – First time to have 12 uniquely designed BDRA folding chairs for sale on the front row

2007 – 12,000 school kits were assembled at the BDRA Gift of the Heart Kit Assembly by over 200 volunteers.

2007 – Auction of "special" meals: "Tina's Secret Garden," "Poolside Brunch," and a Progressive Dinner via limousine

2007, Sept. 29 – Endowment Dinner – Under the tent at Jay Witman's home, 657 Fruit-

Jo Anne Boyer and the cake she made to celebrate the 30th Anniversary of the BDRA in 2006. It was sold by the piece along with a dip of ice cream for $2.50.

ville Pike, Manheim, PA. Cost: $25. (Jay hosted this one-time event in memory of his mother, Anna Mary Witman, who died March 15, 2006. All proceeds went to the Endowment Fund of the BDRA.)

2008 – Tenth Anniversary of Theme Baskets at the BDRA. In first 9 years, over 1,400 gift baskets had been donated, raising over $128,000.

2008 – First appeal for jars and/or bags of loose change. Change was also collected at the Auction from those attending.

2008 – Fourteen BDRA front row folding chairs were offered for sale

2008 – First Coin Auction

2008 – First time that the Baked Goods and Produce Stands closed at 3:30 p.m. and any remaining items were donated to local charitable organizations.

2008 – "Special Meal" Auction with hosts

Randy & Tina Weaver offering a 7-course meal in "Tina's Secret Garden;" Main Hall Auction Committee serving a dinner at the home of Earl & Charlene Fahnestock; York First COB sponsoring a Progressive Dinner visiting 3 homes

2008, October 19 – "An Afternoon of Favorite Hymns," was held at the Sight & Sound Millennium Theatre, Strasburg. Featured were a 300 member choir with orchestra and Myron Augsburger as speaker.

2009, June 7 – Death of Jay Witman, one of the Auction originators, and its main leader and motivator since the beginning

2009, August 7 – Northeast Golf Tournament/ Mechanic Grove Golf Tournament held at the Tanglewood Manor Golf Club, Quarryville. Cost: $65 pp. Raised $12,500.

2009, September – Publication of the book, *The Story of an Auction—For the Glory of God*, the history and stories of the BDRA for the first 32 years, with Vivian S. Ziegler as author and compiler

2009 - magazine-style SB with 120 pp. and some pages in color.

❖ ❖ ❖

B. The Fundraising/ Kickoff Dinners

1993, June 12 – First Fundraiser/Kick-Off Dinner sponsored by Jay Witman and held annually for the next 5 years on the lawn of Jay's home near Manheim, PA. Entertainment: Bob & Libby Kettering, Jeryl Metzler. Guests: 300. Amount raised: $5,700

1994, June 11 – Second Fundraiser/Kick-Off Dinner. Cost: $5 pp. Entertainment: Bob & Libby Kettering. Guests: 400. Amount raised: $9,800

1994, September – Tickets for the first "special table" for eight for the 1995 Fundraiser/ Kick-Off Dinner were auctioned. Those at that table were to be served solely by Jay Witman.

1995, June 10 – Third Fundraiser/Kick-Off Dinner. Jay Witman was hospitalized, so Laura Stoltzfus and Nancy Wenger served the special table of eight in Jay's absence. Entertainment: Joe Detrick family. Cost: $5 pp. Guests: 510. Amount raised: $15,952

1996, June 8 – Fourth Fundraiser/Kick-Off Dinner. Entertainment: "Sounds of Brass". Cost: $10 pp. Guests: 540. Amount raised: $16,400

1997, June 14 – Fifth Fundraiser/Kick-Off Dinner under the big tent. Entertainment: "Conestoga Four." Cost: $10 pp. Guests: 500. Amount raised: $20,000

1998, June 13 – Sixth Fundraiser/Kick-Off Dinner was moved to the Hempfield COB due to an approaching storm. Still had the "special" table. Entertainment: The Conestoga Valley Middle School trumpeters (Barrett Clark, Gene Clark, and Jonathan Groff) and the Midway COB Men's Chorus directed by Arlene Keller. Guests: 625. Amount raised: $20,000

1999, June 12 – Seventh Fundraiser/Kick-Off Dinner was held at Hempfield COB. Entertainment: Men's Chorus from Midway COB, directed by Bob Kettering (in the absence of Arlene Keller) Jay Witman was absent due to health reasons and the special table was served by Lloyd Groff, Helen Groff, and Candy Myer. Cost: $12 pp. Guests: 450. Amount raised: $16,000

2000, June 10 – First time the Fundraiser/Kick-Off Dinner was held at Yoder's Restaurant in New Holland. Cost: $12 pp. Entertainment: Joel and La Breeska Hemphill. Guests: 425

2001, June 9 – Kick-Off Dinner at Yoder's. Cost: $14 pp. Entertainment: The Kevin Spencer. Guests: 495

2002, June 8 – Kick-Off Dinner at Yoder's. Cost: $15 pp. Entertainment: Jeff & Sheri Easter. Guests: 400

2003, June 28 – Kick-Off Dinner at Yoder's. Cost: $15 pp. Entertainment: Palmetto State Quartet. Guests: 490

2004, June 12 – Kick-Off Dinner at Yoder's. Cost: $15 pp. Entertainment: The Hoppers. Guests: 792. Amount raised: $47,463 (One donor underwrote the cost of the dinner.)

2005, June 11 – Kick-Off Dinner at Yoder's. Cost: $18 pp. Entertainment: The Crabb Family. Guests: 624. Amount raised: $28,159

2006, June 10 – Kick-Off Dinner at Yoder's. Cost: $20 pp. Entertainment: The Hoppers. Guests: 675. Amount raised: $34,189

2007, June 9 – Kick-Off Dinner at Yoder's. Cost: $25 pp. Entertainment: Nielson and Young, duo-pianists. Guests: 435. Amount raised: $22,892

2008, June 14 – Kick-Off Dinner at Yoder's. Cost: $25 pp. Entertainment: Mercy's Mark. Guests: 460. Amount raised: $18,652

2009, June 13 – Kick-Off Dinner at Yoder's. Cost: $25 pp. Entertainment: Collingsworth Family. Guests: 432. Amount raised: $20,474

2010, June 12 – Kick-Off Dinner at Yoder's. Cost: $25pp. Entertainment: The Whisnants.

C. The Praise Dinners

1996, May 2 – First Memorial Dinner sponsored by the Wenger Foundation as a tribute to Renee A. Layser, deceased. Guests: 780. Total funds raised for the BDRA: $110,000

1997, April 24 – Second BDRA Dinner (now known as PRAISE dinner) attended by 450 people @ $100 each. Speaker: David Ring and Southern Gospel music by The Canaanland Boys. Co-sponsored by the Wenger Foundation, Mel & Gloria Burkholder, and Donald & Frances Layser. Total raised: $45,000.

1998, May 14 – Third PRAISE dinner. Guests: 320. Entertainment: Southern Gospel groups, "Common Bond" and The Canaanland Boys. Co-sponsored by the Wenger Foundation, Donald & Frances Layser, and Jay N. Crouse, excavating. Amount raised: $31,878 to be divided between the BDRA ($19,076) and the Lebanon Valley Youth for Christ

1999, April 23 – Fourth Annual PRAISE dinner. Guests: 440. Entertainment: Glenn Faus, humorist and executive director of COBYS. Amount raised: $56,231. BDRA received $14,024

2000, April 20 – Fifth Annual PRAISE dinner. Guests: 525. Entertainment: The Trio – Kirk Talley, Ivan Parker, Anthony Burger. Amount Raised: $52,658. BDRA received $16,248.

2001, April 19 – 6th Annual PRAISE dinner. Guests: 660. Entertainment: Ken Davis, Christian comedian, and "Sanctuary," Southern Gospel quartet. Amount raised: $65,752. BDRA received $12,437.

2002, April 18 – 7th Annual PRAISE dinner. Guests: 680. Entertainment by the Nashville Gospel Brass. Amount raised: $70,068. BDRA received $13,477.

2003, April 17 – 8th Annual PRAISE dinner. Guests: 500. Amount raised: $55,510.

From 2003 through 2008, the amount raised at each of the PRAISE dinners was divided between the following four charities: COBYS Family Services, Evangelical School of Theology, Friendship Community, and On Fire Youth Ministry.

2004 – 9th Annual PRAISE dinner. Guests: 630. Amount raised: $71,160.

2005 – 10th Annual PRAISE dinner. Guests: 800. Amount raised: $87,170.

2006 – 11th Annual PRAISE dinner. Guests: 840. Amount raised: $92,415.

2007 – 12th Annual PRAISE dinner. Guests: 775. Amount raised: $87,680.

2008 – 13th Annual PRAISE dinner. Guests: 700. Amount raised: $76,535.

From 1996 through 2008, the 13 PRAISE dinners raised a total of $902,057 and from that amount contributed $230,262 to the BDRA.

Praise Dinner 2010 will be held Thursday, April 29, at the Lebanon Expo Center. Cost: $100 pp. Entertainment: The Allen Family.

D. The Faith Dinners

2004, March 27 – First FAITH Dinner sponsored by SOPA District was held at York First COB. Cost: $7.50. Guests: 292. Program: The Philip Nell Family, High Rock Gospel Grass, and Sisters of the Moonlight. Amount raised for the BDRA: $4,700. Planning Committee: Sally and Bob Bingaman, Ruth and Bob Henry, and Irene and Elvin Molison.

2005 – Second FAITH Dinner held at York First COB. Amount raised: $6,823

2006, April 1 – Third FAITH Dinner was held at York First COB, sponsored by the York First congregation. Guests: 350. Entertainment: The Miracles Quintet. Amount raised for the BDRA: $10,000.

2007 – No FAITH Dinner was held this year.

2008, March 29 – Fourth FAITH Dinner held at York First COB, sponsored by four SOPA churches: West York COB, Madison Ave. COB, Black Rock COB, and York First COB. Guests: 225. Entertainment: Victoria Smith. Amount raised for the BDRA: $6,500.

2009, April 25 – Fifth annual FAITH dinner held at the New Fairview COB. Guests: $275. Entertainment: Sandy Heisey (Florin COB). Amount raised for the BDRA: $10, 679.

❖ ❖ ❖

E. The Quilt Auctions

(Records for the years not listed were not found by the compiler.)

1984 – 72 quilts. Highest-selling quilt ($925) was made by Lititz COB

1986 – Highest price ($7,000) for Lizzie Longenecker's quilt

1987 – 105 quilts. Highest price ($5,500) for never-used *Long Star* quilt donated by Anna Lutz, Lititz, and a close second was a Lizzie Longenecker quilt which sold for $5,000.

1988 – Highest price ($10,600) for a quilt made by Lizzie Longenecker, White Oak COB centenarian.

1990 – 118 quilts. Top price ($6,300) was paid for 101-year-old Lizzie Longenecker's *Trip Around the World* quilt. Next highest was $3,100 for a *Mariner's Compass* quilt.

1993 – 130 quilts and wall hangings

1999 – $53,900. Highest-selling quilt ($2,100) was a *Rose of Sharon* quilt made by Florin COB quilters. Highest wall hanging was *A Summer Garden* for $2,400.

2004 – $39,750
2005 – $42,725
2006 – $36,150
2007 – $37,425
2008 – $43,905

F. The Heifer/Livestock Auctions

Amounts listed are the net proceeds. Records for the years not listed could not be found by the compiler.

1982 – First Heifer Sale with 42 head selling for $46,565

1984 – Total: $45,000 (35 heifers)

1986 – Total: $67,465 (75 heifers)

1987 – Total: $84,700 (85 animals)

1988 – Total: $70,000

1989 – Heifer sale made over $82,000 (Included two llamas)

1990 – Total: $88,602 (70 heifers)

1993 – Total: $73,000

1994 – Total: $68,000

1995 – Decision was made to hold the livestock sale Friday evening and move the Heifer Sale to Friday noon. Net proceeds from both sales totaled $85,597

1996 – Total: over $70,000

1999 – Total: $82,620 (64 animals)

2004 – Total: $105,715

2005 – Total: $113,761

2006 – Total: $70,763

2007 – Total: $110,982

2008 – Total: $91,117 (60 head)

(Note: The Heifer Sale Committee retains a portion [around $10,000] each year as seed money to buy young heifers to feed for the next year's sale.)

❖ ❖ ❖

G. The Shenandoah District Disaster Auction (SDDA)

Net Proceeds from the First Sixteen Years of the Shenandoah District Disaster Auction

1993 – $124,096.46
1994 – $111,149.11
1995 – $111,139.16
1996 – $115,654.17
1997 – $151,288.29
1998 – $139,110.29
1999 – $138,827.31
2000 – $149,623.78
2001 – $180,150.04
2002 – $181,102.42
2003 – $188,927.85
2004 – $196,725.21
2005 – $215,013.25
2006 – $210,710.08
2007 – $215,748.09
2008 – $205,281.05

(2009 SDDA SB, p. 52)

At the SDDA in Harrisonburg, VA, on May 15-16, 2009:

1348 tickets were sold for the Friday evening oyster/ham dinner
90 gallons of oysters were fried and eaten
193 pancakes and 333 omelets were eaten on Saturday morning
290 lunch tickets were sold for Saturday lunch
26 units of blood were given
$190,000 was raised

(SDDA Website)

The motto giving inspiration and motivation to the SDDA.

CHAPTER FIFTEEN

Acknowledgements

"Our Father, Thou hast given so much to us. Give us but two things more:
a grateful heart and a warm, helping hand." Unknown

J UST AS HAVING a successful BDRA each year involves many persons, writing this book was also a group effort. My role was multifaceted: compiling, collecting stories and statements from all the sale booklets since 1987, conducting numerous personal interviews, gleaning facts from completed information questionnaires, and then using all that information in writing stories related to the Auction.

Although Jay Witman, a major source of information, cooperated fully with me as long as he was physically able, it became impossible for him to share the many wonderful stories and insights which are now forever lost. However, I am grateful for all he was able to contribute, and for his willingness to allow me to see a facet of his character which I had not realized–how he loved Jesus and sought to serve Him. Our interviews began with prayer and I could feel God's presence as I recorded Jay's faltering words.

He was not a perfect person, as he readily admitted, and he had his personality quirks as we all do, but Jay's perseverance in following his goal of giving glory to God and helping those facing disasters was an inspiration to many. His physical difficulties along the way reminded many of these verses in 2 Corinthians 4:8-10:

"We are pressed on every side by troubles, but not crushed and broken. We are perplexed because we don't know why things happen as they do, but we don't give up and quit. We are hunted down, but God never abandons us. We get knocked down, but we get up again and keep on going. These bodies of ours are constantly facing death just as Jesus did; so it is clear to all that it is only the living Christ within who keeps us safe." (TLB)

Thank you to the following persons for lending me their copies of SBs printed through the years: Landis and Audrey Myer, Belinda Graybill, and Jay Witman. They were my major information source, although some writers whom I quoted may note that I condensed, rewrote, and at times simply used a sentence here and there from their articles. I'm hoping that some who open this book and see their SB article, poem or story in print again will be happily surprised that it has taken on a new life, and can once more be a challenge to fresh readers.

Thank you to all those who took the time to meet with me for personal interviews and/or returned the completed information sheets. Although we requested information and stories from anyone at various times, the response was very sparse. I discovered that one factor causing this is that many people, who have been active in making the BDRA a success, are very humble and prefer working anonymously. This attitude is commendable, but it also made the collection of these stories difficult. I kept hearing: "I didn't do that much; many others did more than I did." Or they would say, "We didn't keep a record of that; we just gave."

Thank you to the BDRA Board of Direc-

tors who commissioned me to take on this task. Although it seemed overwhelming at first, and I knew that it was beyond my own strength and ability, I was encouraged by their faith in me. The Apostle Paul's declaration in Philippians 4:13 was also a motivation for me: *"I can do all things through Christ which strengtheneth me." (KJV)* This printed book in your hands is a silent witness once again to answered prayer and the fact that *"with God, nothing shall be impossible." (KJV)*

Thank you to John Minnich, the photographer at the BDRA who provided many of the photos in this book—at no charge. Since Jay Witman spent much time in the Minnich home as he was growing up, John and Jay were almost like brothers, so each understood how the other thought. The pictures themselves speak of John's excellence as a photographer, having the gift and ability to be at the right place at the right time.

A big thank you to David Farmer who took time from his own busy writing agenda to proofread this work and suggest necessary corrections and improvements. I have appreciated his willingness to share his knowledge of the English language and felt privileged to receive his input.

Finally, thank you to my husband, Earl K. Ziegler, who encouraged me in this project by being a proofreader and critic, making phone calls, preparing meals, and enduring long hours alone while I was busy working. His support and sharing meant more than I can put in words.

Vivian S. Ziegler
Author and Compiler
September, 2009

CHAPTER SIXTEEN

Directions to the Brethren Disaster Relief Auction (BDRA)

at the Lebanon Area Fairgrounds
Cornwall & Evergreen Roads
Lebanon, PA 17042

From Route I-81:
- ➢ Exit 30/Lebanon
- ➢ Travel east (south) on Route 72
- ➢ Go through the City of Lebanon
- ➢ Turn left @ Sheetz (Rocherty Road)
- ➢ Go 1/3 mile east on Rocherty Road
- ➢ Fairgrounds are on right side of road by intersection of Rocherty and Cornwall Roads

From the Turnpike I-76:
- ➢ Exit 20/Cornwall
- ➢ Travel west (north) on Route 72
- ➢ Turn right @ Sheetz (Rocherty Road)
- ➢ Go 1/3 mile east on Rocherty Road
- ➢ Fairgrounds are on right side of road by intersection of Rocherty and Cornwall Roads

From Route 422:

➢ Turn east (south) onto Route 72

➢ Turn left onto Rocherty Road

➢ Go 1/3 mile east on Rocherty Road

➢ Fairgrounds are on right side of road by intersection of Rocherty and Cornwall Roads

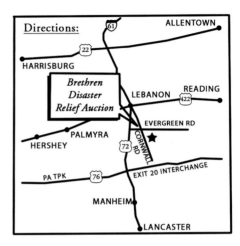

Addendum

O<small>N</small> J<small>UNE</small> 7, 2009, the BDRA lost the visionary motivator, Jay M. Witman, who helped get it started, kept it going and inspired us all to do bigger and better things "to the glory of God." In private conversations, when he referred to the Auction, he emphasized, "It's not about me. It's about Jesus." He would wave his arm toward the priceless collection of one-of-a-kind articles he had accumulated after a lifetime of auctioneering and say, "This is just junk. What *really* matters is serving Jesus and helping others."

No one was surprised to hear of his death. Everyone who knew him realized that he had been plagued by physical illnesses for the last forty years. It seemed he went to the hospital more often than the normal person goes to a dentist! Many observed that by sheer perseverance, courage, and his strong faith, he appeared to surpass the nine lives usually attributed to a cat! Death seemed to beckon him many times, but he stubbornly refused to succumb.

Several weeks before he died, his nephew, Clarke and his wife, Sarah, visited Jay in the hospital and found him sleeping in his room. Not wanting to waken him, they left and came back several hours later. This time, to their surprise, he was walking laps around the hospital halls! Clarke complimented him and said he was pleased that he appeared to be a bit stronger and added, "It will be good to get you back home again."

Jay responded, "If I get there, that'll be fine, and if I don't, that's cool, too. I am ready to go "home."

Clarke observed, "His peace in facing death was comforting to all those who were close to him, to all those who loved him."

Only Jay could accomplish putting bookends on either side of the BDRA Kickoff Dinner, regularly scheduled for the second weekend in June, which this year was June 13th. Jay passed away on June 7th, the Sunday before the Kickoff Dinner, and his Memorial Service was held the day after the Kickoff Dinner, on Sunday afternoon, June 14th.

At his Memorial Service, held in the White Oak COB, one of the ministers, J. Marvin Shenk, read from Psalm 1, Ecclesiastes 7:1-4, John 14, and Psalm 90:12. Commenting on the way that Jay, the son of Amos B. and Anna Mary Johns Witman, from a young age, seemed raring to take on the world, Rev. Shenk observed that he enjoyed doing things with a flare.

At the age of ten, he accepted Jesus Christ as his Lord and Savior and was baptized on May 5, 1963. As a young boy, he already had a deep desire to help mankind. Hoping to become an overseas missionary, he had that dream shattered by his many health issues. Following his father's death when Jay was a teenager, he spent much time with and was influenced greatly by the Earl and Marian Minnich family who played a great part in shaping him into the person he would become.

In the fall of 1970, he graduated at the top of his class from the Reppert School of Auctioneering in IN. After graduating from Manheim Central High School in 1971, he studied at the Stevens Trade School in Lancaster, majoring in real estate appraising and graduating in 1976.

His career in auctioneering began in 1971 with Wilbur H. Hosler and by 1973, he was cofounder of the Hat and Gavel Auction Co. in Lititz. After being a partner in the J. Omar Landis Auction Service, Ephrata, Jay became the founder and owner of Witman Auctioneers, Inc. and Tents for You, both in Manheim. He sold for several automobile auctions in MD, NJ, Ephrata and Lancaster, conducted many public sales and called for many charitable auctions from Boston to Miami. Most notable was the Atlantic Northeast District COB Disaster Relief Auction he cofounded 32 years ago in 1977.

Seventeen years later, he assisted the Shenandoah District in Harrisonburg, VA, in establishing a similar disaster auction.

Among antique dealers and his colleagues in the auctioneering business, Jay was recognized and respected as a person who spoke bluntly, to the point, and "told it like it is." He was opinionated and left no uncertainty about where he stood on issues. Although not everyone agreed with the way he said and did things, he was respected as being honest and forthright. A former employee of ten years confirmed, "Jay always treated me like a person."

A member of the White Oak COB, Jay was instrumental in organizing the Manheim Prayer Breakfast and was an active supporter of Gideons International, Hope International and other charities. In addition, he served as a Northeast Advisory Board Member for the former Lititz Springs Commonwealth National Bank, a member and presiding president of the Manheim Historical Society, and a past member of both the Lancaster and Manheim Chambers of Commerce. As a former member of the Rotary Club of Manheim, he conducted many Rotary International auctions through the years and was a Rotary Paul Harris Fellow. Because of his own physical problems, he became a member of the Crohn's and Colitis Foundation of America.

Jay liked things done well. His spotless white suit exemplified that. Through his leadership, the reputation of the BDRA changed from handling used, flea-market, ordinary items to selling quality, first-class, top-of-the-line items. He hated eating from paper plates, and there is a story that sometimes around the Minnich family table, everyone but Jay ate from paper plates. Jay used china!

In addition to collecting antiques, he enjoyed cooking and took pleasure in maintaining a weed-free flower garden. His nephew, Clarke, shared that he was often allotted the job of mowing Jay's lawn and that Jay had very definite ideas about the edges of the lawn being perfectly straight. Just a short time before his death, Jay returned home from one of his many hospital stays and that same afternoon was pulling weeds at his house!

He is survived by three brothers, Clair E., husband of Bonnie Witman of Pine Grove, PA; Dale A., husband of Pamela Witman of North Waterboro, ME; and Luke R., husband of Cristel Witman of Manheim, PA; and a sister, Lois F., wife of Dale Hernley of Elizabethtown, PA.

With the same zeal with which he lived his life, Jay prepared to meet his God. His favorite hymns, *Jesus Loves Me* and *Just As I Am*, both expressed his amazement and humility in the realization that Jesus truly loved him. Almost as a response to that, another favorite hymn was *How Great Thou Art*, and this was often the number he requested all the BDRA attendees in the Main Hall to stand and sing around noontime on Saturdays.

At his Memorial Service, Jim Myer read from Psalm 112, which has often been referred to as a word portrait of a righteous man comparable to Proverbs 31's description of an ideal woman. In the NIV we read:

> *"Wealth and riches are in his house, and his righteousness endures forever. Even in darkness light dawns for the upright, for the gracious and compassionate and righteous man. Good will come to him who is generous and lends freely, who conducts his affairs with justice. Surely he will never be shaken; a righteous man will be remembered forever.*
>
> (Psalms 112:3-6)

Although the accumulation of wealth and articles of value motivated Jay in his early business career, as he grew older, endured physical

suffering and grew closer to his Lord, his values changed. In his later years, he set an example of giving and encouraged others to increase their capacity to share and to give.

Because of that change, Jim Myer also spoke on 2 Corinthians 9. From this chapter, he zeroed in on verse 7b, *God loves a cheerful giver,* and emphasized three points:

1. A cheerful giver plans ahead – verses 1-2
2. A cheerful giver thinks big – verses 5-6
3. A cheerful giver knows he can't outgive God – verses 10-11

He concluded by saying that generosity, giving cheerfully, leads us to thanksgiving as described in verses 11 and 15, and shared that some of Jay's last words were, "God is so good!"

Although the writing of this book was commissioned more than a year ago, Jay had shared confidentially with Duane Ness at that time that he didn't want this book to be printed until the final chapter of Jay Witman had been written. He had sensed that the end was not far away long before others truly sensed that his health was failing for the last time.

In his last weeks, realizing that the end was near, Jay instructed Duane Ness on his thoughts and goals for the auction, and his dreams and intentions for the September, 2009, BDRA. In addition, several craftspersons are preparing special handmade selections of their work in Jay's memory to be auctioned for disaster relief.

Since Luke had been his business partner for 29 years and his biological brother, many professional, community and church friends have offered their condolences to him.

While they didn't always agree, in Jay's death, Luke says he has lost a "mentor, business colleague, counselor, brother, and a very dear friend." Although appreciative for each expression of comfort, Luke has pondered: "Why do we wait until a person has died to let them know how much we appreciate them?"

During the dinner following the Memorial service, Clarke Witman shared that during Jay's last few weeks, he noted a definite change in him: He went from a perfectionist, who fussed about keeping the edges of his gardens and lawns straight to a "man who's seen Jesus."

Today he is pain-free and with the Lord he loved.

Index

Buffenmyer, Jay, 158
Burger, Anthony, 243
Burke, Edmund, 17
Burke, Edward, 211
Burkhart, Gloria, 106
Burkholder, Gloria, 122, 173-174, 242
Burkholder, Mel, 70, 173, 174, 242
Burkholder, Melvin S., 71, 122
Bush, Barbara, 208
Bush, George W., President, 42, 231, 214
Byler, Betty Sue, 59

- C -

Campanella, Kathleen, 207
Canaanland Boys, 242
Carter, Jimmy, President, 215
Carter, Velma, 41
Cascioli, Lucy, 135
Cassel, Amos, 89
Cassel, Charles D., Elder, 89
Cassel, Keri, 61
Cassel, Miriam, 89
Castro, Fidel, 128
Chinworth, Jim, 37
Chronister, Keith, 58
Clark, Barrett, 241
Clark, Frank, 235
Clark, Gene, 241
Cleaver, Harry J., 217
Cleaver, Jim, 217
Cleveland, Grover, 41, 139
Clinton, Bill, President, 232
Cochran, Thad, U. S. Senator, 233
Collingsworth Family, 242
Common Bond, 242
Copenhaver, Rachel, 138
Copenhaver, Ron, 92
Copenhaver, Verna, 138
Copenhaver, Wendy, 92
Covey, Leona, 230
Covey, William, 230

Cox, Grace, 97
Crabb Family, 242
Crawford, Deanna, 109, 200, 215, 219
Cronkite, Walter, 161
Crosby, Fanny J., 1, 201
Crouse, Jay N., 242
Cryan, Robert, 84
Custer, Jan, 8

- D -

Dagen, Miriam, 95
Davis, Ken, 243
de Perrot, Steve, 44
Dean, Geri, 232
Detrick, Ben, 117-118
Detrick, Joe, 14, 70, 241
Detrick, Venona Bomberger, 118
Dibert, Don, 79-81
Dibert, Doris, 79, 81
Dibert, Kevin, 216
Diehl, David, 117-118
Diehl, Thomas, 117
Diffenbach, Allen, 58
Diffenderfer, Harold W., 69-71, 238
Diffenderfer, Nancy, 189
Diller, Ann, 115, 125-126
Diller, Carl, 58
Dochat, Bill, 231
Dravecky, Dave, 69
Duble, Lois, 204
Durnbaugh, Donald F., 30

- E -

Earhart, Stanley, 127
Easter, Jeff, 242
Easter, Sheri, 242
Ebersol, Isaiah, 144
Ebersol, L. B., 158
Ebersol, Linda, 144
Ebersole, Doug, 58

Ebersole, Nelson, 58
Eckert, Harold, 210
Edwards, Karen, 18
Eldreth, David, 75
Erwin, Nancy, 129, 131
Eshbach, Theresa, 112
Eshbach, Warren M., 112, 209-220, 233
Eshelman, Effie, 126, 127, 128
Eshelman, Glenn, 218
Eshelman, Jim, 126, 127
Eshelman, Shirley, 218

- F -

Fahnestock, Carol, 146
Fahnestock, Charlene, 67, 77, 178, 241
Fahnestock, Earl, 178, 241
Fahnestock, Fern, 142
Fahnestock, Linda, 62
Fahnestock, Nancy, 142
Fahnestock, Verda, 81
Farmer, Carol, 73, 178-179
Farmer, Dave, 178, 179
Farmer, David, 248
Faus, Glenn, 221, 242
Faus, Sheryl, 221
Fields, Ann, 50
Fitzkee, Carolyn, 199
Fitzkee, Don, 62-63, 145
Fogelsanger, Doris, 114
Foltz, C. Ned, 44, 75, 81
Foltz, Gwen, 44, 81
Ford, Henry, 40
Ford, Tom, 117, 200
Forney, Verna, 233
Forry, Charles M., 192, 193
Forry, Virginia, 193
Foster, Betty, 210
Foster, Earl, Pastor, 213
Frantz, Michael, 43
Fuchs, Becky, 113
Fuller, Millard, 215
Fyock, Joan, 199

Hollingshead, Larry, 101-102
Holmes, Bernice, 228
Holsinger, George, 201
Holsinger, Janice Longenecker, 64-65, 195
Holsinger, John, 65, 195
Hoover, Alan R., 158
Hoover, Barbara, 59
Hoover, William, 59
Hope, Ruth-Anna, 49-50
Hopkins, Evan H., 208
Hoppers, The, 242
Horst, C. B., 92-94
Horst, Doris, 96-97
Horst, Harold, 98-99, 106
Horst, Miriam, 98-99, 106
Hosler, Bonnie, 63
Hosler, Ken, 63
Hosler, Wilbur H., 59, 252
Hostetter, Randy, 148
Huffaker, Perry, 199
Huffman, Nelson R., 193
Hufford, Scott, 159

- J -

Jackson, Andrew, 133
Jacobs, Ina R., 125
Jenkins, Dave, 59, 177
Jenkins, Jesse O., 177
Jenkins, June, 177
Jenkins, Thelma, 177
Joanou, Grace, 87, 139
Johns, Susanna, 139
Johnson, Bruce, 50
Johnstone, Mary Ann, 165

- K -

Kauffman, Elizabeth, 109
Kautz, Gregg, 69
Kautz, Mary Lynn, 68-69
Keener, Anna M. Gantz, 92, 110
Keener, Barbara, 110
Keener, Clarence, 93

Keener, Clarence A., 92, 110
Keener, Clarence, Jr., 92
Keener, Clarence L., 110
Keener, Clarence, Sr., 109
Keener, Nancy, 110
Keener, Ruth Arnold, 110
Keener, Thelma Haldeman, 110
Keeney, Del, 106
Keeny, Kenneth, 59
Keeny, Shane, 215
Kegerreis, Ed, 92
Keller, Amy, 179, 180
Keller, Arlene, 117, 241
Keller, Arlene S., 199
Keller, Chris, 179, 180
Keller, Cindy, 199
Keller, Cody, 179
Keller, Dan, 199
Keller, David, 124
Keller, Jane, 199
Keller, Kirby K., 153-154
Keller, Mikaila, 179
Keller, Norman, 199
Keller, Sue, 3, 32, 169, 170, 171, 172
Keller, Thom, 3, 32, 169, 170, 171, 199
Kensinger, Janice L., 27
Kettering, Bob, 117-118, 201, 241
Kettering, Harold, 107
Kettering, Henry, 111
Kettering, Joe W., 24
Kettering, Libby, 118, 241
Kettering, Maybelle, 111
Kettering, Robert D., 4, 13
Kettering, Robert K., 5, 117-118
King, Bernard N., 149
King, Fern, 92-93, 95-96
King, H. F., 24
King, Henry, 110
Kirst, Mildred, 145
Kitchen, Otis, 194
Klein, Edward, 208
Kleinfelter, Randy, 116

Kleinfelter, Stanley, 116
Kleinfelter, Whitey, 116
Kline, Carole, 132, 133
Kline, Connie, 127
Kline, David, 43, 124, 132-133
Kline, John, 35, 107
Kline, Patrick, 43, 132, 133
Kline, Randal V., 25, 59
Kline, Thelma, 96
Kline, Verna, 97, 100
Kneasel, Alvena, 180, 181
Kneasel, Lee, 180, 181
Knight, Anna, 227
Knight, Jessica, 227
Knight, Joseph, 227
Knight, Willie, 227
Kniss, John N., 86
Kniss, Ruth, 86-87
Koppenhaver, Greta Layser, 120
Koppenhaver, Michael, 120
Koser, Dave, 65
Kover, Floy, 138
Krall, Ethel, 135, 136
Krall, Leroy, 135, 136
Kreider, Betty, 44, 110-111
Kreider, Breanna, 104-105
Kreider, Brenda, 123
Kreider, Carol, 80
Kreider, Carroll, 65, 122-123, 150
Kreider, Carroll Hall, 195
Kreider, Carroll L., 151
Kreider, Clair, 25, 110-111
Kreider, Clair E., 116
Kreider, Eleanor, 122
Kreider, Florence May, 91
Kreider, J. Everett, 59
Kreider, Jane, 108
Kreider, Jim, 59, 122
Kreider, Kay, 44
Kreider, Ken, 65, 80, 122, 150, 195
Kreider, Linda, 59
Kreider, Lloyd H., 59
Kreider, Mabel, 50
Kreider, Mary, 130
Kreider, Russel, 105